MOTIVATED IRRATIONALITY

MOTIVATED IRRATIONALITY

DAVID PEARS

CLARENDON PRESS · OXFORD

Oxford University Press, Walton Street, Oxford OX2 6DP

Oxford Glasgow New York Toronto
Delhi Bombay Calcutta Madras Karachi
Kuala Lumpur Singapore Hong Kong Tokyo
Nairobi Dar es Salaam Cape Town
Melbourne Auckland
and associated companies in
Beirut Berlin Ibadan Nicosia

Oxford is a trade mark of Oxford University Press

Published in the United States
by Oxford University Press, New York

First published 1984
Reprinted (new as paperback) 1986

British Library Cataloguing in Publication Data

Pears, David
Motivated irrationality.
1. Irrationalism (Philosophy)
I. Title
153.4'3   B824.2
ISBN 0-19-824662-5
ISBN 0-19-824909-8 (Pbk.)

Library of Congress Cataloging in Publication Data

Pears, David Francis.
Motivated irrationality.
Includes index.
1. Irrationalism (Philosophy)--Addresses, essays,
lectures. 2. Ethics--Addresses, essays, lectures.
I. Title.
B824.2.P43 1984   128   83-17458
ISBN 0-19-824662-5
ISBN 0-19-824909-8 (Pbk.)

Printed in Great Britain
at the University Printing House, Oxford
by David Stanford
Printer to the University

To Rosalind

PREFACE

Most of the work for this book was done at Santa Monica in the autumn of 1979 and again in the autumn of 1981. It began as a course given at the University of California, Los Angeles in each of those two years and profited from interchanges with my pupils there. Several papers were extracted from this material and given in various places between 1980 and 1982.

It is impossible to acknowledge all the points made on those occasions, but two discussions were especially helpful. One followed the reading of a paper on self-deception to which Bernard Williams replied at the Maison des Sciences de l'Homme in Paris. The occasion was a meeting of the Working Group on Rationality organized by Jon Elster in January 1982. The other discussion was started by a paper arguing that conscious *akrasia* is, in general, easier than conscious irrationality in belief-formation, read to a Symposium of the Aristotelian Society at Southampton University in July 1982 and answered by David Pugmire. In Oxford informal discussion of early drafts of several chapters in Freddie Ayer's Circle produced some important criticisms and suggestions.

The book was put together in the summer of 1982, first in Provençal sunshine at Castagniers and then in Oxford *vervecum in patria crassoque sub aere*. I hope the difference does not show.

I take this opportunity to thank Dorothy Cuninghame and Elsie Hinkes for their sympathetic reading of my handwriting and accurate typing. If the book illustrates any of the faults that it describes, it will do so in other ways.

10 November 1982
The Rockefeller Centre,
Villa Serbelloni,
Bellagio.

POSTSCRIPT

I had thought this book was finished, but some of its leading ideas were presented on various occasions in the first few months of 1983 and several points made in the subsequent discussions necessitated changes in the text. The most extensive revisions were in Chapters V and VII, which deal with the most difficult problems.

A paper based on Chapter V was read to the Philosophy Colloquium of the University of California at Berkeley and at the University of Western Washington at Bellingham. A paper based on Chapter VII was read to the Philosophy Colloquium of the University of California at Los Angeles and to the Israel Colloquium for the History, Philosophy and Sociology of Science at the Van Leer Jerusalem Foundation. Chapters VIII-X provided material for the Bar-Hillel lectures at the University of Tel Aviv.

The analysis of the relation between Donald Davidson's functional theory of systems and the version of the theory developed in Chapter V is partly based on discussion with him at Berkeley, and Chapter VII, which has been almost completely rewritten, owes a lot to the discussion of the related paper in Los Angeles, and to Edna Ullmann-Margalit's reply to it in Jerusalem.

19 April 1983
Mishkenot Sha'ananim,
Jerusalem.

CONTENTS

I

METHOD

There are several different ways of approaching the topic of irrationality and identifying the problems that it raises. Philosophers have written at length about it and it would be possible to begin by following the course of their discussions of irrational behaviour and irrational belief. Another way would be to start from the writings of psychologists who have tried to record and explain the varieties of human irrationality in thought and action. Both these approaches ought to lead to the heart of the matter with the maximum speed and the minimum risk of entanglement in irrelevant details. It seems sensible to tread in the footsteps of those who have located the problems and tried to solve them.

But who should be chosen as the guides, philosophers, or psychologists? That makes a bigger difference to the discussion of this topic than might have been expected. Psychology was a part of philosophy until about a century ago, but there is already a great divergence between the two ways of treating irrationality. Philosophers are interested in the concepts involved in descriptions of irrationality and in the limits set by them to what can be said to happen. Consequently, they go straight for the most extreme cases and try to establish whether they fall inside or outside the bounds of the possible. Can a person really deceive himself or act knowingly and without compulsion against his own better judgement? Psychologists, on the other hand, are less concerned with the hard conceptual line dividing the possible from the impossible. Their attention is all on the phenomenon of irrationality as they actually find it and their aim is to explain how it occurs. So their question is not, 'How can these things happen?' but, rather, 'How do these things happen?'

There is no doubt that these two approaches are compatible with one another. The prevalent view of the relation between philosophy and science is that philosophers demonstrate *a priori*, from the concepts themselves, what is possible and what is impossible, whereas scientists focus on to the phenomena that fall under the concepts and try to establish *a posteriori*, from the facts, which of them occur, and to explain their occurrence. So it looks as if the choice between the two approaches raises no questions of principle but is simply a matter of convenience. Which of them offers the best way of beginning to understand the subject?

However, the situation is not as simple as it looks, because the line of demarcation between philosophy and the disciplines whose concepts it analyses cannot be drawn so firmly. It is more like a buffer zone into which incursions can be made from both sides. If the discipline is a science, as it is in this case, the concepts analysed by philosophers will have been developed to fit phenomena discovered by scientists, and that makes it necessary both for the analysis to take account of the empirical facts and for the conceptualization of the empirical facts to take account of the analysis. This give and take between philosophy and the disciplines whose concepts it studies complicates the analytical investigation of any topic, because it means that, wherever we start, we shall not stand on a firm base that is exempt from subsequent alteration. If we start from the apparent implications of a concept, we shall have to check them against its actual use, and, if we start from its actual use, we must be prepared for the possibility that some of its applications might have to be adjusted to bring them into line with its real implications.

An example is needed. We cannot take the concept of self-deception and assume, with many psychologists, that it must be in good working order because there is general agreement about its application. But equally we cannot take the apparent implication of this concept, that a person deceives himself with full knowledge of what he is doing, and argue, on the side of many philosophers, that, since this is impossible, there is no such phenomenon as self-deception. What is needed is a balanced judgement and a due regard for the claims of denotation and connotation, which will avoid both the combination of literalism and paradox that is typical of much sceptical philosophy and the lax conceptualization of much psychology.

The same need may be felt in the analytical investigation of other subjects. If we believe, as we must, that Zeno's arrow reaches its target, we want to know what is wrong with the argument purporting to prove that it cannot reach it. Somehow or other the two sides must be reconciled in cases of this kind. However, the need is especially acute when the subject is irrationality and there are two factors that make it so.

One is the marked tendency of philosophers to reject extreme forms of irrationality because it seems to them that the description of them demonstrates their impossibility without further argument. Here there is often a certain confusion between what might happen in the heat of the moment and what might happen if the same process were as cool as its philosophical description. Philosophers project into ordinary thought and behaviour the rationality of their own analyses of ordinary thought and behaviour. Their prejudice is common among bystanders, who forget what it is like to be a participant: 'How can they fail to avoid faults that are so obvious to us?'

The second factor that makes the need for reconciliation especially acute in this area is something on the other side. When psychologists are confronted by apparent irrationality, they readily accept it at face value because they assume that the psyche is divided against itself. However, though this may well be true, it really is necessary to know what it means. By what criterion is division established, and how are the two resulting parts related to one another? Does it depend on consciousness and unconsciousness, as Freud had it, or on something else? Until these questions are answered, the suggestion is no more than a schema for possible explanations, easily adopted because it is so deficient in content. The speed with which psychologists move away from the hard paradoxes of philosophers is directly proportional to the emptiness of this excessively general explanatory schema and its lack of commitment to anything at all precise. Incidentally, this is a point at which philosophical analysis could well contribute to the construction of scientific theories.

If there is such a big divergence between the philosophy of irrationality and the psychology of irrationality, it makes a substantial difference which of them is chosen as a guide to the topic. Those who follow philosophy will be likely to reject the more extreme forms of irrationality and to reduce the territory of the possible, while those who follow psychologists will be likely to expand it because they think that they have a way of accommodating the extreme cases within it.

Perhaps, then, it would be best to follow neither. Instead, it might be possible to start by collecting examples of irrationality in a way that was not influenced by any theory or any theoretical tendency. There is much to be said for attempting this neutral approach to the topic. The first look at any phenomenon really ought not to be through the restricting lens of a theory. There is also another disadvantage in accepting the guidance of technical treatments of irrationality, which is that most of them concentrate on a limited range of cases. Philosophers get hooked on two central concepts, self-deception and acting flagrantly against one's own better judgement, neglecting the broad range of related phenomena which ought to be included in any comprehensive classification of types of irrationality. Psychologists, on the other hand, are influenced by the latest theory, and in the last thirty years their attention was at first concentrated exclusively on 'hot' cases, in which the irrationality is motivated, and then, by reaction, on 'cold' cases, in which its source is purely intellectual.[1] It would be better to collect examples from the widest possible field.

That will be the procedure followed here. The first task will

[1] See R. Nisbett and L. Ross, *Human Inference: Strategies and Shortcomings of Social Judgment*, Englewood Cliffs, New Jersey, 1980, Ch. 10.

be to try to achieve a simple but comprehensive classification of different types of irrationality. The inquiry will then concentrate on motivated cases, but not before they have been separated from unmotivated cases. The ideas of philosophers and psychologists will be used, but only after the initial classification has been made.

It may be objected that this procedure cannot really be followed, because it is never possible to classify phenomena without the influence of any theory. Nobody can divest himself of the traditional theories that are expressed in the ordinary descriptions of familiar cases. Naturally, these are not the theories of technical psychology, but they are none the less theories, belonging to what is sometimes called 'folk-psychology'. The attempt to see things straight in their complete individuality would be like the attempt to paint without a style.

This may well be true, but one must start somewhere reasonably firm, and it is as well to start with the minimum load of theoretical commitment.

II

IRRATIONALITY

A driver passes a sign that says 'Self-service' and misreads it as 'Self-sacrifice'. Perhaps he is just short-sighted, or there may be another, more interesting explanation: he may be a selfish person who tries to disguise his egoism as altruism. The difference between the two explanations seems clear: the first cites a kind of incompetence, while the second cites a wish, which operates in a way that Freud, for one, would not have found especially circuitous. Either way, this is not a case of irrationality, and the reason why it is not is plain: irrationality is a failure to make proper use of material already in the mind, but in this case the correct reading never gets through to the driver's mind.

A man in love believes that the girl returns his love, when all his evidence shows that she really rejects it. This is a case of irrationality, because the error is not caused by misperception: the significant facts are actually registered in his mind, but only to be misinterpreted later. However, the question asked about the case of misperception can be asked here too. Is the man just bad at interpreting the signs of other people's feelings, so that he might have made the same mistake if he had been watching a well acted scene of unrequited love in the theatre? Or is the explanation not incompetence, but, rather, the wish to be loved?

The questions raised by these two simple examples can be pursued further. First, it is not quite enough to characterize irrationality as failure to make use of material already in the mind. We need to know what counts as material in the mind. This may be perfectly clear in the two examples, but consider a third, intermediate case. The affair goes better and he tells her that he intends to marry her, quite sincerely, because he really thinks that he intends to do so, but later he breaks off the engagement, explaining, of course, that he has changed his mind. However, a friend of his rejects this explanation and says that all along he could tell from certain signs that he never really had the intention. If the friend were right, this would be a case of someone's failing to register his own intention correctly and an intention is something in the mind. Is it then to be counted as a case of irrationality on the ground that he fails to make proper use of something in his mind?

It seems preferable to discriminate between the man's intention and his information about his intention. Both are in his mind, but we may hold that it is only a failure to make proper use of information that counts as irrationality. If we take this line, we shall treat his failure to register his intention like an error in sense-perception and that is a plausible assimilation, provided that there is no implication that people have a method for discovering their own intentions, analogous to using their eyes. The point of similarity is only that in both cases the deficient information ought to have been generated directly by its object.

However, in order to make this suggestion good, we should have to establish what counts as a proper use of information in the mind. A vague answer would be that it is the correct processing of it and, though that is hardly adequate, it is enough to support the idea that the case does not exemplify irrationality, because failure to record an intention is certainly not an example of failure to process information correctly. On the contrary, it is failure to acquire information, in spite of the fact that it is information about oneself, and, not to exaggerate, readily available information.

Another question raised by the first two examples concerns the difference between the two possible explanations of the errors. There certainly seems to be a clear distinction between misperception caused by a wish and misperception caused by short sight, and between misinterpretation of evidence caused by a wish and misinterpretation of evidence caused by general incompetence in a particular field. It is no objection that the distinction looks lame in the third example, because there appears to be no such thing as general incompetence at recording one's own intentions. The distinction itself remains clear enough, or so it seems.

However, there are two qualifications that need to be put in at this point. First, it would be unrealistic to suppose that the two causes of error always operate separately. There must be many cases in which they co-operate in the production of error and some in which the co-operation is unnecessary, because each would have been sufficient by itself, in much the same way that a man facing a firing-squad can be killed by two simultaneous bullets in the heart.

The second qualification is more difficult to get right. Although the two causes can co-operate with one another, they seem to belong to two completely distinct types, and it seems that, between them, these two types cover the whole field, because any error must be produced either by incompetence or by a wish; or, of course, by bad luck, but that is not really an explanation. However, this neat picture may not be quite right. It is possible that the two types of causation do not really exhaust the field, and it is even possible that wishful thinking is a concept without a clear boundary.

Let us approach these questions dialectically, first putting the case for drawing a single line across the field between the two types of cause, with no possibility of any intermediate type, and then putting the case for inserting an intermediate possibility.

The case for drawing a single line is based on Freudian theory. Freud overturned a view of reason, common since antiquity, according to which it is a completely independent force. Evidently, it is a force that is stronger in some people than in others, and, when it comes to action, it is less often frustrated in some agents than in others. But the old idea was that there is no interfering with its inner working. A good analogy would be the engine of a car, which may be more or less powerful and more or less frustrated by what happens beyond the clutch, but, if it itself malfunctions, the trouble is entirely its own. This view was challenged by Freud, who argued that failure of rationality can often be attributed to a wish and gave the support of a theory to something that was already half accepted by popular wisdom. The result was a new scene in which it struck people as absolutely obvious that failures of rationality, like failures to execute movements in the external world, are produced either wilfully or by incompetence and it was naturally assumed that the two causes are entirely distinct.

The case for inserting an intermediate possibility has been developed by cognitive psychologists in the last twenty years. They argue that, even when no wish is operating, a failure of rationality may not be produced by incompetence. For in many cases of this kind the person is perfectly capable of processing the information correctly and even understands the principles governing its correct processing, and yet he goes wrong. A neo-Freudian would have to attribute such errors to bad luck, but the new suggestion is that reason itself has certain bad habits that produce them. For example, salient evidence is given more weight than it is worth, and a person's first formulation of a theory is obstinately retained even when further evidence is telling heavily against it. So just as Freud reduced the province of chance by pointing out the extended operations of the will, these psychologists reduce it still further by pointing out certain bad habits or perversions of reason itself.

There is strong experimental evidence that this is right.[1] If so, it is a mistake to argue that, whenever a failure of rationality cannot be attributed to incompetence, it must be attributed to a wish. It does not, of course, follow that such faults are never attributable to wishes, but only that the scope of Freudian theory is restricted. So in an investigation of motivated irrationality care must be taken to ensure that the cases discussed really are examples of wishful deviation.

[1] See R. Nisbett and L. Ross, *Human Inference: Strategies and Shortcomings of Social Judgment*, pp. 12-13 and Ch. 10.

This, incidentally, is an illustration of the hazards of trying to see a phenomenon straight, without any theoretical prejudice. We started with the intention of building up a classification of types of irrationality with a minimum commitment to theory. It was objected that there must be a popular theory underlying our ordinary descriptions of different cases. That seemed acceptable, because it would be a minimal theory and its long survival might even be taken as an indication of its truth. However, it has now become apparent that, even after the popular theory has been modified by Freud, it is wrong on an important point. We have to insert an intermediate possibility between causation by incompetence and causation by wishes.

It might be thought that this still leaves a firm line around the area of wishful causation, even if this type of causation does not confront a single alternative. However, that is not really so. For suppose we ask what the wishes are for. A review of the three examples shows that the driver wished to disguise his egoism as altruism and that the man in love wished to be loved and, later, to be respected for his intention or his honesty. Now these are all personal wishes, probably accompanied by emotion and, therefore, hot. But we cannot say that the perversions of reason never involve any wish. Reluctance to abandon a first hypothesis obviously involves one. True, we are assuming that the problem itself is purely intellectual and that the person has no prior stake in a particular solution, but, once he has formulated his first hypothesis, he will wish to retain it, and this wish is personal and may even be accompanied by emotion. Susceptibility to salience is another matter. It would be an obvious mistake to suppose that people attach too much weight to salient evidence because they prefer it, or prefer to be swayed by it. So there seems to be a gradation here rather than a clear-cut difference between hot and cold cases.

The question about the various possible objects of these biasing wishes is worth pursuing in another direction. In the second example the man wished to be loved, but his immediate goal was the belief that he was loved. What use would that be to him if the belief were false?

The first point that needs to be made in response to this question is that irrationality does not necessarily lead to a belief that is false. Irrationality is incorrect processing of information and, if the information that is fed into the mind is itself false, the incorrect processing may lead to a true belief. That would be a case of one error cancelling another, as sometimes happens when a column of figures is being added. For example, the girl might really love him, but secretly, and a jealous rival might send him a forged letter purporting to come from her and dismissing him, and then he, mistakenly believing that the letter was written by her, might discount it in his usual irrational way, but this time he would arrive at the truth.

However, that only scratches the surface of the problem. What needs to be explained is why the man's immediate goal is a belief which, in relation to his evidence, is likely to be false, when his ultimate goal is the real thing, being loved. Obviously it is not the improbability of the belief that attracts him, but its exhilarating effect. So the explanation must start from the fact that achievement of the real thing would not produce any satisfaction if he were unaware of it. The belief is the intermediary, the messenger with the good news, and, when actual achievement causes satisfaction, it is the belief in achievement that is the immediate cause. This causal linkage makes it possible for him to take a short cut to satisfaction: he simply manufactures the belief without the real thing.

Naturally, he himself would not describe what he was doing in this way, because, if he did, he would be brought up short by the thought that, even if it were possible to combine a belief with the knowledge that it was false, it would hardly produce much satisfaction. In any case, to believe that she loves him is to believe that it is true that she loves him, which would scarcely be possible if he knew that the belief was false. So when his ultimate goal, the real thing, leads him to go for the belief as an immediate goal, his plan is devious and masked. However, the masking is not always total, because he will always be capable of realizing, and will sometimes actually realize, that the belief is likely to be false, and it remains to be explained why this does not bring him up short. But that is a problem that may be postponed for the moment.

The solution to the present problem is put neatly by Freud. [We want to know how anyone can aim at belief in the real thing instead of the real thing itself. Freud's answer is that the normal procedure, governed by the reality principle, would be to alter the world and let the altered world produce the satisfying belief, but that, when the alteration required in the world is too difficult, wishful thinking, governed by the pleasure principle, goes straight for the belief.[2]]

There is also another direction in which it is worth pursuing the question about the possible objects of biasing wishes. In the examples presented so far the wish has not been for a belief directly connected with an action in prospect. The driver's misreading of the notice was a side-effect produced by the displaced operation of his general wish to disguise his egoism, and the immediate object of the wish of the man in love was in the first case a belief that gave pleasure and in the second case a belief that eliminated discomfort. But now consider a new kind of case in which the wish is for a belief that would make it easier to yield to a temptation. The driver goes to a party and he judges it best to stop at two drinks in spite of the pleasure to be had from more, because there is nobody else to take the wheel on the way home. Nevertheless, when he is offered a third drink, which, we may suppose, is a double, he takes it. How can he? Easily, if the wish for a third drink biases his deliberation at the party before he takes it. For example, he might tell himself, against the weight of his evidence, that it is not dangerous to drive home after six measures of whiskey, or he might forget, under the influence of his wish, how many drinks he had already taken. Either way, his wish for a third drink would be diverted to the im-

[2] See S. Freud, *The Interpretation of Dreams*, Harmondsworth, 1976, pp. 719-21.

mediate goal of altering a belief that stood in the way of his taking it, but in this case the result is a realistic plan which is likely to achieve the real thing, a third drink. Again, we may postpone the question, how such a plan can be formed and carried out.

Although these two examples belong to the same general type, there is an important difference between them, a difference marked by a line that has already been drawn. If the guest persuaded himself that doctors are just wrong about the amount of alcohol that can be taken without loss of judgement or slowing of reactions, he was going against the evidence in his possession and merely making a wishful guess at the facts. That would be a clear case of incorrect processing of information and so, by the suggested criterion, a clear case of irrationality. But the verdict might be different, if he forgot how many drinks he had had.

Misperception of things in the external world has been distinguished from irrationality. Forgetting is difficult to classify because, like misrecording one's own intention, it lies somewhere between misperception and irrationality. Now, if the earlier argument was right, misrecording an intention is not an example of irrationality, because it is not a case of failing to process information correctly, but, rather, a case of failing to register information. Forgetting is a little closer to irrationality, because the forgotten information has been registered in the mind. However, it has to be retrieved before it can be processed correctly or incorrectly, and forgetting it is failing to retrieve it when it is needed. So it is natural to refuse to count forgetting as an example of irrationality and to point to a certain analogy between it and misperception. It is like a momentary failure of perception, or like leafing through books in a library but failing to find a quotation.[3] Again, it is essential to keep this analogy scaled down to its small kernel of truth, which is merely that the information is not available

---

[3] Cf. Descartes, *The Passions of the Soul*, Art. XLII.

for processing and that the simple use of a faculty, in this case memory, could make it available.

* * *

In this chapter the ideas of philosophers have hardly been used. Some use has been made of psychologists' experimental results, but the main undertaking has been to build up from examples, presented with the minimum of theory, a simple classification of different types of irrationality. The theme, an unsurprising one, has been that irrationality is incorrect processing of information in the mind. This fault was distinguished from two others which, at first sight, look quite like it, misrecording something that is in one's mind, such as an intention, and forgetting. A start was made on the task of classifying the causes of irrationality. The neo-Freudian assumption, that it must be caused either by a wish or by incompetence, was rejected and attention was drawn to reason's own perversions.

It was then argued that a review of the possible objects of biasing wishes shows that there is no clear-cut distinction between hot and cold cases but that there are some indubitable cases of each type at each end of the spectrum. Freud's suggestion about the specification of the immediate goal of wishful thinking was adopted, and wishful thinking for pleasure or the elimination of discomfort was contrasted with the kind of wishful thinking that attacks a belief standing in the way of surrender to a temptation.

In the next chapter a move will be made towards the ideas of philosophers.

III

SELF-DECEPTION AND ACTION
AGAINST ONE'S OWN
BETTER JUDGEMENT

Philosophical investigations of irrationality have two distinctive features, not unconnected with one another. They approach the topic through the concepts of self-deception and of action done knowingly against one's own better judgement and they move very quickly to the limits of the possible. Their interest in drawing a line between what is possible and what is impossible leads understandably to their choice of these two concepts as a starting-point, because they both have an air of paradox about them, as if their natural habitat was somewhere very near the boundary of the possible. Self-deception may even be an impossible achievement and the same may be true of conscious action against one's own better judgement. Naturally, the two concepts are important in their own right and in any case they would need to be related to the types of irrationality distinguished in the last chapter. The need is increased when they are singled out by philosophers for special attention.

When someone acts against his own better judgement, reason is not in control of his actions. Another way of putting the point would be to say that he is not in control of them. The equivalence between these two ways of describing what happens in a case of this kind depends on a very natural theory about the identity of the agent. The true agent is the authority within the visible agent. He identifies himself with this authority and we are simply following suit when we say indifferently that his reason is not in control of his actions or that he is not in control of them.[1]

[1] Cf. Aristotle, *Nicomachean Ethics*, 1168b28-33.

This identification is a matter of some consequence. If we go along with it, we shall encounter a problem. When someone acts against his own better judgement the usual reaction is exasperation: 'What more could reason have done to keep him on the rails?'[2] If his deliberation could not have been better, there was nothing more that reason could have done. So the verdict will be that reason could not have prevented the derailment. But now if we substitute him for his reason in this verdict, we shall be in trouble, because we shall have to conclude that he could not have prevented the derailment.

The guest at the party can be used again to illustrate this problem. He deliberated irrationally in the first version of the story, because his desire for the pleasure of unrestricted drinking led him to conclude, against the weight of his evidence, that it is really all right to drive after six measures of whiskey. Now suppose that his deliberation could not have been better, because it was not flawed in this way or in any other way, and his conclusion was that it would be wrong to accept the third offer of a double. Yet he accepted it. How could he? If at this point we identify him with the authority within him, we are likely to suppose that, since that authority could not keep him on the rails, he could not keep himself on the rails. In other words, people who act consciously against their own better judgement cannot help it and intentional actions of this kind must be the result of irresistible compulsion.

This line of thought will be examined in Chapter X. It is certainly a natural development of the identification of the true agent with the authority within the visible agent. But the conclusion, that actions done consciously and without compulsion against one's own better judgement are beyond the pale of possibility, may well turn out to be false. If so, the identification will have to be rejected or qualified in some way that will block that particular inference from it.

The Greek word for the behaviour of the guest at the party

---

[2] Aristotle uses a proverb: 'When water makes someone choke, what can it be washed down with?', ibid. 1146a35.

in all three versions of the story is '*akrasia*'.[3] It means 'lack of control' and the idea is that the agent, or the agent's reason, is not in control of his actions. So the use of the word in all three cases presupposes that the true agent is his reason, the authority within him. Aristotle compares an agent in *akrasia* to a city with a good legislature but an inefficient executive.[4]

We are by now so accustomed to the idea that the true agent is his reason that we hardly find it necessary to argue for it. It is so obvious that reason ought to control the guest's appetite for drink at the party that it would hardly make sense for his host to ask him to control his rational desire to remain sober enough to drive home safely. However, the obvious can be explained and in this case the explanation is not far to seek: reason happens to be our most reliable guide to action. This is because reason is much more adaptable than its rivals, emotion and appetite. Reason alone allows us to spread out the fan of alternative possible developments that depend on our agency and to simulate them in thought without the commitment or risk of actual experiment.

Perhaps creatures without reason could be said to manifest *akrasia* only if their appetites were not controlled by the most reliable guide that they possessed, which would presumably be the system of primitive emotions, like fear and anger, triggering the stereotypical strategies of avoidance or aggression. As a matter of fact, this would be an extension of the concept of *akrasia,* which Aristotle did not apply to animals,[5] but there is a point in extending it. Preoccupation with our own species may prevent us from grasping the general principle that the true agent is always the best guide within the visible agent, whatever it may happen to be, and the point made by the extension of the concept of *akrasia* is that its opposition to reason in us is only a special case of the general principle.

Akrasia is not quite the same thing as acting against one's

---

[3] See p. 2 for the first two versions, in both of which there is a fault in his deliberation, and p. 6 for the third version, in which there is no fault in his deliberation.
[4] Ibid. 1152a19-23.   [5] See *Nicomachean Ethics*, 1147b3-5.

own better judgement. The two concepts coincide in the third version of the story about the guest at the party, because he actually judges it better to refuse the third offer, but nevertheless accepts it, consciously and without compulsion, if indeed that is possible. However, in the other two cases he does not actually formulate the judgement. So all that we can say is that he acts against what would have been his judgement, if in the first case he had processed his information correctly, and if in the second case he had remembered how many drinks he had already taken.

The relation between *akrasia* and motivated irrationality is more complicated. In the second version of the story the culprit is forgetfulness. If the argument used in the last chapter was convincing, forgetfulness is not an example of irrationality, because irrationality is incorrect processing, and information that is forgotten is not available for processing of any kind. Therefore, *akrasia* produced by motivated forgetfulness is not an example of motivated irrationality.

But suppose that there is no forgetfulness and that what goes wrong is that the guest fails to perceive that the second offer is a treble. He has only had one double and, though another would be a reasonable supplement, a treble would take him beyond his limit. Here his misperception does not count as irrationality for the same reason that forgetfulness does not count as irrationality. However, there is little doubt that it does count as *akrasia* because Aristotle, who is our authority for this concept, almost certainly allowed that *akrasia* may be caused by misperception.[6]

This raises two interesting questions of interpretation. When *akrasia* is caused by misperception, did Aristotle require the misperception to be motivated? And more generally, why did he allow cases of *akrasia* that are not cases of irrationality? The answer to the first question may be that he never thought of the possibility of motivated misperception of facts, like the fact that the drink is a treble. The answer to

[6] Ibid. 1146b35-1147a7.

the second question must be that, even when the first thing to go wrong is not an example of irrationality, he still counts the whole performance as *akrasia*, because reason is not in control of the action. It makes no difference in his eyes that reason is not in control only because it does not receive the support that it normally receives from the senses. It is clear that, on this view of the matter, the question, whether the misperception was motivated or not, loses its importance.

We may now go back to the first version of the story about the guest at the party: the desire for the pleasure of the third drink biases his reasoning and he concludes that it is all right to take a third double and so he takes it. It has already been explained that this is one of the two main types of motivated irrationality, namely the type in which a desire quietly removes the intellectual obstacle to its own fulfilment. Two things now need to be emphasized about this type of motivated irrationality. First, the word 'motivated' is being used attributively in the diagnosis of the fault, because the point is not just that the action is motivated and irrational, but, rather, that the fault committed at the point where the irrationality began was itself motivated. For the agent's irrational belief, that it is all right to drive home after six measures of whiskey, is the beginning of the whole episode and it is a piece of wishful thinking. Second, this initial fault is motivated by the very same desire that is then fulfilled by the action. There is, of course, another way in which the initial fault might have been motivated: it might have happened that the rebellious desire inherited a situation in which, by pure coincidence, the obstacle to its fulfilment had already been removed by another desire. But the diagnosis 'motivated irrationality' implies that it is the same desire that biases the agent's belief and then produces his action. That must be the usual way in which this sort of thing happens, because the coincidence of two different desires co-operating blindly must be very rare.

There is no doubt that Aristotle would have counted this type of motivated irrationality as *akrasia*, but the interesting question is why he would have taken that view of it. In the light of the discussion of the third version of the story, in which the guest failed to perceive that the second offer was a treble, it might seem that, strictly speaking, it was enough for the Aristotelian diagnosis of *akrasia* that reason was not in control of the action, because it did not receive the support that it normally receives from deliberation. For that was the basis of the diagnosis in the case of misperception, and it seems not to have occurred to Aristotle to make the additional requirement that the misperception itself must be motivated. However, there is a significant difference between the two cases: deliberation, unlike perception, is a function of reason and so it would not be at all surprising to find Aristotle making the additional requirement, that the fault in deliberation must itself be motivated. That would produce a very natural picture of the drama within the agent. The war waged by desire against reason culminates in his visible *akrasia*, but it begins within him as a pre-emptive attack on his deliberation, before he goes into action.

However, there is a gap in Aristotle's theory of *akrasia* at this point and it makes it difficult to tell how strong a requirement he was actually making when he diagnosed this type of case as *akrasia*. What is lacking in his account is a step-by-step description of the causation of irrational action. When he is analysing rational action, he does give a step-by-step account of its causation, because that is what his theory of practical reasoning really is. But when he is analysing irrational action, he is content with a very general description of its causation by rebellious desires. It is, therefore, difficult to deduce what he thought about the details of the process, and, in particular, it is uncertain how firmly he adhered to the view that nothing can interfere with reason's internal affairs. Reason is certainly frustrated, but did he think that the desire achieves its victory by attacking reason on its own ground and by disrupting its internal operations?

There is, of course, in the *Nicomachean Ethics*, a lengthy account of what physical appetite does to reason in cases of *akrasia*,[7] but it is almost entirely concerned with the Socratic paradox. How can the agent's knowledge, in this case his knowledge that it is better to refuse the third offer, be outmanoeuvred by his appetite? Aristotle suggests various ways in which the agent's knowledge might be weakened so that it became an easier victim, but he never actually says that it is his appetite that makes it an easier victim. Now we might think that he just takes it as obvious that the cause of the changes in the knowledge that increase its vulnerability is the appetite. But that is only because we see the whole scene through neo-Freudian eyes.

Aristotle himself may well have regarded reason as an independent force and assumed that appetite cannot interfere with its internal affairs. True, he does say that it is only perceptual knowledge of particular matters that is dragged around by appetite because it is intrinsically more vulnerable. But though it is tempting to take this to mean that appetite manipulates some of the internal operations of reason, it is much more likely that it only means that appetite drags reason towards *akrasia* without listening to its protests. On the other hand, it is certainly his view that there is something wrong with the way in which reason makes its protests, some deficiency in timing, urgency, or clarity, and we may ask whether he can really have supposed that in cases of *akrasia* appetite is always lucky enough to inherit a situation in which, by pure coincidence, its opponent has been weakened in one of these ways? However, he does have a possible reply to this. He could claim that it would not be a coincidence, because reason would be generally weaker in such people and so it would not have to become weaker for the special occasion of *akrasia*. This would be parallel to the idea that misperception is caused by a general weakness of the senses rather than by the special onslaught of a wish.

There is also another shortcoming in his theory of *akrasia* which makes it difficult to tell how strong a requirement he

[7] Bk. VII, Ch. 3.

would have imposed on this kind of case when he diagnosed it as *akrasia*. We supposed that the guest drew the irrational conclusion that it was all right to take the third drink, instead of the rational conclusion that it was better not to take it. Now Aristotle's concern with the Socratic paradox led him to concentrate on deficiencies in the agent's knowledge of the rational conclusion and to give sketchier answers to the various questions that might be asked about the irrational one. The first and most radical doubt is whether the irrational conclusion needs to be evaluative. Perhaps it is enough that appetite is locked on to pleasure[8] in much the same way that a missile is locked on to its target, so that all that is needed is some weakening in the opposition offered by reason. If so, in order for *akrasia* to occur, it would be necessary that the agent should realize that he would get pleasure from the forbidden action, but there would be no need for the conclusion that it is all right to do it, still less need for the conclusion that it is better to do it. In fact, Aristotle does seem to have regarded both these conclusions as unnecessary for *akrasia*.[9] It follows that the neo-Freudian question about interference with the internal operations of reason does not arise at the point where he offers a positive theory about the way in which the irrational conclusion is substituted for the rational one. For there is nothing wrong with the conclusion that the third drink would give pleasure. It would. The only thing wrong is acting on it. However, it must be admitted that Aristotle's discussion of these questions is sketchy and the interpretation not at all secure.

Finally, there is the third version of the story about the guest at the party. There is no deficiency in his deliberation and he acts consciously against his own better judgement. This is the limiting case that fascinates philosophers and it will be discussed later. The controversial question is whether such an action can be done without compulsion or whether it

[8] Cf. Aristotle, *De Anima*, 433b-434a.
[9] Aristotle, *Nicomachean Ethics*, 1147a1-5.

always turns out that the agent could not have helped it. There is, of course, no doubt about the classification of non-compulsive conscious defiance of one's own better judgement both as a type of motivated irrationality and as a type of *akrasia*. The only doubt is about its possibility.

At this point it is necessary to revert to something that was said earlier. The proposed translation of '*akrasia*' is 'lack of control', but that really needs more discussion. The literal meaning of the Greek word is 'lack of strength or power', but since the un-negated root is the ordinary word for victory or domination, the implication is that what is lacking is power or control over something else. It follows that those who translate '*akrasia*' as weakness are under-translating the word.[10]

They are also making a further mistake. For Aristotle uses '*astheneia*', the ordinary Greek word for weakness, as the name of one of the causes of *akrasia*, and not as another name for the phenomenon itself. He mentions impetuousness as another possible cause of *akrasia*: the impetuous agent does not give himself time to deliberate.[11] It is quite clear that at this point he is moving to a different level. He starts with the phenomenon of *akrasia*, which is lack of control, and then he goes below the surface in search of its cause and comes up with the suggestion that one of its causes is *astheneia*, weakness. The only excuse for calling *akrasia* 'weakness' is that the word 'weakness' sometimes means no more than 'fault' and *akrasia* is certainly a fault. But that is hardly a justification. It is confusing to use the same word, 'weakness', both as another name for *akrasia* and as the name of one of the possible causes of *akrasia* without explaining the equivocation. Very probably, there is a real confusion here between the phenomenon and its cause. Even if it had only one cause, the distinction between phenomenon and cause should have been preserved.

---

[10] e.g. R. M. Hare, *The Language of Morals*, Oxford, 1952, p. 169.
[11] Aristotle, *Nicomachean Ethics*, 1150b19-28.

There is also a deeper problem here. What Aristotle says about weakness (real weakness, *astheneia*) shows that he regards it as a fault in the executive part of the psyche, which hears but does not carry out the edicts of reason. The weak agent, he says, does not stand by the results of his own deliberation.[12] Now those who translate '*akrasia*' in a way that brings in weakness always translate it as 'weakness of will'. Although this is a mistranslation of '*akrasia*' it may be a fair translation of '*astheneia*', given Aristotle's account of the weak agent. However, it suggests a problem, which surfaces when we ask how weakness of will is related to the kind of weakness of reason that Aristotle seems to count as one of the two possible causes of *akrasia* in his discussion of the Socratic paradox.

This weakness of reason had better be called 'vulnerability of reason' for the sake of clarity and because Aristotle does not actually call it '*astheneia*'. Now there are really two difficulties of interpretation here. First, when *akrasia* is caused by the vulnerability of reason, is that a special case of weakness of will? Second, did Aristotle really think that all *akrasia* involves some fault in the agent's reasoning? Here it must be remembered that *akrasia* is, by definition, not compulsive and so, if an apparent case of *akrasia* turns out to have been compulsive, it was not really *akrasia*.

The second question will be discussed in Chapter X. It is not easy, because Aristotle's remark about weak agents suggests that conscious last-ditch *akrasia* seemed to him to be a real possibility, while his treatment of the Socratic paradox suggests the opposite.

The first question, about the vulnerability of reason, is a less far-reaching one. How did Aristotle explain the feebleness of reason's resistance? If a fault in reasoning is an example of weakness, it certainly is not a straightforward example of weakness of will. True, the will may have something to do with it, because a strong-minded agent under temptation may

---

[12] Aristotle, loc. cit.

succeed in deliberating rationally only because he makes an effort of will and keeps a grip on his reasoning.[13] But the simple equation of weakness in this area with weakness of will is very wide of the mark. In fact, Aristotle did not explicitly attribute the vulnerability of reason to any kind of weakness. However, that is not too important, because the interesting question is a more general one. Did he see it as a fault of character, or a fault of intellect? Unfortunately, the answer is not clear. When *akrasia* results from impetuousness, there is a fault in the reasoning caused by a fault of character, but no general conclusion can be drawn from that kind of case, because the fault in the reasoning is simple omission. Aristotle gives some tantalizing hints about the way in which fear can undermine a soldier's assessment of the odds just before he goes into battle,[14] but he does not have a general theory about such things. A meeting in the Elysian Fields between him and Freud would be interesting.

Philosophical discussions of irrational belief-formation show the same two distinctive features as philosophical discussions of irrational action. They are dominated by a single concept, which in this case is self-deception, and their whole drift is towards the limits of the possible. So there is a certain parallelism here, or, rather, a certain reduplication of pattern, because the problem of irrational action really contains the problem of irrational belief-formation within itself. There are two reasons for this. The formation of a belief is often an action of a kind, and, more interestingly, many irrational actions are made easier by the irrational biasing of beliefs, as happened in the first version of the story about the guest.

Self-deception is an irritating concept. Its supposed denotation is far from clear and, if its connotation is taken literally, it cannot really have any denotation. Perhaps it is better to postpone consideration of the paradoxes of its connotation and start by asking how it is actually used. First, it is

---

[13] There is a hint of this idea in Eudemian Ethics, 1227b12-19.
[14] Cf. *Nicomachean Ethics*, 1115b29-34.

worth noting that it has a wider extension than the concept of motivated irrational belief-formation. For while both concepts apply to the first achievement of the man in love in the example used earlier, only the concept of self-deception applies to his second achievement: when he persuaded himself in the teeth of his evidence that he was loved, that was both self-deception and motivated irrational belief-formation, but when he persuaded himself that he intended to marry the girl, that was only self-deception.]

These two examples give us some firm ground, and taking our stand on it we may ask why there is any need to dramatize them by giving them the flamboyant name 'self-deception', and why, if they must be called that, philosophers have to take the name so literally. What makes the name especially irritating is that it generates a verbal paradox which obscures the real paradox. The real paradox lies in the irrationality of the man's belief in the first case and the perversity of his belief in the second case, and these faults do not depend on the phrase chosen to describe the way in which he forms his beliefs. The facts themselves are obscure enough without our kicking up a cloud of verbal dust.

Perhaps that is a little unfair. It may turn out in the end that the typical self-deceiver really is divided into two systems related to one another in much the same way that two different people are related to one another in a case of ordinary deception. But though this is a real possibility, it is evident in advance that it is unlikely to be realized in all the different types of case that we would diagnose as self-deception in real life or in literature. However, it is rash to predict the result of an investigation before starting to work on it.

When we form beliefs that go beyond the immediate deliverances of perception and memory, reason is our best guide to truth. In certain cases intuition of one kind or another has its successes, but it is evident that some of its successes must be checked in a more laborious way, so that reason can assess the score and tell us how much trust to put in it on occasions when it is not checked. Nobody would listen to a fortune-teller with a published score of successful predictions no higher than could have been achieved by guesswork. So, directly or indirectly, reason is our best long-range guide in the search for truth.

There is an obvious connection between this fact and the fact that reason is our best guide in action. Successful action is based on true conclusions and rational argument is most likely to lead to true conclusions. Now we can imagine creatures without reason and, therefore, without the ability to use the strategy that we find best for attaining truth. When this speculation was begun a short way back, it was suggested that their best guide would be the promptings of primitive emotions like anger and fear, which for us are second best. This immediately suggests that there is a certain lack of parallelism between our situation and theirs. Reason prevents us from believing the conjunction of two contradictory propositions, but there is no such absolute constraint on the beliefs of creatures without reason. No doubt, it is impossible in many cases for them to act, or prepare to act, on the conjunction of two contradictory beliefs, but they are not in a position to do what we can do, namely simulate the coexistence of the two facts and see in advance, or *a priori*, that it is impossible.

This lack of parallelism is important, because it suggests that there may be a similar lack of parallelism between the way in which action is guided by reason in those who possess it and the way in which it is guided by other mentors in creatures who lack it. The idea would be that it is self-contradictory to act against one's own better judgement in something like the way in which it is self-contradictory to believe the conjunction of two logically incompatible propositions. This would produce a striking contrast between us and creatures without reason, because there would be no such obstacle preventing them from acting against the promptings of their best guide to action. This idea will be examined in Chapter VIII.

The impossibility of believing the conjunction of two

contradictory propositions needs to be connected with the paradox of self-deception and both these things need to be connected with the paradox of irrational belief-formation. The connection between the paradox of self-deception and the impossibility of believing the conjunction of two contradictory propositions is quite straightforward. Those who interpret the phrase 'self-deception' literally take it to imply that the self-deceiver believes that something is not so and yet persuades himself that it is so, just like the deceiver of another, except that the self-deceiver is the victim as well as the agent. From here it is a short step to saying that the self-deceiver must believe the conjunction of the two contradictory propositions. But that is impossible, and therefore, it is argued, self-deception is impossible.

The case of the man who was supposed to deceive himself about his own intention can be used to illustrate this paradox. If he deceives himself about his intention he will, in the typical case, start by knowing what it actually is, but then how can he persuade himself that it is other than it is? He cannot, unless he loses his original knowledge on the way, but, if he does lose it, the persuasion will no longer count as deception. The extreme literalism of this argument is worth noting. It assumes that it is necessary for self-deception that the original belief should persist right up to the end of the process of persuasion that installs the opposite belief. It also makes another questionable assumption, that someone who believes two contradictory propositions believes their conjunction. For it is only belief in the conjunction that is undeniably impossible.

Self-deception about one's own intentions is an example of perverse, but not irrational belief-formation. It is in cases of irrational belief-formation that the paradox of self-deception diverts philosophers from a deeper issue and sends them off in pursuit of verbal superficialities. The deeper issue is the problem of irrationality. How can the man persuade himself that he is loved when all his evidence points to the opposite conclusion? This question can be raised without the assumption that he actually believes that he is not loved, and so, on the literal interpretation of 'self-deception', without the assumption that he is deceiving himself.

As soon as this is said, the literal interpretation begins to lose its plausibility. Surely this man is deceiving himself even if he does not actually believe that he is not loved. This really cannot be doubted and it suggests the possibility of a generalization. [Perhaps we can say that, when self-deception involves irrationality, the irrationality is all that it requires and there is no need for the self-deceiver ever to accept the falsehood of the belief that he manufactures for his own satisfaction.]

In fact, the generalization may not work for all cases of irrational belief-formation. If the evidence had been equally distributed between the two alternatives, that she loved him and that she loved him not, and if he had believed in the first one simply because it gave him satisfaction, that might not count as self-deception, but it would be irrational, because the rational course would be to suspend belief. In order to get a clear case of self-deception, we have to increase the irrationality by supposing that his evidence favours the second alternative, as it did in the original example. From that point on the generalization works very well. The next step is to take a case in which the self-deceiver's irrationality is more extreme, because his premisses are sufficient to establish the falsehood of his adopted belief by logical or mathematical necessity. Finally, at the top of the scale we have him violating logical necessity in the simplest possible way: he believes that something is not so, and yet he adopts the belief that that very thing is so, if indeed that is possible.

There are considerable advantages in arranging the cases in this way. The paradoxes on this scale are the paradoxes of irrational belief-formation and they are the real problem. The limiting case at the top of the scale happens to exemplify the paradox of self-deception, which catches the attention of philosophers, who ask themselves how such a thing can happen and usually end by putting it beyond the pale of possibility. Lower down the scale we find the two less controversial cases of the paradox of irrationality, both of which count as self-deception but neither of which involves the paradox of self-deception. Finally, at the bottom of the scale there is the mildest form of the paradox of irrationality, the case that does not count as self-deception at all.

It might be objected that the second case from the top of the scale is more controversial than the third one. For if someone's premisses actually entailed the opposite conclusion to the one that he drew, how was he able to draw it? Would not his belief in the conjunction of his premisses and his conclusion be just as impossible, or, at least, just as close to impossibility in this case as it would be in the case of simple contradiction at the top of the scale? Unless, of course, he were not competent to spot the contradiction. But the assumption is that the case was one of motivated irrationality without over-determination and, therefore, that he was competent to spot it.

It is important to see that this objection must be mistaken, because there evidently are cases of this kind of irrationality in real life. So here is an example. Someone who is competent at simple arithmetic nevertheless occasionally makes mistakes when he is adding up his own bank deposits and subtracting his payments, and most of the mistakes are in his own favour, but when he is performing the same service for a friend, he makes fewer mistakes and those that he does make do not show the same pattern. This example beats the objection, because this sort of thing certainly happens, but we also need to understand how it happens. The explanation would presumably have to start from the fact that in a complicated case most people cannot achieve the same commanding view of their premisses and conclusion that they can achieve in the case of a simple contradiction.

The paradox of irrationality will be examined in Chapter V. What remains to be done in this chapter is to analyse the paradox of self-deception a little further. This is worth doing both because this paradox is the limiting case of the paradox of irrationality and because it is the case that has caught the attention of philosophers in their nervous quest for the boundary of the possible.

First, there is a tricky question about truth and self-deception. The paradox of self-deception was formulated in the following way: 'How can the self-deceiver believe that something is not so and yet persuade himself that it is so?' But Sartre and several other philosophers formulate it in a different way: 'How can the self-deceiver know the truth and yet persuade himself that it is not the truth?'[15] This version restricts the paradox to the special case in which the self-deceiver's original belief is true.

The reason for imposing this restriction on self-deception is that the successful deception of another person requires that he should come to believe something false as a result of being told it by a deceiver equipped with the true belief. If this is so, there are two ways of failing to deceive another person: one way is for the would-be deceiver to fail to put the belief across, and the other way is for the belief that he puts across to be true, because his own belief happened to be false. So when we impute a successful piece of deception to someone we imply both that his own belief was true and that he put across the opposite belief, which was, therefore, false. The same two implications are naturally read into self-deception and the result is Sartre's version of the paradox.

Those who put these two implications into self-deception are creating yet another difference between it and irrational belief-formation. Two such differences have already been pointed out: to deceive oneself about something in one's own mind, such as an intention, is not to form a belief irrationally, and to form a belief irrationally when the evidence for it and against it is exactly balanced may not be to deceive oneself, because it is a border-line case. The third difference, which is a consequence of Sartre's version of the paradox, is that, when the would-be self-deceiver's original belief is false, he fails to deceive himself in spite of the fact that he does

[15] J.-P. Sartre, *Being and Nothingness*, tr. Hazel E. Barnes, London, 1957, p. 49.

form his belief irrationally. This, of course, is because one error cancels another, as happened in the story about the man, the girl, and the rival who forged the letter.

As a matter of fact, although the analysis of the verb 'to deceive', on which Sartre's version of the paradox depends, is correct, there is also a special use of the verb which focuses exclusively on the process in the deceiver's mind. Using the verb in this way, we say that one person is deceiving another because, whatever the outcome, that is what he is engaged in doing. The characteristic of this restricted sense is that both the implications of success are in abeyance: the deceiver may fail to put the belief across or the belief that he puts across may turn out to be true, but he is, nevertheless, engaged in deceiving the other person.

The sentence 'He is drawing a cat' is a simpler example of the same kind.[16] Even if the result is much more like a dog, it is still true, in the restricted sense, that he was drawing a cat. Perhaps afterwards we would prefer to say that he was trying to draw a cat. If so, we would be using the phrase 'draw a cat' in its extended sense, with the usual implication of success and, because he failed, we could only say that he was trying to draw a cat. However, at the time he could have said, 'Whatever the outcome, I am now drawing a cat' and he would have been right in the restricted sense. This is a simpler example, because there are not two conditions of success, as there are in the case of deception, but only one.

The similarity is that in the case of deception the sentence 'He is deceiving you' may be meant as a description of what someone is engaged in doing, whatever the outcome, or it may be meant to include the success of what he is doing. It is evident that when the word 'deception' is used in the first of these two ways, the third difference between the self-deception and irrational belief-formation vanishes. For the falsehood of the original belief will not rule out self-deception just

---

[16] Cf. Wittgenstein, *Philosophical Investigations*, tr. G. E. M. Anscombe, Oxford, 1953, Part I §§ 683-4.

as it does not rule out irrational belief-formation. The reason for this is plain: 'irrational belief-formation' is the name of the actual process in the person's mind, and the phrase 'self-deception' focuses exclusively on this process when the usual implication of success is in abeyance.

There is also another, more substantial question about truth and self-deception. Is self-deception always a bad thing? The point of the question is that, though truth is a good thing, it is not necessarily paramount and it may sometimes be advisable to sacrifice it to something better. For example, someone who starts with the knowledge that his chances of success in some enterprise are slim may then exaggerate them to himself in order to improve them by increasing his confidence. Or he may suspect that a friend is engaged in some shady activity, and he may deliberately avoid finding out if he really is, because he calculates that, if he keeps his image of him untarnished, that will be likely to have a good effect on him.

These examples raise a number of issues. First, there is a big difference between avoiding the collection of evidence that might lead to a true but damaging belief and manufacturing a belief that goes against evidence already collected. The second is a central case of self-deception, but the first is more marginal. Depriving another person of evidence counts as deceiving him only when the agent knows that the evidence would lead the victim to the belief that he does not want him to form, but, naturally, someone who avoids collecting evidence for the reason given in the last example does not know what its effect would be. If he were certain of its effect, it would make no difference whether he collected it or not, and so the assumption was that he had a suspicion about his friend, but no certainty.

There is also a question about the connection between self-deception and faith. When people exaggerate their chances of success in order to improve them, the goal is, as far as it goes, a good one, and that seems to be enough to make such cases examples of faith. But are they also examples of self-deception, good self-deception, of course, but still self-deception? That is going to depend on the precise content of the manufactured belief, because it may be formulated in a way that allows it to make itself true, or it may be formulated in a way that leaves it in the same position as the majority of beliefs, namely unable to make itself true.

If the belief is 'I shall succeed', and if it actually produces that effect, then it is arguable that it fails the extra, Sartrean test for self-deception, because it will make itself true in the end. On the other hand, if the belief is 'I would succeed even if I had no belief in my own success', then, like the majority of beliefs, it cannot make itself true, and, if it is false, it certainly passes the extra, Sartrean test for self-deception.

However, Sartre's extra test for self-deception is less important than the basic test. So let us drop his requirement, that the manufactured belief should be false, and concentrate on the basic requirement, that it should be formed irrationally. Which of the two beliefs passes this test for self-deception?

Again, it is arguable that the first belief fails it, and the case for this verdict is an interesting one. The belief is simply 'I shall succeed' and the agent calculates that it will make itself true and he is right. So he has a perfectly rational plan for achieving what he wants, namely success, and he does not have the irrational idea of founding his belief on the situation that exists before its formation. This, therefore, is a rational kind of faith and not the self-deceptive kind. But again, things turn out differently for the second belief, 'I would succeed even if I had no belief in my own success'. For this belief is in the same position as the majority of beliefs: it ought to be founded on independent evidence, which does not include the existence of any degree of belief in success. But, in fact, the independent evidence goes against the belief. It is, therefore, irrationally formed and so it certainly qualifies as the self-deceptive kind of faith.

There is, however, a complication. The point just made, that the agent with the simple belief 'I shall succeed' has a perfectly rational plan, can be put in a different way: 'Truth is not paramount'. For when people say this, they are thinking of truth that already exists independently of any belief in it, and the rational plan of the agent with the simple belief could be formulated like this: 'Independent truth is not paramount and I am going to sacrifice it for something more valuable, namely truth resulting from my belief in it.'

Now the rationality of this plan was the nerve of the argument for not classifying this as a case of self-deception. But it is now becoming clear that there is something to be said on the other side. Perhaps he is deceiving himself in order to attain truth resulting from his belief in it. He, of course, would deny this, on the ground that he did not have the irrational idea of founding his belief on the situation that existed before its formation. But the ordinary function of a belief is to be true and not to make itself true, and to be rational and not to make itself rational. Beliefs are just not made for such heavy work. So though he does not try to found his belief on the situation that exists before its formation, there is a certain strangeness in his not doing so. He is giving his belief a most unusual function. It is like using an announcement of a man's death in *The Times* to kill him, calculating that it will make itself true, because, when he reads it, he will die of shock. There is, therefore, a case for taking the belief in success at its face value and insisting that it really ought to be true and rational independently of its own existence.

If we take this line, we shall have to say that the man's faith is self-deceptive on the ordinary level but rational on a higher level. The point will be that independent truth and the rationality that offers the best chance of attaining it are not paramount. Consequently, it may sometimes be rational to sacrifice them both for some other goal. There is no paradox here, because the rationality that is sacrificed is strictly related to independent truth and the rationality of the sacrifice is more broadly based.

This split-level analysis of rationality is evidently needed in straightforward cases of self-deceptive faith. In such cases the belief obviously has no chance of making itself true, and so there is no need to specify the truth that is sacrificed as 'independent truth'. What happens in such cases is that truth and ordinary rationality are sacrificed for some other good consequence expected from the belief and the word 'faith' merely endorses the correctness of the calculation on which the sacrifice is based.

Although Sartre's treatment of the paradox of self-deception diverts him from the more important underlying paradoxes of irrationality, it does raise an interesting question about the division of a person into different systems.[17] Suppose that the man who believes that the girl loves him says so without any reservations but shows by his behaviour that he really believes the opposite. This is a more extreme case than the original one, because in that case all that was wrong was that his evidence pointed to the negative belief and it was evidence of a kind that he was competent to assess. What is now being added is that his behaviour shows that he really holds the negative belief. It is important that the reason for ascribing the negative belief to him is not that we label his case 'self-deception' and then follow out the implication of the name, but, rather, that what he does gives us good reason to ascribe the negative belief to him in spite of his sincere expression of the positive belief.

Since it is hardly possible for him to accept the conjunction of two contradictory propositions, they must somehow be kept apart in his mind. Freud's theory about the way in which they are kept apart is that the one that gives satisfaction remains in consciousness, while the other one is kept out of consciousness. Sartre's criticism of this is that no such theory can possibly work. His main argument is that the censor, which keeps the unwanted belief out of consciousness, will be conscious of that very belief and so it will have the additional task of keeping it out of its own consciousness; but if that is the mechanism of repression, the problem of self-deception will break out again within the censor, and so on to infinity.

[17] Sartre, *Being and Nothingness*, pp. 52-3.

This is not a convincing argument. The natural objection to it is that the consciousness out of which the censor has to keep the unwanted belief is only the main system of desires and beliefs which runs the daily life of the person. There is no reason why the censor itself should not be conscious of the existence of the unwanted belief in the unconscious. This would be entirely compatible with its consciousness of the existence of the opposite belief in consciousness. In fact, the censor might even share the unwanted belief with the unconscious. Of course, if it did share it, it could not form the opposite belief, but it is no part of Freud's theory that it should form the opposite belief.

If this objection to Sartre's criticism is going to be made good, it will be necessary to distinguish between 'consciousness' as the name of the main system, which controls a person's life, and 'consciousness' as the name of a relation between any system and the elements to which it reacts, even when they belong to a different system within the person. If we want to play with obscurity, we can combine the two uses of the word in a single sentence, 'The unconscious is conscious of a belief that belongs to consciousness.' But we shall then have to explain that this only means that the belief produces an effect in the unconscious, and we shall have to reject the inference that it must, therefore, belong to the unconscious as well as to consciousness.

This last point is crucial. For, if whenever a system reacted to a belief belonging to another system within the person, it followed that it too must contain it, there really would be contradictions of the kind that Sartre thought he saw not only in Freud's theory but also in every other theory that seeks to explain the phenomena by dividing a person into different systems. However, the development of this point will have to wait until more has been said, in the next chapter, about the various strategies of irrational belief-formation.

* * *

This chapter has introduced some of the leading ideas of philosophers about irrationality in thought and action. They approach irrationality in thought through the concept of self-deception, and irrationality in action through the concept of consciously acting against one's own better judgement, and in both cases they move very swiftly towards the limit of the possibilities.

In cases of irrational action it is natural to identify the true agent with his reason, because reason is the best guide within him. The identification seems to imply that, if reason can give no more help when someone acts consciously against his own better judgement, then he himself cannot help it. This conclusion was questioned but left unrefuted.

The Greek concept of *akrasia* was introduced and related both to action against one's own better judgement and to motivated irrational action. '*Akrasia*' means 'lack of control (by reason)' and it is not the same thing as weakness, which, according to Aristotle, is one of its possible causes. Since we are indebted to him for the analysis of the concept of *akrasia*, some of the details of his discussion were examined in depth.

Four cases were considered. The last one, acting consciously and without compulsion against one's own better judgement, may not be possible, but it certainly would be an example both of *akrasia* and of motivated irrationality. In the second case the agent's error started with forgetfulness and in the third one it started with misperception. Neither of these two cases was counted as a case of irrationality, and in both alike the agent never got as far as formulating his better judgement. However, Aristotle did count the third case as *akrasia*, not because he thought that the misperception was motivated, but because reason did not receive enough support from the senses and so was not in control.

In the first case the agent's rebellious desire biased his deliberation so that he concluded that it was all right to indulge it. In this case too he never got as far as formulating his own better judgement, but it was counted as a case of irrationality. It was also argued that Aristotle would have counted it as a case of *akrasia*. But here too his criterion may not have included the fact that the agent's rebellious desire biased something, namely in this case his deliberation, but may simply have been that reason did not get the usual support from deliberation and, consequently, was not in control. In the end some doubts were expressed about this interpretation. Aristotle's views about the irrational conclusion that replaces the rational one in such cases were also interpreted tentatively.

The first question raised about irrational belief-formation was whether the self-contradictoriness of believing the conjunction of two logically incompatible propositions is matched by the self-contradictoriness of acting against one's own better judgement. The question was left unanswered for the time being and the paradox of self-deception was put on stage. If self-deception requires the opposite belief to the one that is irrationally formed, how can it possibly occur?

It was argued that this largely verbal paradox has diverted the attention of philosophers from the more serious problem of the paradox of irrationality: How can anyone form a belief which goes against evidence already in his possession? Cases of this sort of irrationality were arranged on a scale of increasing severity, and the paradox of self-deception was shown to be the limiting case at the top of the scale.

Two questions about self-deception and truth were then raised. Was Sartre right to restrict self-deception to cases in which the original belief is true? And is self-deception always a bad thing?

The answer to the first question was that we may, but need not, require that successful deception should be based on a true belief and so should produce a false belief in the mind of the victim, whether the victim is another person or the deceiver himself.

The answer to the second question was that there are two types of faith. One type is certainly self-deceptive, but the good consequence of the belief may justify the sacrifice of truth and the rationality that offers the best chance of attaining it. In the other type the belief is formed because it will make itself true and its truth is desired. This is a rational plan and, arguably, not self-deceptive. However, there is a case for regarding this type too as self-deceptive. It is the normal function of beliefs to aim at independent truth rather than at truth depending on their own existence. It would, therefore, be possible to argue that, when a belief is formed because it will make itself true, its formation is irrational, and consequently self-deceptive on the ordinary level, in spite of being rational on a higher level.

Finally, Sartre's treatment of the paradox of self-deception was examined. Freud had sought to resolve the paradox by dividing a person into different systems. Sartre's criticism of this kind of theory was rejected and a general condition was laid down for any viable theory of systems: it must be possible for an element to belong to one system within a person and to pass information about itself to another system within him and yet not to belong to that other system.

IV

GOALS AND STRATEGIES OF MOTIVATED IRRATIONAL BELIEF-FORMATION

It is as well not to push an inquiry too quickly towards the limits of the possible, but to spend more time surveying the centre of the field. The ordinary non-controversial possibilities need to be analysed and distinguished from one another. That is just as much the task of philosophy as the more controversial demarcation of the frontier, which is usually begun all too soon. So an attempt will now be made to describe the various goals and strategies of motivated irrational belief-formation and to relate them to one another in a comprehensive classification.

It is, of course, an empirical question which of the possibilities are realized, how often, and in what circumstances. However, since there would be little point in describing abstract possibilities without reference to actual human experience, a minimal answer to the empirical question will be presupposed. There is, after all, little doubt about the existence of certain simple goals and strategies. Uncertainty begins only when more complex possibilities are described, and there is a real question whether they are ever realized, and, naturally, the doubts increase when the questions become more specific. If we want to know how often the various possibilities are realized and in what circumstances, we can no longer rely on anecdotal evidence but must take account of the findings of psychologists.

The suggestion has been made that the truth of our own beliefs is not a paramount goal for us and that in certain cases it may be rational to sacrifice it to some other goal. However, truth always retains some magnetism when a person is forming a belief, and so, if he is pulled in another direction, that will always require an explanation. If the deviation was not caused by incompetence, the culprit must have been either a wish or one of the perversions of reason, and, if it was a wish, either it operated openly as an acknowledged preference for another goal or it operated surreptitiously. In general, there must be some force producing a fault that the person is competent to avoid, because, though the truth of one's own beliefs may be discounted, it is a goal with an attractiveness that cannot fall to zero. If we or our ancestors had not felt its force, we would not be here to discuss the matter.

Incidentally, that produces a striking difference between self-deception and the deception of others. It is possible to deceive someone else for no ulterior motive purely out of devilry, because the desire to impart truth to others is not in-eradicable, whereas the ineradicability of the desire for the truth of one's own beliefs makes it impossible to deceive oneself simply for the sake of deceiving oneself and an ulterior motive is always required.

Is this the case on any level? Don't the most basic but many people prefer to have comfortable beliefs not going too deeply into truth?

That said, an instant qualification is needed. So far, the assumption has been that in self-deception the motivation is always provided by a wish for some desirable goal. But is there always a desirable goal? And is there always a wish for it or are we sometimes merely programmed to go for it?

Consider self-deception caused by fear or jealousy. These emotions often lead people to form intrinsically unpleasant beliefs against the promptings of reason. Now that in itself does not pose any problem, because in self-deceptive *akrasia* we have already found an example of wishful thinking for the sake of an ulterior goal, namely making it easier to yield to a temptation to act against one's own better judgement, and in a case of that kind there might be something that made the belief or its formation intrinsically unwelcome. For example, a politician who was biasing his beliefs publicly in order to make it easier for him to yield to a temptation, might well feel ashamed of the lengths to which he was obliged to go. In the case of fear we may conjecture that the ulterior goal is avoiding the danger, and that it is best achieved by exaggerating it and so making quite sure of taking the necessary steps. Similarly, we may say that the exaggerated speculations of jealousy, which are intrinsically unpleasant, are the best way of making sure of eliminating all rivals. In both cases the belief is a kind of bitter medicine.

So far, so good. We have a goal in each of the two cases and we can explain why the wish goes for the intrinsically unpleasant belief. The strategy is perfectly rational, but, of course, it is not a strategy of the plastic kind that is characteristic of reason. It is a rigid, stereotypical strategy characteristic of emotion.

However, at this point we encounter a difficulty. When fear makes someone run away, it causes him to want to run away, and when anger makes someone hit out, it causes him to want to hit out. But neither fear nor jealousy causes people to want, in the ordinary open way, to form exaggerated beliefs. What, then, is the justification for postulating a wish in these cases?

This is a difficulty for the original thesis, that all self-deception involves a wish. If it does involve a wish in these emotional cases, it is not a wish that is felt by the subject. We would have to postulate that it is kept in the background and operates surreptitiously. This is not altogether implausible in itself, because in clear cases of wishful thinking, though the subject is aware of the wish, he is often unaware of its operation. Also, even in clear cases the wish does not produce a plan, 'Now I must bias the belief.' So there are differences even between ordinary cases of wishful thinking and wishful running away or hitting out.

However, there is something special about the way in which fear and jealousy cause exaggerated beliefs. It is not only that, if a wish really is the culprit, it is never felt as a practical wish, like the wish to hit out or run away, so that it could never serve as a peg on which to hang an ordinary rational plan. That in itself would not place such a very big gulf between these cases of wishful thinking and ordinary cases. But when we add that there is nothing intrinsically attractive about the immediate goal, the formation of the exaggerated belief, it becomes difficult to see any difference between the hypothesis that such exaggerated beliefs are wishful and the hypothesis that in these cases nature has simply programmed us to react in exaggerated stereotypical ways in order to achieve a desirable ulterior goal.

So there is a certain difference between these emotional examples of self-deception and typical examples of motivated irrational belief-formation. In typical examples the wish for the ulterior goal is focused on to the step that has to be taken in order to achieve it, namely the formation of the necessary belief, but this does not happen in fear and jealousy. There is, presumably, a wish for the ulterior goal, safety or the elimination of a rival, but nature takes over at this point and sets up an emotional programme that ensures its achievement. The plan is nature's and not the person's, and that is why the formation of the intrinsically unpleasant belief is not felt to be the object of the wish.

These exceptional cases are important not because they are cases of self-deception without wishful thinking but because they are clear examples of the advantages of automatization. However, if we want to understand the strategies of motivated irrational belief-formation, it is best to start with typical cases. There are several different strategies and they need to be analysed in detail. Each will have a different structure and the criteria for diagnosing one structure rather than another in a particular case will have to be specified. Let us make a fresh start with a new example.

A girl has a lot of evidence that her lover is unfaithful, but she does not believe it. Two possible kinds of explanation each of which might fit this case have been mentioned: she finds it too painful to accept the belief, or she realizes that they ought to break up now but is tempted to continue the relationship and knows that it will be easier for her to do so if she can preserve her belief that he is not having an affair with someone else. The first explanation would make it a case of simple self-deception and the second would make it a case of self-deception in the service of *akrasia*. There is, of course, also a third possibility, that she is simply not competent to assess the evidence against her belief, perhaps because he is too clever a dissimulator.

But how do we know that the true explanation is not something else that was mentioned earlier? May it not be that, though she is competent to assess the evidence, she was led astray by one of the perversions of reason? Perhaps the evidence against his unfaithfulness was more vivid or salient than the evidence for it. That may even have been his doing, because it is common for dissimulators and advertisers to use strategies that exploit human tendencies only recently explored by cognitive psychologists.

Experiments have established not only that these tendencies exist but also that they are extraordinarily prevalent.[1] Just as Freud had shown that many faults attributed to incompetence or chance are really motivated, so too these experiments have identified a further range of faults that neither belong to the province of chance nor are the result of ordinary incompetence. For people make them without the incitement of any wish in areas in which they are quite capable of proceeding correctly and even understand the principles of correct procedure. Of course, we may, if we like, classify them as a special kind of incompetence, but the important point is that they are not the kind of incompetence that we attribute to a person who finds a task beyond him.

Another possible example of a fault caused in this kind of way that was mentioned earlier was hanging on to the first hypothesis that one formulates to account for a phenomenon even when the evidence is piling up against it. That is not a likely explanation of the girl's mistaken belief about her

[1] See R. Nisbett and L. Ross, *Human Inference: Strategies and Shortcomings of Social Judgment*, Ch. 10, and the articles by A. Tversky and D. Kahneman in the early 1970s which were the first to give the hypothesis a firm scientific basis: e.g. '*Subjective Probability*: A Judgment of Representativeness', *Cognitive Psychology* 1971 and 'On the Psychology of Prediction', *Psychological Review* 1973.

lover, because she has too much else at stake. However, there are other bad tendencies that reason exhibits in the construction of theories and one of them might well provide the explanation of this case, namely the habit of attributing a person's behaviour to a particular disposition when its real source is something quite different.

That sounds vague, but it can be made more specific, and, since this is a very important perversion of reason, and it has not yet been introduced, it is worth analysing it in some detail.

The first point that needs establishing is that an agent whose behaviour manifests a disposition acts rationally, because his action conforms to his general preferences and his assessment of the facts. For example, he orders Sauternes, because he likes sweet wine and knows that Sauternes is sweet. That is rational. So when a spectator attributes an agent's behaviour to a disposition, his error may be to attribute rationality where no rationality exists, because in fact the man was distraught and picked a wine off the list at random. That is the first form of the error of attributing a person's behaviour to a particular disposition, when its real source was something quite different.

The error can also take a second form. The spectator may fail to take account of the circumstances of the action and he may choose an obvious disposition to explain it, when really it issued from a less obvious one. For example, the man chose Sauternes not because he liked sweet wine, but because he thought that his guests liked it. In this case too the action is rational, because again it issues from a disposition, but the spectator's mistake is to pick the wrong disposition, an egoistic preference rather than an altruistic deferment to the preferences of others. Cognitive psychologists have labelled the second form of this error 'the Fundamental Attribution Error'.[2] It is, of course, important not to lose sight of the first

    [2] See L. Ross, 'The Intuitive Psychologist and his Shortcomings', in *Advances in Experimental Social Psychology*, ed. L. Berkowitz, vol. 10, New York, 1977, and 'Afterthoughts on the Intuitive Psychologist', in *Cognitive Theories in Social*

form of the error, whether or not it is brought in under this label.

It may be wondered how any of this could be applied to the case of the girl and her lover. In fact, there are two different ways in which it might be relevant. First, she might attribute his solicitude to enduring affection for herself, when in fact it was a pretence adopted by him to conceal the true state of affairs. That would be a straightforward example of the second form of the error. It is in a simple kind of way a very telling example. For he is actually exploiting her tendency to make the second form of the error just as he might have exploited her tendency to be overimpressed by salient evidence. Simulation, like literature, has to be convincing, and so it not only needs to be realistic at the objective level but also needs to allow for the subjective tendencies of the audience at which it is aimed.

The second way in which the girl's case might be explained by these perversions of reason is more interesting and it introduces an important factor that has not yet been mentioned. So far, the assumption has been that we know that she believes that her lover is faithful. But how do we know this? Most probably because she tells us that that is what she believes. But that raises the question how she herself knows. May it not be that she is making the error, in its first form, about herself, and inferring that, because she is continuing the relationship, she must believe that he is faithful, because that is the only way to make sense of her own behaviour and to represent it to herself as rational? Self-attributions of beliefs, attitudes, and even desires may be based on this kind of rationalization more often than is commonly supposed.

There is a striking difference between this error and the previous one. In the previous case the girl made a mistake in interpreting her lover's behaviour, but in this case she would

Psychology, ed. L. Berkowitz, New York, 1978, and L. Ross and C. Anderson, 'Shortcomings in the Attribution Process: On the Origins and Maintenance of Erroneous Social Assessments', in *Judgments under Uncertainty: Heuristics and Biases*, edd. A. Tversky, D. Kahneman, and P. Slovier, New York, 1980.

be making a mistake in interpreting her own behaviour. She
would be attributing to herself a belief that would make it
rational, but one that she did not hold at the time, because
what she actually did was to continue the relationship in spite
of the opposite belief, that he was unfaithful.

Now it might be objected that people cannot really make
mistakes about their own beliefs; they can lie when they
report them, but they cannot make mistakes about them. But
there are two answers to this. First, the essential part of the
girl's mistake would be about her past belief and nobody
doubts the possibility of that kind of mistake. Second, we
have already encountered an example of a mistake made
about something in the person's mind at the time when he
makes it. The man in the earlier story sincerely said that he intended to marry the girl when in fact he did not. It would be
easy to multiply examples of this kind. The controversial
question is not whether such mistakes occur, but to what
extent self-attributions of this kind, correct or mistaken, are
inferential.

Before that question can be tackled, there are two points
about the example that need to be emphasized. First, it is now
being interpreted as an example of rationalization and it is
essential that there should be something for the girl to rationalize. So she must either be promoting the continuation of the
relationship or, at least, she must have formed the intention
to continue it. There is at this point a clear difference between
this kind of case and a case of self-deception in the service of
akrasia. When someone manufactures an irrational belief in
order to facilitate *akrasia*, he obviously needs to manufacture
it at a time when he has not yet acted or even formed an intention. For these are the performances that will constitute
his *akrasia* and they can hardly be facilitated by a piece of
biasing that post-dates them. Conversely, the girl's rationalization can hardly ante-date her performances. This point
about timing is important and more will be said about it later.

The second point that needs to be made about the example
is that it is being taken as a case of cold and impartial ration-

alization, because it is being explained as the result of a perversion of reason. It is easy to miss this point, because people do sometimes rationalize their intentions or actions out of self-respect. They do not like the idea of being irrational, or perhaps what they do not like is being judged irrational and they are driven by shame rather than by guilt. Indeed, this would be a possible explanation of the girl's rationalization. However, the present assumption is that her rationalization is not powered by any personal motive, because with complete impartiality she rationalizes other people's behaviour in exactly the same way. Her error is produced by a perversion of reason.

The controversial question can now be taken up. To what extent are self-attributions of this kind inferential? The alternative would be to say that people are able to make them because beliefs, intentions, and suchlike register themselves directly in their possessors' minds. Or it might be reasonable to compromise between the two accounts and to say that direct registration and inference both play a part.

In the earlier analysis of self-deception about such matters the argument was that it does not count as irrationality, because the correct information has never been recorded in the mind of the self-deceiver. That would be a completely convincing argument, if such self-attributions were entirely based on direct registration rather than on rationalization of behaviour, and if direct registration could not be construed as inferential. The argument would have to be modified if the first of these two conditions were not met, and abandoned if the second one were not met. For if self-attributions of this kind were to some extent based on rationalizations, self-deceptive cases would to that extent count as examples of irrationality, and if even direct registration were in some way inferential, they would always count as examples of irrationality.

Philosophers who have been influenced by Wittgenstein attach great weight to the direct registration of beliefs, intentions, and suchlike, and they sometimes suggest that it is incorrigible.[3] That must be an exaggeration, because, when this kind of record is checked against behavioural evidence, it may be rejected not only by others but also by the person himself. Cognitive psychologists who are influenced by the ideas of Attribution Theory sometimes go to the other extreme and claim that inference is the only basis of such self-attributions.[4] That cannot be so. Their claim is partly the result of a misunderstanding: they suppose that the record of a belief is a datum from which the belief is inferred whereas in fact it is the internal expression of the belief. But it is also a great exaggeration of the extent to which a person has to wait and see what he does in order to find out what he intends or believes.

Fortunately, there is no need to choose between these two extremes. We can recognize the great importance of the immediate self-monitoring of beliefs and intentions and we can explain why knowledge acquired in this way is not inferential. At the same time we can allow that this source is not always reliable and that the subject himself can appeal against it successfully to the behavioural evidence that is available to spectators too. However, the earlier classification of self-deception in this area does now need some qualification. When people base such self-attributions on behavioural evidence, their self-deception, if they do deceive themselves, does to that extent count as irrationality.

The point of bringing these perversions of reason into an investigation of motivated irrationality is that they provide a powerful alternative explanation. Their remarkable prevalence has altered, or should alter our view of the operations of reason. However, we do not have to confront the phenomena with the determination not to identify the culprit as a wish until we have tried out all the possible cold explanations. All that is necessary is that we should be on guard against the

---

[3] See, e.g., N. Malcolm, *Problems of Mind*, New York, 1971.
[4] R. Nisbett and L. Ross go a long way in this direction and may even go all the way. See *Human Inference: Strategies and Shortcomings of Social Judgment*, p. 203.

dogmatic neo-Freudian assumption that the culprit must be a wish.

Let us suppose now that the effect in the case of the girl really is produced by a wish and let us focus on the various possibilities on the hot side of the matter. It has just been observed that, if the wish biases her belief in order to facilitate *akrasia*, it must do so before the action is done and even before any intention is formed.[5] So much is obvious. What is not so obvious is how much biasing is needed. Can the vague thesis, that enough is needed to make it easier to yield to temptation, be made more precise?

We have been supposing, admittedly a little unrealistically, that the only reason why the girl wishes to believe that her lover is faithful is that that will make it easy for her to yield to the temptation to continue the relationship, which she would otherwise judge it better to terminate. Since it is hardly likely that that would be her only reason for wanting to believe that he is faithful, let us say that it is her main reason. Now, from the point of view of the temptation, her judgement, that it would be better to break off the relationship, appears as a barrier that needs to be lowered. So the question is whether there is any way of quantifying the amount by which it needs to be lowered.

In this particular example, the barrier in the way of *akrasia* is lowered by a single, ungraduated move: instead of believing her lover to be unfaithful and, therefore, judging it better to break off the relationship, she believes him to be faithful and, therefore, judges it all right to continue it. It would be possible to introduce degrees of unfaithfulness at this point, but it is better to switch to a parallel example in which there is a more realistic way of quantifying the amount by which the barrier needs to be lowered.

---

[5] This possibility is mentioned by E. Aronson, 'Dissonance Theory', in *Current Perspectives in Social Psychology*, edd. E. P. Hollander and R. G. Hunt, Oxford, 1976, p. 321, but without any discussion of the details of the conflict, because his main interest is in rationalization after the action.

Some students of social psychology are asked to tell a lie to their class-mates. The lie is said to be a necessary part of an experiment and they are offered a small payment for taking part in it. The payment to a particular student can be increased to the point at which he tells the lie and the sufficient sum of money will then provide a measure of the amount by which the barrier needed to be lowered in his case. Naturally, it is not supposed that everybody has his price for lying, but the measure will work for those who can be bought. The assumption is that they are all, in general, opposed to lying and that is why what the money measures is the amount by which the barrier standing in the way of *akrasia* needs to be lowered.

As a matter of fact, a famous experiment was once carried out along somewhat similar lines.[6] The students were not tested individually to discover the smallest payment for which each would tell the lie, if he had a price for telling it. There was no auction of immorality, but, instead, they were divided into two groups, one of which was offered a larger payment for telling the lie than the other. Since not all the students in each group then told the lie, the experiment up to this point would only reveal that some could be bought for the lower price and some for the higher price, but it would not reveal whether either could have been bought more cheaply.

However, in fact, the experiment went further than this. For it was designed to discover whether those who told the lie felt cognitive dissonance after they had told it. Now cognitive dissonance is, roughly, what people feel when they encounter two things that they find hard to accept together. So the question was whether the liars found that their lie did not square with their earlier beliefs and the idea was that this would be revealed by their later reactions. If they rationalized the lie by altering their beliefs about it and then back-dating their altered beliefs to the moment when they told it, they would be

[6] See L. Festinger and J. Carlsmith, 'Cognitive Consequences of Forced Compliance', *Journal of Abnormal Social Psychology* 1959.

trying to reduce the cognitive dissonance that they felt in retrospect.

The result was interesting. Those who were paid the smaller sum of money tended to whitewash their lie more and those who were paid the larger sum of money tended to whitewash it less. The whitewashing took the form of describing the lie and its circumstances in a way that made it appear less serious. The liars were not actually asked what they thought about the lie before they told it, but their earlier attitudes and beliefs were reconstructed from those of a control group who did not take part in the experiment.

The experiment was difficult to evaluate because it contained too many variables, but, precisely for that reason, it gives us a commanding view of the wide range of possible explanations. One of the possibilities on the hot side is that the students altered their. beliefs about the lie before they told it and even before they decided to tell it. That would make it a case of irrational belief-formation in the service of *akrasia*, and so it would be structurally similar to the case of the girl, if she persuaded herself that her lover was faithful to her in order to make it easier for her to continue the relationship against her own better judgement, or, rather, against what would have been her better judgement.

Interpreted in this way, the experiment would have a distinct advantage over the case of the girl. For it would allow us to measure the amount by which the barrier standing in the way of *akrasia* needed to be lowered. When the payment was smaller, the barrier started off higher, and needed to be lowered further and so more whitewashing of the lie was required; but when the payment was larger, the barrier started off lower, and so it did not need to be lowered so far by whitewashing the lie.

Another hot possibility is that the students told the lie against their own unbiased better judgement, and the alteration in their beliefs did not occur until after they had told it. This might be explained in several different ways. The obvious explanation would be that they could not live with the belief that they had done something wrong. This would make the case quite like that of the girl, if she persuaded herself that her lover was faithful simply because she could not live with the opposite belief.[7] However, there would be a certain structural difference between the two cases: in the experiment the intolerable belief would be about the students' own actions, but this would not be the case with the girl. However, this difference would be removed if we supposed that she continued the relationship against her own better judgement and then found it necessary to alter her belief about her lover, because she could not live with the belief that she had done something so imprudent. Even this is not quite the same, because continuing a relationship is an action that goes on over a long period of time, unlike the kind of lie that the students told.

It is important to notice that there are two different beliefs that an agent may form after his action. He may simply change his mind about the precise nature of his action and hence about the wrongness of it. That is the minimum amount of whitewashing that had to be done by the students who had told the lie. But there is also the possibility, already mentioned, that they went further and claimed that they had actually held the changed belief before they told the lie. That would be an example of mistaken rationalization, and since we are now looking at the hot side of things, we may suppose that the wish that powered it was the wish to be rational, which, by the usual short circuit described so well by Freud, directly produced the belief that they had been rational, when in fact they had not.

There are two complications at this point. Since their actions would have been rational only if they had held the changed belief before acting, the belief produced by the wish was a false belief about a belief. Second, this point really needs to be put more accurately. Strictly speaking, it was only

---

[7] Both would then be cases of 'sweet lemons', the name given by cognitive psychologists to the kind of wishful rationalization that is the opposite of 'sour grapes'.

a necessary condition of their acting rationally that they should have held the changed belief before acting, but not a sufficient condition. For if they had held it then, although it would have made sense of their action, it would have been formed irrationally in the service of *akrasia*. So this piece of rationalization would really only be a self-attribution of partial rationality. But, of course, to the students themselves it would seem to be a self-attribution of complete rationality.

At this point it is necessary to take a closer look at Attribution Theory, and so what follows will be another digression into the territory of cold cases. The possibility has been mentioned that the girl might rationalize her continuation of the relationship not from any hot, personal motive, but coldly and impartially. That is a real possibility and it is the one that is emphasized by Attribution Theorists.[8]

Let us see how it would be realized in the case of the students. There are really two different errors that they might make. They might assume that they had acted rationally when they told the lie, whereas in fact they had acted irrationally. That would be the first form of the error described earlier. Alternatively, they might attribute their action to an obvious disposition, whereas in fact it was attributable to another, less obvious disposition. That would be the second form of the error described earlier, the one labelled 'The Fundamental Attribution Error'. Each of the two errors would have to be a cold one that they would be just as likely to make if they were trying to interpret other people's behaviour rather than their own.

The first of these two errors is easy to understand, if conscious last-ditch *akrasia* is a real possibility. The students would tell the lie consciously and without compulsion against their own better judgement and then later they would rationalize what they had done by minimizing its seriousness and

---

[8] This interpretation was applied to the behaviour of the students in the experiment by D. Bem, 'Self-perception: An Alternative Interpretation of Cognitive Dissonance Phenomena', *Psychological Review* 1967.

attributing it to the disposition to tell trivial lies for financial gain.

The second of the two errors is less easy to understand, but it is the one that Attribution Theorists pin on the students.[9] In order to understand it, we need to identify another variable in the experiment. When a professor asks students in his class to take part in an experiment, they are under some pressure to comply. It is, therefore, entirely possible that the disposition that produced the lies was simply the disposition to co-operate in such a situation. Now that would not be an obvious disposition, because it would be triggered by the background of the drama rather than by any of the salient events that began to develop against that background. It was, therefore, easy for the students to pass over that disposition when they asked themselves afterwards why they had told the lie, and natural for them to go straight for a disposition triggered by some striking event in the classroom. One obvious candidate would be the disposition to do something for the reward that was so surprisingly offered.

However, the reward would not seem to them to be quite enough to explain a lie to their class-mates, especially when it was the smaller of the two payments. So they would attribute to themselves the belief that the lie was not such a serious one, projecting the whitewash into the past in the way already explained. They would also use more whitewash when the payment was small than when it was large. However, according to Attribution Theory, all this would be done coldly and impartially. There would be no personal motivation and, if they had been spectators interpreting the behaviour of other students, they would have made the same attributions.[10]

This interpretation of the students' rationalization of their lies has received strong support from experiments.[11] How-

<hr />

[9] See H. Kelley, 'Attribution Theory in Social Psychology', in *Nebraska Symposium on Motivation*, ed. D. Levine, vol. 15, Lincoln, 1967.

[10] H. Kelley, loc. cit.

[11] See R. Nisbett and L. Ross, *Human Inference: Strategies and Shortcomings of Social Judgment*, pp. 120-2 and pp. 199-207.

ever, it would be naïve to infer that it completely supersedes all hot explanations of such phenomena. For one thing, that would presuppose that the irrationality always occurs after the action when it manifests itself in the agent's biased belief about his earlier view of the rightness or wrongness of what he did. But that is obviously not so. It is a common human experience, presumably confirmable by experiment, that the irrationality often occurs before the action, when it manifests itself in the agent's biased view of the rightness or wrongness of what he is still contemplating doing. The timing of the biasing in self-deceptive *akrasia* is critical.

It is tempting to reinforce this argument by claiming that there is a second type of case which must be given a hot interpretation. There is a well-established phenomenon that cognitive psychologists call 'spreading'.[12] Someone who has made a difficult decision is likely to feel uncomfortable about it, because it was too close-run an event, and so he will tend to exaggerate the considerations that favoured it and to minimize the considerations that went against it. This spreading is a type of rationalization and the usual explanation of it is that it is reassuring because it makes it seem more certain that the decision was not mistaken. Britain's decision to enter the Common Market produced many examples.

On the other hand, it must be admitted that it is possible that spreading is an example of cold rationalization, because it may also occur when someone else's difficult decision is being explained. If it does occur in such cases it only manifests a preference for explanations of actions that are obviously self-sufficient and complete.

However, spreading certainly also occurs before decisions which in the nature of the case are likely to be close-run events, and then its function must be to make the decision easier. These cases are very like irrational belief-formation in the service of *akrasia* and they cannot be given a cold interpretation. The certainty, that these two types of irrationality

12 See E. Aronson, *The Social Animal*, San Francisco, 1972, pp. 111-24.

are not cold, is important, because it puts the existence of some hot cases beyond any doubt. This is, perhaps, clearest in self-deceptive *akrasia*. For though an agent under temptation may be influenced by his idea of his own future state of mind if he succumbs (a useful argument for moralists), he can hardly engage in advance in cold, impersonal rationalization of a prospective action which he has not even made up his mind to perform.

Once the existence of these hot cases has been accepted, it is implausible to maintain that after the action there is never any heat in the rationalization. It would be difficult to believe that, if the girl continued the relationship and rewrote the history of her recent past, she could not be motivated by the wish to have done the right thing or by the wish to have acted rationally. The furthest that it would be plausible to go in that direction would be to claim that hot motivation always needs the support of cold tendencies,[13] but even that seems to be an underestimation of the power of wishes.

In cases like that of the students, cognitive psychologists usually describe what occurs after the action as 'change of attitude'. Strictly speaking, what occurred in that case was a change in factual belief, which produced a change in attitude towards the particular lie, but not, of course, towards lying in general. For what they said to themselves afterwards was that there were mitigating circumstances, and, therefore, the lie was not a serious one. Nor was that all that happened. They also backdated their new factual belief and attributed it to themselves at the moment of lying. So there was a new belief about the circumstances of the lie accompanied by a belief about that belief, and a new attitude to the particular lie accompanied by a belief about that attitude.

That raises an interesting question about the connection between holding a particular belief or attitude and believing that one holds it. It is evident that the two things are very

---

[13] This is the view taken by R. Nisbett and L. Ross, *Human Inference: Strategies and Shortcomings of Social Judgments*, p. 228.

closely connected. But how closely? Attribution Theorists must be right in thinking that a belief need not monitor itself correctly and that the person who holds it may come to believe that he holds it by an inference from his own behaviour. It certainly will not follow that he does hold it, because the inference may easily be mistaken, especially when it is about his past. However, it can happen that, as soon as he draws the conclusion about his past, it automatically makes itself true in the present and future. So, the belief that one holds a belief functions in a different way from the belief that one has a duodenal ulcer. Ulcers do not monitor themselves accurately, and so a person's belief that he has one is less likely to make itself true in the present and future than his belief that he holds a particular belief, and, when it does make itself true, it does so mainly by an entirely different mechanism, namely anxiety.

It is worth looking more closely at the mechanism by which the belief that one holds a belief or attitude makes itself true. It seems to work in the following way. Because beliefs normally monitor themselves accurately, it is an almost irresistible assumption that, if one believes that one holds a belief, that must be because one really does hold it and it is monitoring itself in the usual way. We tend to hang on to this assumption even when the self-ascription of a belief is mainly or entirely inferential, unless, of course, we are absolutely clear that we are using an inference. The next thing that happens is that we rationalize the assumption that the belief is monitoring itself in the usual way by actually acquiring the belief. This objective rationalization is possible only when the rationalizing object is in the mind. The operation of a somewhat similar mechanism is familiar in sense-perception: people often think that they can see something that is not there for them to see, because they have inferred that it must be there, and then in a certain sense they really do 'see' it.

Let us now return to the hot side of things and enquire what the most common strategies of self-deception are. One of them is to act as if the desired belief were true. That tends to generate the belief by a rather complex causal linkage which includes the mechanism that has just been described. There is no paradox in the fact that a mechanism that occurs in cold cases can be exploited in hot cases, but the process is complex and it does need to be analysed.

It is normal for belief to lead to action, but it is possible for action to lead to belief. The man who orders Sauternes does so because he wants sweet wine and believes Sauternes to be sweet, but if he made a slight mistake and ordered a wine that was *demi-sec*, he would be likely to believe it to be sweeter than he would otherwise have believed such a wine to be. He might even find it sweeter when he tasted it, but that would be a case of misperception rather than self-deception. Now there are limits to rationalization and it would be unlikely to occur if he made a big mistake and ordered a very dry wine. However, the limits are greatly extended in matters that require a subjective judgement, and especially in personal relations and in the whole field of self-knowledge. It is the familiarity of this kind of rationalization that makes it possible for people to exploit it in their own cases by acting in order to generate the belief that would normally support the action.

There are two distinguishable stages in this strategy. First, the self-deceiver acts and by acting makes himself believe that he had the belief that would have justified the action. Next, by the mechanism already described, the justifying belief becomes a permanent feature of his life. Both stages are rationalizations. The self-deception will then reinforce itself in those common cases in which a later admission of the falsehood of the justifying belief would be more painful the longer the self-deception had continued.

This strategy of self-deception reverses the usual order of things, because the person acts in order to produce the belief that would normally support the action. So he is really using the double linkage of rationalization in exactly the same way that he would use any ordinary causal linkage in the external world. That is why there is no paradox in the fact that a mechanism that occurs in cold cases can be exploited in these hot cases. The mechanism is familiar in cold cases and then it is put to work in hot cases in the service of the wish to believe.

It is often difficult to tell when this strategy is being used or, more generally, to apply the distinctions that have been drawn between the different motives for self-deception. The first distinction drawn was between cases in which the self-deceiver's goal is simply to eliminate an uncomfortable belief and cases in which his goal is to make it easier to give in to a temptation by eliminating a belief that stands in the way. It is not always possible to assign a particular case to one type or the other, because the two goals can be combined. In fact, that is the most likely explanation of the case of the girl who persuaded herself that her lover was faithful. She wanted to continue a role and the belief was part of the role as well as a way of facilitating the other, practical part of it. Even if in fact her only goal had been the elimination of the intolerable belief, that he was unfaithful, it might not be easy to tell that that was so. For she might be using the strategy of continuing to act as if she believed him to be faithful in the hope that that would generate or fortify the belief, and in that case it would be hard to tell whether the belief was her only goal and the action merely a means to it, or the action itself was another, independent goal. The analytical treatment of hot cases in no way implies that these mixtures are uncommon or that the different types of case are easy to tell apart.

Acting as if something were so in order to generate the belief that it is so is not the only strategy of self-deception. It also has two others. It operates directly on the contents of the mind and it controls what gets into the mind. So the points at which self-deception conducts its operations can be used to set up an exhaustive classification of its strategies. Either it filters input into the mind, or it biases the processing of what is already in the mind, or there is the strategy that has just been examined, operating through output.

When the processing of information already in the mind is biased, there is seldom anything that the self-deceiver does in

order to bias it. Sometimes, no doubt, he will avoid working out the implications of a belief, but usually the biasing is
the direct effect of the wish and there is nothing that could
be regarded as a plan. Freud gives a good description of
what happens in cases of this kind: the normal sequence of
achievement, belief in achievement, and satisfaction is short-
circuited. But, of course, telling someone that is not the same
thing as telling him how to do it. If a person cannot move his
ears, there is nothing for his will to latch on to and it is the
same here. The description of a successful piece of wishful
thinking is not a piece of practical instruction.

True, there are some positive things that a would-be self-
deceiver might think of doing in order to make it easier for
him to bias the processing of information in his mind. He is
not restricted to avoiding working out the implications of his
beliefs. He can also use alcohol or drugs. However, these do
not count as methods of self-deception, because using them
on someone else would not count as deceiving him.

There is at this point a fairly clear contrast with the other
two strategies of self-deception. The first one was filtering input into one's own mind. Depriving another person of relevant evidence is sometimes a way of deceiving him, and so it
is not surprising that controlling the input of information
into one's own mind counts as self-deception. It may seem
questionable whether the third strategy, acting as if the
desired belief were true, ought to count as self-deception,
because there is no exactly parallel way of deceiving another
person. For when someone acts as if the belief that he wants
to install in another person's mind were true, it is the action
of the deceiver and not of his victim that is rationalized. The
deceiver can hardly perform his victim's action for him.
Perhaps the closest approximation to deceiving someone else
in this way would be to hypnotize him and suggest that he do
the action that would then be rationalized by the belief that
we want to implant in him. However, the parallelism does not
really have to be so exact in order to justify the classification
of the third strategy as a method of self-deception.

The fact that there is no positive method of biasing the processing of information in one's own mind is really very striking. A person's beliefs adjust themselves directly to his evidence and a wish cannot simply stand between his evidence and his beliefs like a policeman directing traffic. This is not just because a wish cannot interfere openly. It is also because the process that the wish has to influence presents a smooth, unanalysable surface. There are no interstices and nothing to catch hold of. If someone said 'I want to believe this and so I shall believe it', he would be understood to be making a prediction about himself, rather than announcing a plan. If we are going to identify and ascribe a strategy in cases of this kind, we shall have to ascribe it to a sub-system within the person. Such a sub-system would confront the rest of the person in something like the way in which the whole person confronts another person. It might even notice the weaknesses in the rest of the person and devise strategies to exploit them. This is an important possibility, and it will be the topic of the next chapter.

The first strategy of self-deception does not let things get so far as the other two. It filters input into the mind by avoiding looking for evidence where it seems likely that it will go against the favoured belief and by looking only where it seems likely that the evidence will support it. If there is any paradox in self-deception when it is done in this way, it will be the paradox of irrational action, because it is a kind of *akrasia* to avoid maximizing relevant evidence and to go for unfair samples.

* * *

In this chapter the various possible goals and strategies of motivated irrational belief-formation have been related to one another and classified. Any useful classification of the possibilities must be applicable to the known facts and in this case the facts are common knowledge supplemented by the often surprising findings of cognitive psychologists.

Although truth is not a paramount goal for us when we are forming beliefs, it always has some magnetism and so, when it is defeated, its defeat always requires an explanation. The explanation may simply be incompetence, or perhaps some other goal was preferred either openly or surreptitiously. There is also the important third possibility that truth and the rationality that offers the best chance of attaining it have been defeated by one of the perversions of reason. Several of these perversions were mentioned and illustrated by an ordinary example. One was the tendency to attach undue weight to salient evidence; another was the tendency to assume that a person's actions always issue from his dispositions in a rational way; and a third was the tendency to select the most obvious disposition to explain a person's actions.

Attribution Theorists have established by experiment that the last two tendencies distort our interpretations not only of other people's behaviour, but also of our own. However, it would be a mistake to suppose that self-attributions of beliefs and attitudes are entirely based on inferences from behaviour. The immediate records that beliefs and attitudes produce in our minds are almost always available and, in general, indispensable.

The prevalence of the perversions of reason is important and, when a case of irrational belief-formation is being examined, it is always a real possibility that one of them is the culprit. Consequently, when incompetence has been ruled out, we should never jump to the neo-Freudian conclusion, that the culprit must be a wish.

One of the two types of hot case, self-deception in the service of *akrasia*, was then examined in detail. In an example of this kind the biasing of the belief must occur before the action and even before the formation of the intention. This point about timing is crucial.

The question raised next was 'How much biasing is needed?' The answer was sought in the result of an experiment in which a professor asked some of his students to tell a lie to their class-mates and offered them money for telling it. If they biased their beliefs about the seriousness of the lie before telling it, their lying was an example of self-deceptive *akrasia*. The barrier standing in the way of the lie was lowered partly by the payment and partly by their biasing of their own beliefs. Consequently, a smaller payment led to greater biasing and *vice versa*.

If, on the other hand, the biasing occurred after the lying, it was an example of rationalization, hot or cold. If it was a hot case, the lie was being whitewashed. At the very least, the students found that they needed to believe afterwards that it was not wrong. But if they wanted to claim any degree of rationality at the time of the action, they would have to back-date their new belief.

If the rationalization was cold, the case was interpretable in the way in which Attribution Theorists interpret it. Either they told the lie consciously and without compulsion against their own better judgement and then made the mistaken assumption that their action had issued rationally from a disposition: or else they made the mistake of choosing the obvious disposition, to work for a reward, instead of the real culprit, which was the less obvious disposition to comply with their professor's requests.

Next it was argued that the common human experience of self-deceptive *akrasia* is important, because it establishes beyond any doubt that there are hot cases of irrational belief-formation with the structure that was set up in the experiment on the students. For cases with this structure could be cold only if the biasing occurred after the action. This argument was then extended to 'spreading' when it occurs before the action and makes the decision in an evenly-balanced predicament easier. The mechanism of rationalization was then examined and an answer suggested to the question, why the inferential belief that one holds a belief should lead one to form the latter belief.

Finally, three different strategies of self-deception were distinguished and analysed. The first was the strategy of controlling the input of information into the mind. The second was to bias the processing of information already in the mind. The third was to act as if the desired belief was true. The third strategy exploits the mechanism of cold rationalization, which occupies the central position in Attribution Theory.

V

PARADOXES AND SYSTEMS

The problem of the paradoxes was postponed for later treatment and it must now be confronted. The difficulty lies in the various forms of the paradox of irrationality and not in the paradox of self-deception. Even if we did not have a word like 'self-deception', with an apparently over-demanding connotation, we would still have to deal with the problem posed by its actual denotation. What happens in cases denoted by it is, at the very least, that the self-deceiver forms a belief unsupported by his evidence under the influence of a wish. Often he does something worse: he forms a belief in the teeth of evidence that gives inductive support to another, incompatible belief. Or, worse still, his belief is logically or mathematically incompatible with information possessed by him when he forms it and perhaps even used by him as its basis. The limiting case on this scale, set up in Chapter III, is believing the conjunction of two logically incompatible propositions, which is what is required by the connotation of the word 'self-deception', if it is taken quite literally.

Here, on the threshold of the problem, we encounter a variable. There are different degrees of irrationality exhibited on the scale and we may wonder which, if any of them, require us to adopt the apparently drastic hypothesis that a person really consists of two separate systems. One would be the main system, which controls his daily life and includes the favoured but irrational belief and the information that makes it irrational; and the other would be a sub-system, which includes the cautionary belief, that, given his information, it was irrational to form the favoured belief. The point of the hypothesis is that the cautionary belief would have prevented the formation of the irrational belief if only it too had belonged to the main system, but, unfortunately, it could not intervene, because it was confined to the sub-system. But is this hypothesis really needed to explain all the degrees of irrationality on the scale, even the minor ones? Perhaps it is not needed at the bottom of the scale, where it may be enough to observe that it is a common human failing to form beliefs unsupported by the evidence. Schisms within a person do not seem to be as common as that. It is only further up the scale, where the irrationality is more extreme, that it becomes impossible to explain it in this facile way and so, perhaps, necessary to suppose that there are two independent systems operating within a single person.

Now a person divided into two systems is in some way like two people. But in what way? That depends on the kind of division that is postulated, and there is more than one way in which the line between the two systems can be drawn. So here we have a second variable, in the solution to the problem rather than in the problem itself. This variable too has to be given a precise value. It is no good suggesting that a person is divided into two different systems unless the principle of division is definite and clear. One possibility, a very natural one, is to follow Freud and let the main system include everything accessible to the person's consciousness, while the sub-system includes everything else that is needed to explain his speech and behaviour.[1] _unconscious_

Another option would be to draw the line between main system and sub-system in a way that reflected the interaction between the attitudes, desires, and beliefs of a person rather than his consciousness of them.[2] If, for example, his belief, that it would be irrational to indulge in a particular piece of wishful thinking, did not intervene in the main system and prevent him from indulging in it, then that belief would be

[1] In *The Psychopathology of Everyday Life* Freud uses this theory to explain a wide range of errors in thought, speech, and action, many of which are examples of motivated irrationality.

[2] D. Davidson takes this line in 'Paradoxes of Irrationality' in *Philosophical Essays on Freud*, edd. R. Wollheim and J. Hopkins, Cambridge, 1982.

assigned to a sub-system, even if he were conscious of it. When the line between the two systems is drawn in this way, the result is a functional theory, because it is the actual functioning of the belief that decides on which side of the line it should be placed.[3] The belief is cautionary and its proper function is to intervene and stop the irrationality, but what it actually does is to sit on the sideline and let it happen. This way of assigning elements to systems is quite different from Freud's way. It would be like judging a person's citizenship by the country in which he operates rather than by the country in which his existence has been registered.

There is nothing unusual about having a variable in the solution to the problem of irrationality. It merely shows that more than one theory can be expressed in the words, 'This person is divided into two different systems'. Such ambiguities are common and their resolution produces two or more distinct theories, which can then be put into competition against one another, in order to discover which gives the best explanation of the phenomena.

However, it really is difficult to manage a variable in the problem itself. The solution has to fit the problem and, if the problem is indeterminate, the fit is going to be hard to achieve. A person buying shoes needs to have a definite opinion about the size of his foot and it is much the same here. It really does seem to be necessary to make certain of the magnitude of the problem before trying to solve it. So we may feel that we ought to begin by trying to find out which of the degrees of irrationality on the scale are impossible without a schism within the person.

But, unfortunately, that is not a firm or neutral starting-point, because it is uncertain what counts as a schism. If we adopt the functional theory, we shall say that there is a schism whenever there is irrationality that the person is competent to avoid, even if it is a low degree of irrationality. For if someone

---

[3] The reason for calling this theory 'functional' is not the usual one, namely that the function of a belief makes it the belief that it is, but, rather, that its function governs its assignment to a system within the person.

is competent to avoid a piece of irrationality, the relevant cautionary belief will be somewhere within him, and, if it does not intervene and stop the irrationality, it will be assigned to a sub-system automatically by the functional criterion. So the thesis, that no degree of avoidable irrationality is possible without a schism, will be true by the definition of the word 'schism'.

On the other hand, if we adopt the Freudian view of schisms, that they divide what is conscious from what is kept out of consciousness, we shall avoid that kind of circularity only to run into a different difficulty. The circularity will be avoided because we shall have an independent criterion for assigning elements to a sub-system. The new difficulty will be that it is only the most extreme degree of irrationality that seems to be impossible without this kind of schism. Consequently, if we confine the inquiry to degrees of irrationality that are impossible without a Freudian schism, we shall be confining it to a very small corner of the field.

It would be prudent to cast the net more widely and to bring the maximum variety of cases of irrationality within the scope of the inquiry, even those that generate the mildest form of the paradox. It is always risky to give in to the temptation, so strong in philosophy, to focus exclusively on the extreme cases. When the two theories of systems are tested on the whole range of the phenomena, it may well turn out that we do not have to make an exclusive choice between them. At least, we ought not to start with the prejudice that they must be incompatible rivals. They certainly seem to have very different structures and it may be that each applies in its own way to a different part of the field and the two parts may even overlap.

At first people find it hard to think of a better explanation of irrationality than Freud's, because his idea dominates the scene and prevents them from seeing past it to other possibilities. If someone forms a very irrational belief, it seems obvious that he cannot consciously believe that it is very irrational, and, if it is only mildly irrational, it is still likely that the conscious belief, that it is mildly irrational, will undermine it. A belief is likely to be undermined even by the less damaging fact, that it is caused by a wish, unless that fact is kept out of consciousness. Of course, the subject need not be unconscious of the existence of the wish and its supposed fulfilment may well make him happy, but the causation of the belief is something that really is better kept out of his consciousness.[4] The Freudian explanation seems sufficiently versatile to deal with all the phenomena. What more could we ask for?

One modification, which certainly must be demanded, has already been discussed. Freud thought that everything in a person's consciousness proceeds rationally within the limits of his competence, unless it is disturbed by a wish. That has been shown to be mistaken, because there is also another source of disturbance, the perversions of reason. Let us, therefore, modify Freud's claim and say that, whenever reason goes off the rails and the derailment is not attributable to incompetence, the culprit will be either a wish or a perversion of reason. This is a theory about the productive causes of irrationality. It may be called 'the mixed theory' because it includes both types of productive cause and it is certainly an improvement on Freud's hot theory.

It is worth observing that Freud's theory of systems is primarily concerned with the permissive cause of irrationality. It tries to identify the thing that allows irrationality to occur, and the suggestion is that its permissive cause is some failure of consciousness. Now the task of identifying the permissive cause of irrationality is quite different from the task of identifying its productive cause. Freud could have been right in thinking that its permissive cause is always a failure of consciousness in spite of being wrong in thinking that its productive cause is always a wish.

---

[4] Freud distinguishes between cases in which both the existence and the operation of the wish are kept out of consciousness and cases in which only its operation is kept out of consciousness. See *Introductory Lectures on Psycho-Analysis*, tr. J. Rivière, London, 1922, pp. 50-1 and 182-3.

The next question to ask is whether Freud's theory of systems succeeds in identifying the permissive cause of the two types of irrationality covered by the mixed theory. Evidently, this is a double-barrelled question. The explanation might be more successful with one of the two types than with the other. It might, for example, explain the possibility of irrationality produced by the perversions of reason more successfully than the possibility of irrationality produced by wishes. Anyway, the two types of case have to be examined separately.

Freud's theory of systems derives its explanatory power from a plausible principle: If a person consciously believed that the belief that he was forming was irrational, that would prevent him from forming it, whereas, if the same cautionary belief were not conscious, it would not prevent him from forming it. Actually, it is a bit more complicated than this, because the belief that a belief is caused by a wish, or by a perversion of reason, also has an inhibiting tendency and it would have to be treated in the same way.

However, the essence of the principle is simple. It has two parts, one concerned with the non-permissiveness of a conscious cautionary belief and the other concerned with the permissiveness of an unconscious cautionary belief. It is as if the cautionary belief were a policeman, obstructive when on duty but permissive when off duty. Of course, the presence of the cautionary belief somewhere within the person follows from the assumption that he is competent to avoid the particular piece of irrationality, but the question is, where, exactly, within him it ought to be placed.

The next thing that needs to be done is to explore the differences between Freud's theory about the productive cause of irrationality and the mixed theory. The basic difference is that the mixed theory adds the perversions of reason to the wishes that Freud took to be the only productive causes of avoidable irrationality. Consequently, when Freud's theory of systems is combined with the mixed theory, it has two different processes to explain by finding their permissive causes, the biasing effect of wishes and the biasing effect of the perversions of reason. So much is obvious.

What is, perhaps, less obvious is the effect of the difference between the two types of biasing covered by the mixed theory. Suppose that two people form a belief that is mildly irrational and recognized as such by both of them, and suppose that one of them forms it wishfully while the other forms it as the result of one of the perversions of reason. Each will be worried not only by the irrationality of his belief but also by the unreliability of its causation. However, a mildly irrational belief might still turn out to be true by a piece of luck. Also, though the perversions of reason are bad guides, it could happen coincidentally that, for example, a salient but weak piece of evidence did point to the true conclusion. Similarly, a desired belief might just happen to be true. Suppose that the two people are aware of all this. Then there is likely to be a difference between what happens next in the two cases. If the operation of the perversion of reason is detected and its result is recognized as irrational, it will be likely to collapse completely, but if the operation of the wish is detected and its result is recognized as irrational, it may still retain some of its power to fascinate and delude. This difference will turn out to be important later in the analysis of last-ditch *akrasia*.

It is mentioned here for another reason. It shows that Freud's theory of systems gives a better account of the conditions that allow irrationalities to be caused by the perversions of reason than of the conditions that allow the same irrationalities to be caused by wishes. It may seem surprising that Freud's idea, that the permissive cause of irrationality is some failure of consciousness, should work best outside the area in which he himself used it. However, the explanation is not far to seek. He used it in cases where the productive cause of irrationality is a wish, but it simply is not true that mild cases of wishful irrationality are always stopped by consciousness of their nature and causation. It is more plausible to suppose that serious cases are always stopped, although, as will be shown in a moment, even in serious cases consciouness is often an insufficient obstacle. But it is quite certain that mild cases are not always stopped by consciousness.

On the other hand, it is entirely understandable that a perversion of reason should cease the moment that a person becomes conscious of it. This is because cold illusions have no residual force after they have been unmasked. They are like the illusions of reason described by Kant,[5] except that they are much less grand and they distort perfectly ordinary processes of thought. Of course, one of these perversions of reason will not lose its general grip on a particular thinker just because its operation on a particular occasion has been unmasked. All that is stopped in such a case is the particular operation and the particular piece of irrationality. However, that really is stopped, because the unmasking of the particular trick leaves it with no residual power.

The mixed theory also differs from Freud's theory about the productive cause of irrationality in other ways, not all of which need to be discussed in detail here. For example, Freud was mainly concerned with the unconscious, which is a permanent reservoir of deeply repressed wishes and thoughts, but in ordinary hot cases of irrationality it is usually only the operation of the wish that is kept out of consciousness and not its existence as well. Also, in such cases there is no deep repression in the unconscious, but only shallow repression in the preconscious,[6] and even that only needs to last as long as is necessary for the particular piece of self-deception. It is as if the self-deceptive wish established a temporary camp for a siege rather than a permanent army of occupation. There is also a further difference, which does matter in this investigation: self-deception often involves a complex strategy which is, from the point of view of the wish to believe, entirely rational, even if it is based on the preconscious, but the Freudian unconscious is a much more chaotic structure of wishes and thoughts.

[5] Kant, *Critique of Pure Reason*, Transcendental Dialectic, Introduction.
[6] See Freud, *Introductory Lectures on Psycho-Analysis*, pp. 249-50.

The deficiency that has just been pointed out in Freud's theory of systems needs to be described carefully and its effect needs to be measured accurately. Otherwise it will be easy to draw the exaggerated conclusion that, because there are many hot cases of irrational belief-formation in which failure of consciousness is not necessary, therefore it is only at the top of the scale of irrationality that the theory has any explanatory power. It is important to see why this would be an exaggeration.

One point that was made against the theory was that the consciousness that a belief is being produced by a wish is not sufficient to prevent it from being formed and so lack of that consciousness is not a necessary permissive cause of its formation. Another point was that consciousness of the irrationality of a wishful belief in relation to information in the believer's mind is still not sufficient to prevent it from being formed, so that even lack of this consciousness is not a necessary permissive cause of its formation. This suggests two questions. First, can we identify cases at the top of the scale where it really is necessary for the believer to be unconscious of the irrationality of his belief? If so, they will be hot cases to which the Freudian theory of systems really does apply. However, that might be a rather meagre defence of the theory. So the second question will be, whether we can somehow extend its explanatory power further down the scale to milder cases of irrationality.

The first question is more difficult than might be supposed. It is, of course, obvious enough that the really mild cases at the bottom of the scale are not stopped by consciousness. More interestingly, it is possible for a person to persist in a consciously irrational belief further up the scale, when he possesses inductive evidence against it. An example will illustrate this point: someone receives a telegram containing such bad news that he disbelieves it, not just momentarily, but with persistent incredulity, although he knows that the source is generally reliable. (It is in the nature of inductive evidence that it allows people the latitude to refuse to make their beliefs conform to it even though they are perfectly aware of what they are doing,[7] and, when a powerful wish is operating, the refusal may go to considerable lengths.)

Even near the top of the scale, in the area of self-contradiction, the persistence of the belief will not always require any failure of consciousness. If someone appears to believe each of the two propositions in a contradictory conjunction, we cannot immediately infer that one of the two beliefs must be preconscious. For we must first ask whether the two beliefs keep their distance from one another in his mind. If each has its place in a different role played by him, they need never meet or come into conflict and each could be believed consciously. In such a case the consciousness of each belief is a reflection of it and the reflections, like the beliefs themselves, are simply kept apart. Consciousness does not automatically involve the lateral movements that produce collisions.

The only thing that cannot happen is that two contradictory beliefs should be caught in the same focal consciousness and both survive. It really is impossible to believe the conjunction of two contradictory propositions. In this case it is hardly necessary to add that it is impossible only if the cautionary belief is in the person's consciousness, because it always will be unless he is drunk, drugged, or insane. In other more complicated cases, the additional stipulation will be needed, because the cautionary belief might simply not occur to him. For example, it might not occur to him if he were reviewing an argument or a mathematical computation too complex for him to survey in one glance.

This is a meagre result. It appears that, even when no use is made of the storage space of the preconscious, almost nothing is impossible. On the other hand, it is arguable that

---

[7] D. Davidson argues that in practical reasoning a similar kind of latitude always allows a person to reject the singular value-judgement that is supported by his premisses without contradicting himself. See 'How is Weakness of the Will Possible?' in *Moral Concepts*, ed. J. Feinberg, Oxford, 1970, reprinted as Essay 2 of *Essays on Actions and Events*, Oxford, 1980. This kind of latitude is discussed in Chs. VI and VII.

Freud's theory of systems does cover the point that has just been made about mental distance. For he allows that preconsciousness may only be temporary, because a belief may be confined to the preconscious only when its incompatible rival is in consciousness, and that would be one kind of example of mental distance. However, his theory could hardly be stretched to cover the other kind of example, in which both beliefs would occur in the same mental sequence but not in the same focal consciousness. In any case, the explanatory power of his theory would still be very restricted in hot cases, because in such cases the explanation would succeed only at the top of the scale of the paradoxes. True, it would come into its own in cold cases, because in that area it would succeed lower down the scale, but he never applied it to cold cases. However, it is possible that there is some way of extending its scope further down the scale in hot cases. That was the second question that needed to be considered and it will now be taken up.

There is indeed a way of achieving this extended scope for Freud's theory of systems, but only at a price. It works perfectly as a theory about the permissive cause of the extreme cases of irrationality that would be impossible without it, and it can be extended to cases that would only be difficult without it, provided that it is recognized that the extension involves some reduction in its explanatory power. The recipient of the telegram did not find it impossible to maintain his irrational belief, but he must have found it difficult. It would have been easier for him to maintain it, if the cautionary belief had lapsed from his consciousness. Even at the bottom of the scale, where a belief is formed without any supporting evidence or with equally balanced evidence, it will be easier to maintain if these facts are kept out of the believer's consciousness. The distribution of a person's belief tends to adjust itself automatically to his evidence within the limits set by his competence, just as water on an uneven surface tends to find its own level and distributes itself in perfectly adapted pools. It is hard work propping up an ill supported belief and it is certainly made easier by the lapse of the cautionary belief from consciousness.

This is an obvious way of extending the scope of the Freudian theory of systems down the scale of wishful irrationality. Philosophers, who approach the subject by way of the paradoxes, naturally think first of cases where the irrationality would have been impossible, if the cautionary belief had not been kept out of consciousness. There are, however, far more cases where a failure of consciousness is an important luxury rather than a necessity. In these cases the Freudian theory of systems still has considerable explanatory power, although, it must be admitted, less than in the extreme cases that could not occur without a failure of consciousness.

So far, attention has been focused on the first half of the principle on which Freud's theory of systems is built. If a person's cautionary belief, that the belief that he was forming was irrational, were conscious, it would prevent him from forming the irrational belief. The suggestion is that this needs an amendment: his conscious cautionary belief would tend to prevent him from forming the irrational belief, by making its formation more difficult, but only in the limiting case impossible. However, there is also the other half of the principle to be considered: if the same cautionary belief were kept out of consciousness, it would not prevent him from forming the irrational belief. That is equally important, because there would be no point in banishing the cautionary belief from consciousness if it remained equally obstructive in the preconscious. Freud's theory about the permissive cause of irrational belief-formation presupposes not only that the cautionary belief is obstructive in consciousness but also that it loses its power to obstruct when it lapses from consciousness.

So much is obvious. What is not so obvious is that on this side too Freud's theory of systems provides a less than perfect explanation of the phenomena. For if the lapse of the cautionary belief from consciousness did provide a complete explanation of its non-intervention, that would be because preconscious beliefs are always powerless to produce their normal effects in consciousness. To put the point in the way in which it was put earlier, a preconscious belief would always be shut up in its sub-system and it would never be able to use the sub-system as a base for operations in the main system. But this is not universally true preconscious beliefs. Therefore, on this side too, although Freud's theory of systems has some explanatory power, it has less than is commonly supposed.

As a matter of fact, it is an understatement to say that it is not universally true that preconscious beliefs are powerless to produce their normal effects in consciousness. The fact is that actions are often controlled by preconscious beliefs. This kind of control can even be illustrated by a development of the example of wishful thinking that was supposed to be explained by the denial of its occurrence. The girl who persuaded herself that her lover was not unfaithful might avoid a particular café because she believed that she might find him there with her rival, and yet she might not be conscious of this belief. This is really very puzzling. On the one hand, we explain her irrational belief, that her lover is faithful, by saying that her cautionary belief, that this belief is irrational in relation to her evidence, is kept out of her consciousness. On the other hand, we seem to destroy the force of this explanation by suggesting that her choice of cafés is governed by another, preconscious belief, which must be producing its normal effect in consciousness, if there is anything in the suggestion. How can we have it both ways?

It is important to appreciate the scale of this difficulty. It extends far beyond cases like this one, where a suppressed belief guides the believer's actions. A large part of our lives is governed by information that is not emotionally unacceptable but is simply handed over by consciousness to the archivist because it would clutter its office and impede its daily business. Even the elaborate processing of sensory input is often governed by principles which are learned without ever surfacing in consciousness. For example, table-tennis players are usually unaware that they rely on the sound of the ball hitting the table for the timing of their returns. It would be easy to multiply examples, and the point that needs to be appreciated is the scale of the phenomenon and the variety of the cases in which consciousness is bypassed. People underestimate it only because it is unobtrusive.

How can Freud's theory of systems be defended against the charge that it appeals to preconsciousness to explain the muzzling of the cautionary belief and yet has to allow that many preconscious beliefs produce their normal effects in consciousness? This time it is not enough to say that the lapse into preconsciousness tends to block the normal effects of a belief in consciousness.

That shift to a tendency was an appropriate response to the previous objection, because the irrationality of a wishfully formed belief is kept out of the believer's consciousness in a large proportion of cases, and because we understand why this is so. It is an empirically verifiable fact that we find conscious irrationality a strain even low down on the scale where it is far from impossible. But the situation in preconsciousness is completely different. We do not know that a large proportion of preconscious beliefs have their normal effects in consciousness blocked. It may well be that the truth is the opposite. Also, even if we were sure, that the lapse into preconciousness did tend to block the normal effects of a belief, we would still lack a complete understanding of what was going on, until we had identified the cause that is present when the blockage occurs and absent when it does not occur. There is a sharp contrast here with our understanding of the obstructive operation of the cautionary belief in consciousness. We have identified the cause governing that operation, namely the varying difficulty of accepting beliefs of different degrees of irrationality. But we have not yet identified the cause governing the operation of preconscious beliefs.

In order to find it, we have to investigate the structure and organization of preconscious Freudian sub-systems. The key to the problem will turn out to be their rationality. They are built around the nucleus of the wish to believe and this wish is the cause that blocks the normal effect of the cautionary belief. In the other case, the girl's wish to avoid a painful confrontation produced the opposite effect: it allowed the preconscious belief to guide her steps to another café. To put the point in Freud's way, the sub-system is dynamic. It is obvious that it is impossible to extend this explanation to cold cases, where the perversions of reason produce illusions that cannot be represented as the work of a rational *homunculus* within the person. So there is a nice symmetry here: Freud's theory about the permissive cause of irrationality works best in consciousness when the productive cause is a perversion of reason, but it works best in preconsciousness when the productive cause is a wish that stops the intervention of the cautionary belief.

The details of this solution can wait. Meanwhile, it is worth stepping back from the problem for a moment in order to get it into deeper focus. We are trying to assess the explanatory power of Freud's theory of systems with a view to comparing it with the explanatory power of a purely functional theory. Freud's line between main system and sub-system separates what is conscious from what is not conscious. Lack of consciousness is supposed to be the permissive cause of irrationality. However, it appears to be neither a necessary nor a sufficient permissive cause. Its lack of necessity does not pose too difficult a problem, because consciousness does tend to block irrationality, and because we know that the operation of this tendency is governed by the varying difficulty of accepting beliefs of different degrees of irrationality. But the fact that preconsciousness is not a sufficient permissive cause of irrationality emerges as a more difficult problem. The only way to deal with it is to change the subject. Instead of concentrating on permissive causes in consciousness, we have to extend the inquiry to the preconscious and identify the productive causes that operate down there and stop the intervention of the cautionary belief.

It really is important that we have to do this. It is so easy to fall into the error of supposing that Freud's account of the permissive cause of irrationality in consciousness is self-contained and essentially correct, so that its shortcomings can be accepted or, if necessary, remedied, without any use being made of his account of its productive cause in the preconscious. But though there is some truth in that idea when he proposes lack of consciousness as a necessary permissive cause of irrationality, it is far from true when he proposes it as a sufficient permissive cause. Why, then, is it so easy to suppose that it is true? There are several things that might explain the illusion.

The main thing is that we see everything from the high ground of our own consciousness and so are led very naturally to overestimate its dominance. We do this in various ways. The simplest way is to play down the frequency of irrationalities that the subject is competent to detect. This is partly attributable to a habit of thought noted by William James:[8] we assume that, because certain mistakes really would be impossible in a psychological or philosophical investigation, therefore they must be impossible in daily life. But the professor's protest, 'Of course, I could not do that' should be countered with 'No, not just at the moment'. There is even a tendency to underestimate the frequency of conscious irrationality in the middle of the scale and at its lower end. This is easily done in a cold investigation. Either the emotion felt by the subject is forgotten or its power is discounted. After all, there is not supposed to be any emotion in the investigation.

Another simple error that is often made is to forget the difference between the total absence of the cautionary belief and its mere absence from consciousness. If it were totally absent, the subject would simply not be competent to avoid the irrationality. If, however, the cautionary belief is merely shifted to the subject's preconscious, there is a real need to complete the theory by asking what it does there, because, it might use

---

[8] 'The *great* snare of the psychologist is the *confusion of his own standpoint with that of the mental fact* about which he is making his report. I shall hereafter call this the "psychologist's fallacy" *par excellence.*' W. James, *The Principles of Psychology*, London, 1891, vol. I, p. 196.

his preconscious as a safe base for operations against his consciousness. If it does not do that, we need to know why it does not do it. This is easily forgotten once it has gone to earth, because we have a natural tendency to underestimate the achievements of the preconscious. Consciousness strikes us as omni-competent and all our achievements seem to be its achievements. But if we really think that, we are simply overlooking the successes of inbuilt automatisms and effortless preconscious tricks.

All these factors contribute to the big mistake of supposing that Freud's theory of the permissive cause of irrationality is self-sufficient and essentially correct, so that there is no need to go to his theory of the productive cause in order to remedy its shortcomings.

Let us shelve Freud's theory of systems for the moment and turn our attention to the functional theory. The functional theory tries to explain irrational belief-formation in the same general way as the Freudian theory but with a big specific difference. It does not make any use of consciousness in drawing the line between main system and sub-system. The main system, according to this theory, consists of all the desires and beliefs in the subject's mind that interact with one another in a rational way to produce further desires and beliefs and eventually speech and action. If one of his desires or beliefs fails to interact in a rational way with any element in the main system, it is assigned to a sub-system.[9]

No use is made of consciousness when the line is drawn in this way. In fact, beliefs belonging to sub-systems, as they are set up by this theory, are often conscious. For example, the girl's cautionary belief, that it is irrational for her to believe that her lover is faithful, would be assigned to a sub-system, because it does not intervene in the main system to block the formation of the irrational belief, but it could well be conscious. Her inductive evidence allows her the latitude

[9] See D. Davidson, 'Paradoxes of Irrationality', p. 304: 'The breakdown of reason-relations defines the boundary of a sub-division.'

to form the irrational belief without self-contradiction and she could be consciously exploiting that fact. Conversely, her belief, that she might find him in a certain café with her rival, would be assigned to the main system, because it produces its normal rational effect there, namely avoidance of the café, but it might well be preconscious, as it was in the case described.

The first point to notice about this theory is that it certainly succeeds in covering all cases of avoidable irrationality. In such cases the irrationality is always the result of the cautionary belief's failure to intervene and stop it and, whenever a failure of this kind occurs, a line is drawn between main system and sub-system. So the functional theory of systems does not suffer from the disadvantage of restricted scope, like the Freudian theory.

However, this advantage is achieved in a way that might be found worrying. It is achieved by definition. A system's boundary is simply defined as a line across which some element in a person's psyche fails to produce its normal rational effect on the elements that control his daily life. That definition guarantees a perfect fit between the functional theory of systems and the phenomenon of irrationality that the subject is competent to avoid, but the trouble is that it seems to deprive the theory of all explanatory power.

Freud's theory of systems did at least identify a permissive cause of irrationality that is not simply tied to it by definition, namely failure of consciousness. This is an empirically discoverable cause and one whose presence can be established independently of its supposed effect, the irrationality, precisely because it is not tied to it by definition. That is why failure of consciousness entered the lists with such high hopes of explaining avoidable irrationality. True, the hopes were dashed when it became apparent how severely the theory's scope is restricted. But the advantage of the functional theory at this point appears to be illusory. For though it achieves the right scope, it achieves it by definition and so it seems to forfeit all explanatory power. Instead of pointing to an independently discoverable cause, it merely exercises its logical powers of definition on the problematical material. Nothing new is produced and all that seems to be offered is a dramatic redescription of the original phenomenon of irrationality.

Can the functional theory of systems be defended against this criticism? One thing is immediately clear. It is necessary that its defence should begin with a disclaimer. The theory is simply not concerned with the permissive cause of irrationality in the main system. It is not intended, and it must be made clear from the start that it is not intended, as a theory about the situation in the main system that makes irrationality possible. This disclaimer is an essential preliminary, because people approach the functional theory through Freud's theory of systems, which really is, in large part, a theory about the permissive cause of irratonality in the main system. So they assume that the functional theory must be a rival in that field, when in fact it is no such thing. The two theories then joust at one another down separate lists and never meet.

It is easy to see that the functional theory is not offered as an explanation of the main system's susceptibility to irrationality, like Freud's theory of systems. For all that it tells us about the main system is that the irrationality occurred there, because the cautionary belief did not intervene effectively. But that is guaranteed by the definition of the concept of 'effective intervention'. So the next question is, 'Why did the cautionary belief not intervene effectively?' But the theory does not make any attempt to explain why it did not intervene effectively by identifying a permissive cause in the main system. This is because it simply is not intended as an alternative to Freud's suggestion, that the necessary permissive cause in the main system is some failure of consciousness. In short, the criticism is based on a misunderstanding and what it imputes as a fault is really the unexceptionable consequence of a different intention.

However, this disclaimer immediately raises the question, what the real intention of the functional theory is. What exactly is it trying to do? The next move in its defence must be to answer this question. If the theory does not get its explanatory power by identifying a permissive cause of irrationality in the main system, it must get it from some other source. But what is the other source?

It might be suggested that it gets its explanatory power from its description of the connection between main system and sub-system. This suggestion is not implausible. For when we postulate a schism within a person in order to explain irrational belief-formation, we naturally model the two systems on persons, crediting each of them with the same kind of internal organization as a whole person. It is their separateness that then seems to explain why a belief that is in one of them does not produce its normal effect in the other, in much the same way that the separateness of two different people would explain why a cautionary belief in one of them would not automatically stop the formation of an irrational belief in the other.

However, this does not really succeed in locating the source of the functional theory's explanatory power, because the separateness of the two systems is really only another piece of theatre. Perhaps the best way to appreciate this is to reflect that the explanation of the imperviousness of one person to the unexpressed beliefs of another would break down if they shared a single body, or if they were in constant telepathic communication with one another. But two systems within a single person do share the same body, and, in particular, the same brain. True, they may be localized in different parts of the brain but at present we have no way of knowing whether this is so or not. Therefore, the line that we draw between them is purely psychological.

What needs to be explained is why the cautionary belief does not produce its normal effect across that line. In default of a physical explanation we might hope for a psychological account of the junction between the two systems which would explain the blockage. But that would be an empty dream inspired by an analogy with no residual content. The criterion used by the functional theory when it draws the line is simply that that is where the blockage occurs. There is then an obvious need to explain the blockage, but it cannot possibly be explained as a consequence of the psychological features of the frontier between the two systems, because it has no more psychological features than were given to it by its original definition. So the source of the explanatory power of the functional theory cannot be located at this point.

There is only one possible remaining source of the explanatory power of the functional theory and that is in the sub-system itself. The sub-system is built around the nucleus of the wish for the irrational belief and it is organized like a person. Although it is a separate centre of agency within the whole person, it is, from its own point of view, entirely rational.[10] It wants the main system to form the irrational belief and it is aware that it will not form it, if the cautionary belief is allowed to intervene. So with perfect rationality it stops its intervention.

The aim of this part of the inquiry is to compare Freud's theory of systems with the functional theory. Part of the comparison will have to wait until the functional theory has been developed in more detail, but part of it can be carried out without more ado. It was pointed out earlier that, when the productive cause of irrationality is a perversion of reason, Freud's account of the permissive cause in the main system is very successful, but that what he says about sub-systems has no application to a case of this kind, because there is no nuclear wish. The functional theory too has no application in this area for exactly the same reason. However, the functional theory is worse off, because it also has nothing to say about the permissive cause of irrationality in the main system. Add up these two deficiencies and the result is that the functional theory really does not have any explanatory power when it is applied to cases of irrationality produced by the perversions of reason.

[10] This is the essential point, presented forcefully by D. Davidson in 'Paradoxes of Irrationality'.

It is true that the functional theory is compatible with Freud's idea, that the permissive cause in the main system is failure of consciousness, which can, therefore, be brought in as an extra explanatory factor when it is needed.[11] However, the search for the source of the explanatory power of the functional theory is bound to concentrate on the theory itself and not on the possibility of adding a different idea to it as a supplement. So it is clear that the functional theory does not have any explanatory power in cold cases. For it is only in hot cases that there is a nuclear wish, around which the sub-system can be built and its internal rationality developed.

More details are needed of the structure and organization of sub-systems marked off by the functional theory. Perhaps it is best to start from a principle that was formulated earlier: a system can react to a belief or desire in another system without necessarily sharing it.[12] The point of this principle is that it allows a system to become aware of an element in another system without taking it over, and that is important in cases where it would lose its own internal rationality if it did take it over.

This principle is needed not only by the Freudian theory of systems but also by the functional theory. For both have to preserve the internal rationality of the sub-system, and it would be impossible to preserve it if the sub-system's awareness of the situation in the main system always forced it to recreate it in itself by a kind of empathy. The way in which the principle prevents this may be illustrated by the case of the refusal to believe bad news. The recipient of the telegram in that example possessed the cautionary belief that the source was reliable and, consequently, that it would be rational to believe the message. However, he rejected it under the influence of his wish, and the question is, how the sub-system, built around the wish, managed to react to certain elements in the main system without losing its internal rationality. That is the result that the principle has to secure.

---

[11] See D. Davidson, 'Paradoxes of Irrationality', p. 305.   [12] See p. 37.

It is certainly necessary for the functional theory that the result should be secured somehow. For the sub-system in a case of this kind is supposed to dominate the main system and manipulate it. This is quite different from the relationship between systems investigated by role psychology. In that kind of case the person moves out of one role into another and each role has certain beliefs that are peculiar to it. There may well be incompatibilities between the beliefs that are peculiar to two different roles but they can easily be preserved from conflict by mental distance. The systems associated with these roles are all on the same level and they do not try to dominate one another,[13] whereas in the case of the refusal to believe the bad news dominance and manipulation are the *raison d'être* of the sub-system.

This imposes an extra requirement on the sub-system in a case of wishful thinking. Like the systems associated with different roles, it has to be internally rational, but unlike them, it has to react to certain elements in the main system in order to dominate it successfully. It must, for example, be aware of the main system's problem, which is that it has evidence pointing to an unwelcome conclusion. Also, if the solution of the problem is at all complicated, it must be aware of the weaknesses of the main system, in order to be able to adjust its strategy to them. Finally, it ought to be aware of the achievement of its goal, the main system's eventual formation of the desired belief, because, if it were not aware of it, it might continue its operations when they were no longer necessary.

[13] 'It is probably no mere historical accident that the word, persona, in its first meaning, is a mask . . . In a sense, and in so far as this mask represents the conception that we have formed of ourselves—the role we are striving to live up to—this mask is our true self, the self we would like to be. In the end our conception of our role becomes second nature and an integral part of our personality. We come into the world as individuals, achieve character and become persons.' R. E. Park, *Reason and Culture*, Glencoe, Illinois, 1950, pp. 294-50, quoted by Erving Goffman, *The Presentation of Self in Everyday Life*, Harmondsworth, 1959, p. 30. The idea that the mask is the true self becomes more interesting when there are many masks. No hierarchy is implied by multiple impersonation.

The need for all this information about elements in the main system evidently threatens the internal rationality of the sub-system. For it has to acquire the information without acquiring the elements themselves, or, at least, without acquiring all of them. This delicately balanced achievement is not easy but it is essential. For if the sub-system accepted the main system's evidence and drew its wishful conclusion, how could it possibly contain the cautionary belief? It is at this point that the functional theory needs the principle that a system can be aware of an element in another system without necessarily sharing it. The element to which the principle obviously has to be applied is the main system's wishful belief. Naturally, the principle is also needed by Freud's theory of systems.

It might be objected that this solves one problem but leaves another, equally difficult problem unsolved. For if the sub-system contains the main system's evidence and the cautionary belief, it seems that it must form the rational belief. But how can it possibly do that, if it is built around the nucleus of the wish to form the opposite belief? This is the reasoning behind Sartre's criticism, that Freud's censor would have to conceal the rational belief from its own consciousness.[14] The criticism can be generalized. Whatever the sub-system, and however it is marked off from the main system, it cannot accommodate the rational belief, if it is built around the wish to form the irrational belief. In fact, it may not even be able to accommodate the evidence and the cautionary belief, because, together, they push it so hard towards the rational belief.

Here it must be remembered that the internal rationality of the sub-system is as indispensable to the functional theory as it is to Freud's theory, because it would lack all explanatory power if it lost it. So how can this new problem be solved?

There seem to be two ways of solving it. One solution would be to apply the principle to the main system's evidence

[14] See pp. 36-7.

and to say that the sub-system is aware of this evidence in the main system but does not accept it. Of course, it would not reject it either. It would merely take note of its presence in the main system and it would not have to choose between believing it and disbelieving it. For it is not concerned with the external world, but only with the conflict between evidence and wish in the main system.

Another solution would be to specify the content of the wish in a more discriminating way. It is natural to assume that the wish that lies at the heart of the sub-system is the wish to believe that the telegram's message is false, but perhaps it is really only the wish that the main system should form that belief. In the main system itself this wish would be equivalent to the wish to form it, but in the sub-system the equivalence would not hold and the wish would assume an altruistic guise. Or perhaps we ought to say that it would assume a semi-altruistic guise in the sub-system, because the object of its benevolence is a system belonging to a person to whom it too belongs.

One thing that recommends the second solution is its perfect appropriateness to the relation between sub-system and main system in a case of wishful thinking. The main system faces a hostile environment, but the sub-system's problem is not the main system's external problem but, rather, the likely effect of that problem on the main system. It is almost as if the main system were the sub-system's environment. The main system finds itself unable to dominate its environment and undo the distressing event reported in the telegram, and so what happens instead is that the sub-system dominates its environment and eliminates the distressing belief from the main system. The distress is shared by the two systems but it is egoistic in the main system and semi-altruistic in the sub-system. What makes the discriminating analysis of the wish so plausible is that it exactly fits this situation. It allows the main system's wish not to form the distressing belief to secede and set up a sub-system in which it becomes the wish that the main system should not form it.

There is, however, a possible objection to this solution. It might be argued that, if the content of the wish in the main system is formulated in a different way from the content of the wish in the sub-system, they are really two different wishes. The model would then be two different people, one of whom wishes to deceive the other in order to make him happy. This certainly gives us a coherent explanation. On the other hand, a case can be made for relaxing the criterion of identity and allowing that it is the same wish in main system and sub-system. For we may then say that this wish secedes from the main system and sets up a sympathetic sub-system without losing its identity.[15]

The error in Sartre's criticism of Freud can be explained from this vantage point. Sartre failed to appreciate the special character of the relationship between sub-system and main system in cases of wishful thinking. The sub-system looks out on to the main system and the main system looks out on to the world. Sartre's error was to assume that both systems look out on to the world and that, consequently, both have the same input, the same aspirations, and the same problems. That is indeed the case when systems are associated with different roles played by a person, but not when they are related to one another as sub-system and main system in a case like the refusal to believe bad news.

It may be objected that this deals with one problem only by creating another one. If the wish belongs to both systems, how are we going to be able to use the functional criterion for drawing the line between them? The reason why the wish was supposed to operate from the sub-system was that its effect in the main system is irrational. So we formulated the theory that it operates across a systemic boundary. But the natural interpretation of that theory is that the wish is confined to

---

[15] This was probably Freud's reason for using the relaxed criterion of identity for wishes and other attitudes. If 'affect' can change its object without changing its identity, the dramatization of the origin of the sub-system is more convincing. It must be admitted that this is not a compelling reason for relaxing the criterion of identity.

the sub-system. How then can it belong to the main system too? More generally, how can any element belong to both systems?

There are a number of problems here and it is best to start with the simplest one. How can an element belong to two different systems? It is easy to see that there is no bar to this dual citizenship when the systems are associated with two different roles played by the same person. There is in a case like that no reason whatsoever to suppose that none of the beliefs in one of the systems could be shared by another one. If someone played one role with one friend and another role with another friend, he would not give them different telephone numbers.

The only reason for finding dual citizenship more difficult in cases of wishful thinking is that a sub-system that only has to dominate the main system needs fewer elements and most of them are problematical. This is because we only have to assign to it the elements that are needed to explain its rational manipulation of the main system and most of those elements are potential trouble-makers. However, that hardly justifies a refusal to assign any element to both systems and, if we find a plausible candidate, we are free to treat it in that way.

It has already been mentioned that in Freud's theory the wish is the essential nucleus of the sub-system. But it also interacts with the main system's irrational belief in an entirely rational way to produce satisfaction.[16] So, at least for the purposes of that theory, main system and sub-system may often be drawn as two intersecting circles and the wish may be placed in their overlap, with the proviso that it takes an egoistic form in the main system but a semi-altruistic form in the sub-system.

The question, whether the same picture is appropriate to the functional theory, is not so easy to settle. We know the result that has to be achieved, but it is not entirely clear how to achieve it. The functional theory must be set up with an internally rational sub-system and a main system in which a

[16] See p. 71.

wish interacts with the irrational belief in a rational way to produce satisfaction. But there may be more than one way of achieving this result, because there may be more than one way of formulating a functional criterion for drawing the line between the two systems.

The formulation that has been proposed here is that, if a desire or belief fails to interact in a rational way with any element in the main system, it is assigned to a sub-system. So far, this has been interpreted as a formula that only requires non-intervention: a desire or belief is assigned to a sub-system when it fails to intervene in the main system in some rational way in which it ought to intervene. This is a negative interpretation of the formula. But it could also be given a positive interpretation. It might mean that a desire or belief is assigned to a sub-system when it does interact with some element in the main system, but in an irrational way. The point is that there is a difference between irrational intervention and failure to intervene rationally and the criterion for drawing the line between main system and sub-system must choose between these two faults.

It is worth dwelling for a moment on the effect of this choice between the negative and the positive versions of the criterion. If we use the positive version, a wish that causes an irrational belief will be assigned to a sub-system simply because the belief is irrational. It will not be necessary to inquire whether the person was competent to detect the irrationality of the belief and avoid it. Its objective irrationality will be sufficient to support the placing of the wish in the sub-system. There will be no need to ask whether the person possessed the cautionary belief which, nevertheless, failed to intervene and stop the formation of the irrational belief. It will not even be necessary for the belief that is caused by the wish to be objectively irrational. For it will be sufficient that its causation by the wish is irrational, even if the person does not realize that this kind of causation is irrational. When this version of the criterion is used, a sub-system will be needed for any kind of irrationality and not just for irrationality that the person is competent to detect and avoid.

If, on the other hand, we use the negative version of the criterion, the theory of sub-systems will only apply to irrationalities that the person can detect and avoid. For a sub-system will be needed only to house an element that belongs to his psyche but fails to produce the effect that it ought to produce, namely inhibition of the irrational belief, and in cases of wishful thinking it is only the cautionary belief that qualifies as an element of this kind. It is this interpretation of the formula that has been used so far and it has been assumed that the theory of systems only has to cover irrationalities that the person is competent to detect and avoid.

Which version of the criterion is used by Davidson in his pioneering article, 'Paradoxes of Irrationality'? According to him, 'The breakdown of reason-relations defines the boundary of a sub-division'.[17] This is because 'in . . . a case of irrationality . . . there is a mental cause that is not a reason for what it causes. So, in wishful thinking, a desire causes a belief. But the judgment, that a state of affairs is, or would be desirable, is not a reason to believe that it exists.'[18]

There is no doubt that Davidson is only concerned with internal irrationality or irrationality that is relative to elements in the person's psyche. But his explanation of his criterion for drawing the line between main system and sub-system leaves it unclear whether he is using the positive or the negative version of it. This is probably because the example of irrationality that he uses does not force him to make an explicit choice between the two versions. In his example the irrationality does not lie in the belief itself but in the fact that it is caused by a wish and, since everybody realizes that wishful thinking is irrational, there does not seem to be any need to ask whether this cautionary belief is in the person's psyche and whether it is, perhaps, its failure to intervene that 'defines the boundary of a sub-division'. If the irrationality had been

---

[17] Loc. cit., p. 304, quoted earlier in this chapter in n. 9.
[18] Loc. cit., p. 298.

the irrationality of the belief in relation to elements in the person's psyche, these questions would have been inevitable, because he might well be incompetent to detect and avoid the internal irrationality.

There are, in fact, several reasons for preferring the negative version of the criterion, which is the one that has been developed in this chapter.[19] First, and most important, it is always conflict that makes us divide a person's psyche into two systems, but there is no conflict between incompatible elements in the psyche of a person who is unable to detect their incompatibility. We may ask, 'How can he believe both these things?', but our scepticism will vanish when we discover that he cannot see that they are incompatible, and there will then be no reason to suppose that they have to be kept apart by being relegated to two different systems in his psyche.

This is connected with another important reason for preferring the negative version of the criterion. Suppose that a desire that causes a belief is relegated to a sub-system simply because it has committed this fault, even if the person does not realize that it is a fault. The relegation will have to be total banishment and the wish will have to be assigned exclusively to the sub-system rather than being placed in the overlap of the two circles. For the intention is to keep the wish and the belief apart for the same general reason for which two contradictory beliefs have to be kept apart, namely because their relationship is objectively irrational. The wish and the belief interact, because the wish causes the belief, but only across a line that marks the irrationality of their interaction.

However, it is very difficult to develop this version of the theory of systems in a coherent way that will accommodate all the facts. For it is also a fact that, after the formation of the irrational belief, this same wish interacts with it in a perfectly rational way and produces satisfaction. Must we say that one irrational interaction between two elements is a suf-

[19] Davidson has told me that this is how his formulation of the criterion should be developed.

ficient ground for the banishment of one of them, and that it is not in any way redeemed by other rational interactions? That would be a harsh punishment for a peccadillo. But a much stronger objection to it is that it is just about impossible to see how a theory constructed on these lines can account for all the facts. For the model for the two systems is two people and so when an element has been assigned exclusively to one system it cannot interact directly with an element that belongs exclusively to the other system.

There are also other, less important reasons for preferring the negative version of the criterion to the positive version. What, for example, should we say about cases of over-determination if we used the positive criterion? It is quite common for an internally rational belief to be formed, in the first instance, as a result of some non-rational association of ideas. Much of our thinking is exploratory and its inventiveness would be considerably reduced if all lateral associations were banned and if linear rationality were always required. Do we really have to postulate a sub-system to house every idea that produces a rational belief by non-rational association?

It might seem that one of these reasons for preferring the negative version of the criterion could be circumvented. When it is argued that in a case of wishful thinking the wish operates irrationally in the sub-system and rationally in the main system, it might be objected that these operations are really carried out by two different wishes. However, this objection is not convincing. For even if we do reject the relaxed criterion of identity that was proposed earlier and refuse to allow that the main system's wish to form the belief is the same wish as the sub-system's wish that the main system should form it, it cannot be denied that the main system shares the latter wish. There will, therefore, always be one causally operative wish that belongs to both systems.

These reasons for preferring the negative version of the criterion to the positive version are cumulatively overwhelming. So we may retain the idea that an element is assigned exclusively to a sub-system if and only if it fails to interact rationally with any element in the main system. This also has another, incidental advantage. It allows the functional theory to be mapped on to Freud's theory about the productive cause of irrationalities that the person is competent to detect and avoid, and so it makes it very natural for us to adopt it.

It will have been noticed that in the development of the functional theory the sub-system has been credited with information about the contents of the main system. This is an essential feature of sub-systems in cases of wishful thinking, but it does prompt the question, whether they should also be credited with consciousness. That is a difficult question. On the one hand, it is easy to see that it is impossible to attribute rationality to sub-systems without the necessary information about their main systems, and that the explanatory power of the functional theory depends on their rationality. Perhaps the evidence for crediting them with rationality is most impressive when there is prolonged and elaborate self-deception. In such cases it seems impossible that the favoured belief should be promoted in the main system by a series of coincidental events. On the other hand, if these events are planned by the sub-system, it must have a lot of information about the main system and it must know how to use it. Should we then attribute consciousness to the sub-system?

This does not pose a general problem for the functional theory, because, unlike Freud's theory, it does not require sub-systems of this kind to be preconscious. However, there are cases at the top of the scale of irrationality where some failure of consciousness is bound to occur, and so Freud's idea about the permissive cause of irrationality in the main system has to be brought in as an auxiliary explanation. In such cases there really is a problem about consciousness and it is a difficult one. How does the sub-system receive and process information unless it has an internal consciousness of its own?

Since this is a general problem for Freud's theory, it is worth looking at his response to it. But, first, it must be pointed out that much of the sub-system's information about the main system will not need to be kept out of consciousness and so it will simply be assigned to both Freudian systems in the way already described. However, that will not be true of all the information required by the sub-system, because some of it will be confidential, like reports in a military campaign. Can Freud explain how this information is received, processed and used by the preconscious, if it does not have an internal consciousness of its own?

As a matter of fact, Freud did discuss the question, whether the unconscious has an internal consciousness of its own.[20] Now the preconscious, like the unconscious, has no direct access to the external world. It cannot, for example, take over the waking person's voice and speak directly about itself, like a dissociated personality.[21] So if it did have an internal consciousness, it would be one that was buried alive. Freud points out that this hypothesis about the unconscious guarantees its own alienation from the phenomena. If it is true, it will ensure that there is no direct evidence to indicate its truth and so it is impossible to argue from the absence of any direct evidence that it is false. All that we can do is to note that the unconscious often operates as if it had an internal consciousness of its own. It seems reasonable to treat the hypothesis that the preconscious might have an internal consciousness in the same way.

But though this is right, it leaves something unexplained. It correctly diagnoses the emptiness of the claim that there is something down there surveying the arrival of elements in the sub-system and the simulated outcomes of different courses of action in order to compare them with one another as we do up here in our main systems. But it fails to specify what takes the place down there of the conscious exercise of reason up here. To put the point in another way, there is no difficulty in understanding how a system reacts to information if it receives it and processes it consciously, but what happens if it

[20] See *The Unconscious*, in *Collected Works*, vol. XIV, pp. 169-70.
[21] See M. R. Haight, *A Study of Self-Deception*, Brighton, 1979, Chs. 3 and 4.

does these things without the accompaniment of consciousness? The problem cannot just be dismissed.

However, it is too big a problem to be taken on here and two moves towards its solution will have to suffice. First, if the sub-system uses information about an element in the main system, it must react differentially to that element. This means that it must at least be the case that, if another element had occupied its place in the main system, it would have reacted differently. For example, when the sub-system terminates its operations in response to the main system's formation of the favoured belief, it must at least be the case that it would have prolonged them, if the opposite belief had continued to occupy that place in the main system. Second, when the sub-system adopts a complex strategy of self-deception, it must be reacting differentially to the outcomes of its various stages. This means that it must at least be the case that, if any of the stages had had a different outcome, it would have been sensitive to that fact and at the next stage, if a different procedure had been needed, it would have adopted it. These minimal conditions are quite strong, but the suggestion is that they can be met without any internal consciousness.

There is another question about Freud's theory of systems that needs to be raised here. Why is there an asymmetry in the passage of information between his kind of main system and his kind of sub-system? Why is it that the sub-system can receive information about the formation of the irrational belief in the main system, but the main system cannot receive information about the cautionary belief in the sub-system?

This is not such an unmanageable question. The answer to it must start from the point reached in the earlier discussion of belief and belief about belief.[22] It was argued that the belief that one has a belief is apt to produce the belief itself, because beliefs are normally self-monitoring. However, the assumption throughout that discussion was that both beliefs belonged to the same system. It would evidently be a mistake

---

[22] See pp. 58-9.

to suppose that a person who believed that a sub-system within himself contained some irrational belief would be likely to take it over in his main system too. Now the sub-system in the kind of case that is being examined here is in just this position: when its campaign of self-deception is completed, it will believe that the main system contains the irrational belief but it cannot take it over without the consequences described by Sartre, if it already contains the main system's evidential beliefs and the cautionary belief.

So far so good. But why can we not argue symmetrically that the main system can become aware of the cautionary belief in the sub-system, but will not take it over because it is incompatible with the conjunction of its evidential beliefs and its irrational belief? The reason why we cannot argue in this way is that the main system would find the cautionary belief entirely convincing as soon as it became aware of it. For the assumption is that the person is competent to avoid the irrationality and so the only reason why the cautionary belief is not in his main system is that it has been suppressed. This explanation rests on a distinction that is essential to Freud's theory of systems, namely the distinction between direct consciousness of a belief in the main system and indirect consciousness of a belief that remains in the sub-system in spite of the fact that 'consciousness' is the name of the main system.[23]

In the course of this examination of the two main theories of systems, Freud's theory and the functional theory, it has become apparent that they are not direct rivals of one another. Freud's theory is restricted to cases that involve some failure of consciousness. At the very most it can only be extended to cover the phenomenon of mental distance. The

[23] The distinction can be put in another way: the main system's awareness of an element in the psyche is sometimes based on experiencing it, but sometimes only based on inference. The need for this distinction shows the inadequacy of Freud's criterion for drawing the line between main system and sub-system in this kind of case. In fact, Sartre's criticism of Freud would have been more successful if it had been less ambitious and concentrated on the fact that Freud's systemic line does not account for all the differences between consciousness and lack of consciousness.

functional theory has a wider application, but, unlike Freud's theory, it is not concerned with the permissive cause of irrationality in the main system. Consequently, it has nothing to say about irrationalities produced by the perversions of reason. Its relevance is only to hot cases and its strength, which it shares with Freud's theory, lies in its account of the internal irrationality of the sub-system.

* * *

This chapter has assessed the scope and success of two different theories that divide a single person into main system and sub-system in order to explain the formation of an irrational belief that he is competent to detect and avoid. The assumption has been that the two theories are compatible with one another, just as the political division of a continent is compatible with its geographical division, and the main point of comparison has been their explanatory power.

Freud's theory identifies the main system as consciousness and the sub-system either as the unconscious or, in the kind of case that is under examination here, as the preconscious. The functional theory draws the line between the two systems in a way that has nothing to do with consciousness; it assigns an element to a sub-system whenever it fails to interact rationally with any element in the main system.

Freud's theory falls naturally into two parts. It tries to explain the possibility of irrationality by identifying its permissive cause in the main system, and it tries to explain the actual occurrence of irrationality by identifying its productive cause in the sub-system. There are two types of irrationality requiring explanation, wishful irrationality and irrationality caused by a perversion of reason. The theory that both can be explained in the Freudian way was called 'the mixed theory'.

Attention was first focused on to Freud's account of the permissive cause of irrationality. It is based on a plausible principle: if a person consciously believed that the belief that he was forming was irrational, that would prevent him from forming it, whereas, if the same cautionary belief were not conscious, it would not prevent him from forming it.

A distinction was drawn between the extreme instability of the perversions of reason and the greater stability of wishful irrationality. Except at the top of the scale, where the irrationality is most severe, consciousness will not put an end to the power of a wish to fascinate and delude, but when irrationality is produced at any point on the scale by a perversion of reason, it collapses as soon as it is detected. It followed that Freud's account of the permissive cause of irrationality works better with the latter than with the former type of case.

Investigation showed that it is only in a small minority of cases that wishful irrationality is impossible without some failure of consciousness. It is even possible for someone to believe each of two contradictory propositions consciously, provided that they keep their distance from one another in his mind, perhaps because they belong to two different roles that he plays. The only really solid impossibility is the impossibility of consciously believing the conjunction of two perspicuously contradictory propositions.

However, Freud's theory about the permissive cause of wishful irrationality may be able to bring the phenomenon of mental distance under the concept of temporary preconsciousness. Also, there is no doubt that it can be extended to cases where it is not impossible, but only difficult to maintain the irrational belief without some failure of consciousness. But the cost of the latter extension is a certain reduction of its explanatory power.

Attention was then switched to the second part of the principle underlying Freud's theory: if the cautionary belief were not conscious, it would not prevent the subject from forming the irrational belief. This was criticized because it is not generally true that a preconscious belief is powerless to produce its normal effects in consciousness. On the contrary, our actions are often governed by preconscious beliefs. For example, the girl who preconsciously believed that she might find her lover with her rival in a particular café might avoid it.

Freud's only response to this criticism would be to draw on the ideas developed in the other part of his theory, which deals with the productive cause of wishful irrationality. The sub-system is built around a wish and it acts rationally when it prevents the preconscious cautionary belief from producing its normal effect in consciousness but allows the girl's preconscious belief about the café to produce its normal effect. It is obvious that this part of his theory does not apply to cold cases of irrationality produced by the perversions of reason.

Various explanations were offered of our tendency to exalt consciousness and to make the mistake of supposing that Freud's account of the permissive cause of wishful irrationality is self-contained and essentially correct, so that its short-comings can be accepted, or, if necessary, remedied without any use being made of his account of its productive cause.

Next, the functional theory of systems was examined. This theory makes no use of consciousness when it draws the line between main system and sub-system. Instead, it assigns an element to a sub-system if it fails to interact in a rational way with any element in the main system.

This criterion for marking the boundary certainly gives the functional theory a wider application than Freud's theory. However, it suffers from the disadvantage of not indicating any empirically discoverable permissive cause of irrationality in the main system. The explanation that it offers is the failure of the cautionary belief to intervene effectively, but that failure is tied by definition to the phenomenon requiring explanation. How then can the theory achieve any explanatory power?

The defence of the functional theory began with a disclaimer. It is simply not intended as an account of the permissive cause of irrationality in the main system. Nor does it get its explanatory power from its account of the connection between main system and sub-system. It followed that it can get it only from its account of the internal structure and organization of the sub-system. The essential point is that the sub-system is an internally rational centre of agency.

This part of the functional theory was then developed in some detail. One principle governing the development was that a system can be aware of an element in another system without necessarily sharing it. This allows the sub-system to acquire the information needed for its strategies without losing its internal rationality, an important achievement, because its *raison d'être* is to manipulate the main system, which is really its environment.

That, however, created a problem about the sub-system's attitude to the favoured belief. If the sub-system is rational, it will reject it, but how can it do that, if it is built around the nucleus of the wish to accept it? One suggested response to this Sartrean objection was that the wish is the wish that the main system would accept it. That squared very well with the evident fact, that the sub-system in a case of wishful thinking is not like the kind of system postulated by role psychologists. The environment that it has to dominate is not the external world, but only the main system. Another response that was suggested was that the sub-system merely takes note of the evidence in the main system without either accepting it or rejecting it.

The first of these two suggestions raised a further problem. How can the wish belong to both systems? An explanation of this dual citizenship was offered within the framework of Freud's theory. The extension of the explanation to the functional theory was more difficult, because it depended on the precise formulation of the criterion for drawing the line between the two systems. One possibility would be to assign an element exclusively to a sub-system if and only if it failed to interact in a rational way with an element in the main system with which it ought to interact in a rational way. Another possibility would be to assign an element exclusively to a sub-system if and only if it interacted in an irrational way with an element in the main system. Several reasons were given for preferring the first of these two versions of the criterion to the second one.

A further question about Freudian sub-systems in cases of

wishful thinking was whether they need an internal conscious-ness of their own. Freud's ideas on this topic were mentioned, and a functional substitute for internal consciousness was suggested.

Finally, an explanation was offered of the asymmetry in the passage of information between main system and sub-system and the explanatory successes and failures of the two main theories of systems were reviewed.

VI

THE LOCATION OF THE FAULT
BEHIND IRRATIONAL ACTION

In all the examples of irrational action discussed so far the fault has lain in the agent's deliberation. The guest misremembered the number of his drinks or else he persuaded himself that it was really all right to drive home after three double whiskeys. The girl continued the relationship against her own better judgement, because she refused to believe that her lover was unfaithful. In these two cases and in the others that have been discussed the derailment began within the agent's reasoning and the original fault was intellectual. It was, of course, a motivated intellectual fault and the wish that produced it was the same wish that then produced the irrational action. For in self-deceptive *akrasia* the rebellious wish uses the simple strategy of removing the intellectual barrier that stands in the way of its own satisfaction. But is there also another possibility? Could it leave the barrier untouched and, without any preliminary lowering of it, simply jump it when the moment for action arrived? That is the difficult question.

This extra possibility, if indeed it is one, was mentioned earlier and the further type of *akrasia* was given a name, 'last-ditch *akrasia*'. Socrates maintained that last-ditch *akrasia* is not a real possibility unless it is unconscious.[1] Aristotle was ambivalent about it,[2] and there is no agreement on the matter

---

[1] See Plato, *Protagoras*, 354E-358D. There is, of course, another possibility, namely that the act is done consciously but under compulsion. In that case it is not usually classified as *akrasia*. The exclusion of compulsive cases will be maintained here because it would be unfair to diagnose a case of compulsion as 'lack of self-control'. The distinction may be difficult, but it has to be drawn.

[2] See Aristotle, *Nicomachean Ethics*, Bk. VII, Chs. 1-10 and *Eudemian Ethics*, Bk. B, Chs. 6-8, both of which will be discussed in Ch. X.

today. On the one hand, it seems obvious that the guest could take a third double whiskey consciously, without compulsion, and without any diminution in his conviction that it would be better to stop at two. On the other hand, his conviction certainly ought to have prevailed and it is arguable that, if it did not, there must have been either an element of compulsion or some intellectual slippage.

This is not an easy matter to settle. One thing that makes it difficult is the influence that early intuitions exert on the later construction of theories. Asked whether Socrates was right or wrong, people consult their intuitions and, whichever way they go, all their subsequent theorizing is likely to support them. The general prevalence of this particular perversion of reason has already been mentioned. It is especially difficult to control in an area in which it is scarcely possible to identify the facts independently of the theory that is chosen to explain them.

When someone reviews his own performance, he will tend to describe it charitably in a way derived from Socrates' theory, 'How can I have acted against my own better judgement? There must be an explanation that will show that my fault was not really so flagrant.' It is, of course, easy to find one and if a friend objects that the chosen explanation, probably compulsion, does not seem to fit the facts, he can retort that there are no firm, independent facts and that the uncharitable view is based on facts seen through the lens of some anti-Socratic theory. It is, perhaps, suspicious that the Socratic theory is the one that people usually apply to themselves, while the anti-Socratic theory is reserved for others, but nothing can really be built on such marshy ground.

The search for firmer ground is likely to be long and arduous, because the question answered so quickly by intuition involves some complex theoretical issues. Verdicts of compulsion are notoriously hard to establish or reject. It is also by no means easy to know how much to expect of a value-judgement. Of course, the judgement that it would be better to stop at two drinks ought to prevail, but what is its average actual power? Can we assume that, if the agent means it, it will be powerful enough to beat anything except compulsion, provided that there is no intellectual slippage? Is that how the mill of prudence or morality grinds out our actions?

Some sort of framework is needed for the discussion of these questions and we can establish one by plotting the various possible locations of the faults that lead to *akrasia*. They can then be surveyed and the first question that needs to be asked about them is 'Which of them lie within the agent's reasoning?' This is an important question, because the answer to it will help to determine the nature of the fault committed at each of the possible locations. It may be thought that it is a question which, unlike many others that arise in this area, will not require much discussion, because it is obvious that the faults examined so far lie within the agent's reasoning, while the fault in last-ditch *akrasia* lies outside it. However, this does not seem to have been the view taken by Aristotle when he said that the action is the conclusion of a piece of practical reasoning.[3]

Suppose that the guest is reflecting on his options before he arrives at the party. He may begin by thinking that, as far as pleasure is concerned, limitation to two drinks is undesirable, but, in relation to his safety on the drive home, it is, on the contrary, desirable. These would be two general value-judgements, each relativized to its own factor, and in his particular predicament they evidently demand an adjudication from him. Let us write them down as the first lines of his argument, a conjunction held together by the adversative word 'but'. Suppose next that he weighs up these two value-judgements and his adjudication is that, in the circumstances as far as he knows them, it would be better to stop at two drinks. That is the second line of his argument, a singular value-judgement about his predicament. Now he still has not finally committed himself, because this singular value-judgement remains relativized in two distinct ways. First, it is explicitly relativized to the circumstances as far as he knows them: the truth, unknown to him, may be that his host's whiskey is as weak as Cypriot brandy. Second, it is implicitly relativized to the two considerations mentioned on the first line of his argument, pleasure and safety: the truth, unknown to him, may be that a new consideration, courtesy, would make it better to accept the third offer. In order to commit himself, he must detach his conclusion from all relativizations and make the outright singular value-judgement that it is better to stop at two drinks.[4] That will be the third line of his argument and after that, perhaps, he will stop at two drinks.

If, notwithstanding, he takes a third, there are several locations within his reasoning at which the fault may have occurred, and two of them are particularly important. One, discussed earlier, is that he exploited the latitude between the second and third lines of his argument and drew the conclusion that it was all right to take another drink. The suggestion was that he just guessed that current medical opinion was mistaken. A more interesting variant of this possibility would be that he just guessed that the relative values of pleasure and safety were not what he was taking them to be. This interpretation of his case does not imply that values are objective in any exciting sense, but only that it is possible to get them wrong, whatever the general criterion of correctness may be. A man can doubt the solidity of his own bank-account without placing unlimited faith in his country's currency.

Another possible fault-location within his reasoning would be between its first line and its second line. Here the fault would not be intrinsic to this particular piece of deliberation, but, rather an inconsistency between his weighing up of safety and pleasure this time and on earlier, similar occasions. To-

---

[4] This analysis of a piece of practical reasoning is modelled, with slight changes, on the illuminating account given by D. Davidson: see *Actions and Events*, pp. 37-41 (a passage in Essay 2, which is a reprint of *How is Weakness of the Will possible?*). Naturally, this particular schema does not fit every case of practical reasoning, but it does illustrate the important problems in the most economical way.

day he puts pleasure first but there is no apparent difference
between today's predicament and earlier predicaments in
which he put safety first. It is evident that this fault too is
made possible by latitude. For he would not be supposing
that all the facts were the same when he reversed the values,
but, rather, that the facts were different in some way that
would justify the reversal. However, his supposition would
be a mere guess completely unsupported by his evidence and
in this case, as in the previous one, the fault would undoubt-
edly lie within his reasoning.

The difficult question is whether, after the argument has
gone through faultlessly to its third line, a fault can occur
between that line and the action without any compulsion and
without any failure of awareness. That, of course, would be
conscious last-ditch *akrasia*. There is also the other question
that has to be asked about the fault at this location, quite
apart from the doubt about its possibility: 'If it did occur
here, ought it to be counted as a fault in the agent's reasoning, on the ground that the action is its conclusion, or does it
lie outside it?'

This does sound like a rather trivial question. To form a
belief is to do something, even if it is not the same kind of
performance as doing an action, and so, when an agent
moves down the lines of deliberation and eventually acts, he
is, in some broad sense, doing things all the time. Also, the
eventual action is the goal of his reasoning and the drama is
not over until it has been performed. If anyone likes to mark
these two points by saying that the action is the conclusion of
practical reasoning, it seems that there is nothing to stop him
from doing so, but equally nothing much to be gained by it.

It is, however, possible to give this thesis more substance.
Aristotle himself probably meant that in cases in which there
is no time to make an outright value-judgement the intentional action takes its place as the conclusion.[5] There are also

---

[5] D. Davidson tentatively adopts a similar view of such actions. See *Actions and
Events*, p. 99, which will be discussed in Ch. IX.

two ways of developing the thesis which give it more sub-stance in all cases of practical reasoning rather than in the sub-class of cases that Aristotle seems to have had in mind. One way of doing this would be to say that the action should be counted as a step in the reasoning because it can be assessed in the same way as the steps that preceded it.[6] The other would be to say that the intrinsic character of the reasoning is affected by the fact that the action is its goal, even though it is done after the reasoning is over.[7]

It might be thought that there cannot be much in the second idea. For even if the judgement, that it would be better to stop at two drinks, is not the final conclusion of a piece of practical reasoning, it is its last verbal stage, and, if the reasoning down to and including that stage were used in ad-vice rather than in deliberation, it seems that its intrinsic character would remain unaltered. In fact, it looks as if it would have exactly the same character even if it were used afterwards in court with a switch to the past tense. We could, of course, refuse to call the reasoning 'practical' in such cases, but the refusal really would seem to be a trivial move. For the reasoning itself seems to be exactly the same whether it is practical or consultative or historical.

However, things are not always what they seem to be and a case can be made for thinking that there is an intrinsic difference between an argument used by an agent in his search for the best thing to do and what appears to be the same argument used by a friend advising him or making a later retrospective judgement about his action. This case will be developed and reviewed in the next chapter.

The first idea, that the action can be assessed in the same way as the steps that preceded it, would take us much further if only it could be made to work. For if the action really could

---

[6] This idea will be examined in Ch. VIII.

[7] This idea is defended by A. Müller in 'How Theoretical is Practical Reason?' which appeared in *Intention and Intentionality, Essays in honour of G. E. M. Anscombe*, edd. Cora Diamond and Jenny Teichman, Brighton, 1979. It will be ex-amined in Ch. VII.

be assessed in the same way as the verbal steps in practical reasoning, it might be possible to argue that last-ditch *akrasia* would be a kind of self-contradiction, and, therefore, a fault that could not be committed consciously. It was pointed out earlier that someone might believe two propositions which he knew to be logically incompatible, provided that they kept their distance from one another in his mind. However, this proviso is not met when they both occur in the same argument, especially if it is a short one. Therefore, if taking the third drink really does contradict the outright value-judgement that it would be better not to take it, conscious last-ditch *akrasia* may turn out to be demonstrably impossible, and, when it appears to occur, the explanation may always be that the act was done under compulsion. Certainly, the proviso about mental distance is not met, because the two moves, making the judgement and doing the action, are juxtaposed. Perhaps a proof of Socrates' theory could be constructed along these lines.

Here, then, is one possibility of finding firm ground beneath the intuition that Socrates was right and it will be explored in Chapter VIII. The action is counted as a step in practical reasoning because it is assessed in the same way as the verbal steps that precede it and conscious last-ditch *akrasia* turns out to be an example of conscious self-contradiction, impossible to achieve without the help of mental distance. Of course, everything will depend on the precise way in which the action is assessed. Will it be capable of truth or falsity? Or will the contradiction have a different kind of basis? If so, it may be hard to demonstrate that conscious last-ditch *akrasia* would be quite as difficult as point-blank self-contradiction.

It must be remembered that the assumption is that the action is not done under compulsion. If it were compulsive, it would not count as *akrasia* and there would be no special difficulty in understanding it. An obsessional belief may come very near to contradicting the believer's evidence and he may know that it does, and similarly the contradictoriness of

an agent's compulsive action against his own better judgement might be perfectly clear to him. *Akrasia* is by definition
non-compulsive and it is only non-compulsive, conscious,
point-blank contradiction in action that would come out as
impossible, if this argument were convincing.

There is also another direction in which firm ground may
be attainable. It may be that an intentional, non-compulsive
action is necessarily based on a supportive outright value-
judgement and it may also be that a value-judgement necessarily produces a conforming action, if it is followed by any
intentional non-compulsive action. Philosophers who agree
with Socrates have often claimed that these two connections
are necessary. It will be convenient to use the name 'forward
connection' for the one that runs from value-judgement to
action, and the name 'backward connection' for the one that
runs in the opposite direction, from action to value-judgement. The question, whether they really are necessary connections, will be discussed in Chapters IX and X.

Something needs to be said about the difference between
claiming that the two necessary connections make conscious
last-ditch *akrasia* impossible and claiming that it is impossible
because it requires the agent to contradict himself by acting.
If the two connections really were necessary, nobody could
say that the guest judged that it would be better to stop at two
drinks, but took a third one intentionally and without compulsion, or that he took a third one intentionally and without
compulsion but did not judge it better to do so. The reason
why nobody could say these things about him is that they
would be self-contradictory descriptions of his case.

That is one claim. The other claim is that, if he made an
outright singular value-judgement and acted against it, he
would be contradicting himself by so acting. That is a different claim, because describing an action is not the same thing
as doing it. It is not the same thing even when the agent describes his own action. So on the assumption that the two connections are necessary, if he contradicts himself by acting
against his own better judgement, that contradiction is not

the same as the contradiction in which he would be involved if he merely described himself as acting against his own better judgement.

One way of appreciating this difference is to see that the two performances would lead people to make quite different protests. If the guest took a third drink after judging it better to stop at two, they would protest that his action was inconsistent with his value-judgement, but, if he reported that he had taken a third drink after reporting that he judged it better to stop at two, anyone who believed in the necessity either of the forward or of the backward connection would protest that his second report was inconsistent with his first one. No doubt, both protests would elicit an explanation chosen from the same range of possibilities, perhaps 'I must have been acting under compulsion'. However, that does not alter the fact that the protests themselves are different, because they have different targets. The first target is acting against one's own better judgement, which is something that only the author of the judgement could be accused of doing, but the second target, reporting an impossible combination of value-judgement and action, is something that anyone could be accused of doing. It is, of course, possible to base the second protest on the first one and to take the view that the report is self-contradictory because it represents the agent as contradicting himself by his action. But there is no need to take this view and, in any case, it merely connects the two contradictions without identifying them with one another.

The point is worth labouring, because it is necessary to understand the different ways in which philosophers have argued for the Socratic thesis that what looks like conscious last-ditch *akrasia* must really be compulsive action. One way is to claim that conscious last-ditch *akrasia* would require the agent to contradict himself by acting, and the other is to claim that it is self-contradictory to describe his case as 'conscious last-ditch *akrasia*'.

It is curious how difficult it is to hold these two things apart in one's mind. They tend to coalesce and produce a blurred image, especially in reflections on practical reasoning.[8] This coalescence is not confined to acting and describing one's action. On the contrary, it also affects wanting to do something and saying that one wants to do it, and it seems to be produced by a well known peculiarity of practical reasoning. Its peculiarity is that it does not develop independently of its subject-matter in the way in which theoretical reasoning develops. If someone infers that there will be an eclipse of the moon tomorrow, his conclusion neither influences, nor is influenced by the later eclipse, because it cannot alter it and is not based on precognition, but this detachment is not maintained by practical reasoning.

Suppose, for example, that someone starts from the premiss that he wants to be in London by 6.00, adds the further premiss that the 4.30 train is the only one that will get him there in time and concludes, 'So I want to catch it'. This conclusion may be influenced from outside the argument by what he finds that he actually wants to do when he reaches it, and no precognition is needed for this influence because the fact is contemporary and available to him. Also, in the opposite direction, the conclusion may influence what he actually wants to do by showing him what he ought to want to do and no psychokinesis is needed for this influence because the effect is produced in his own psyche.

This reciprocal sensitivity is evidently connected with the difference between a piece of practical reasoning and what appears to be the same piece of reasoning used in advice or in a retrospective assessment of the action. But the point to be made about it now is that it tends to bring about a coalescence of wanting to do something and saying that one wants to do it in accounts of practical reasoning and so to produce a blurred image. The trouble that we experience with acting and saying that one is acting really begins further back in the

---

[8] P. H. Nowell-Smith introduced 'logical oddity' both as a property of actions that run counter to the agent's reasons and as a property of reports of actions that run counter to reports of his reasons. See *Ethics*, London, 1954, pp. 72-5, 83-5, and 102-7.

process of reasoning and it needs to be treated in a general way that will cover all its manifestations.

The strategy will be to keep the two arguments for the Socratic thesis strictly separated and to begin with the suggestion that in last-ditch *akrasia* the agent would be contradicting himself by acting.

* * *

Not much has been done in this chapter, because it is intended to set the stage for what is to follow. An earlier example was expanded to include a fuller process of deliberation by the agent and two possible locations of the fault that started his *akrasia* were found within his reasoning. These faults would be intellectual but motivated, and so his *akrasia* would be self-deceptive. The difficult question was then raised: 'Could the fault occur at the last ditch, between his outright singular value-judgement and his action without any failure of consciousness?' Socrates' answer was that that location is not a possible one for the fault, unless there is compulsion and then, of course, it is not an example of *akrasia*.

Another, related question was then considered: 'Is the action the real conclusion of a piece of practical reasoning?' Aristotle's answer, that it is, can be given an interpretation that almost trivializes it, but three interpretations that would make it more substantial were suggested. One was that, when there is no time to make the outright evaluative judgement, the action takes its place as the conclusion. This was probably what Aristotle meant. The second suggestion was that the action is a move in a piece of practical reasoning which affects the character of the verbal steps that precede it. The third was that to act against one's own outright singular value-judgement is to contradict oneself in a way that is just like drawing a contradictory conclusion in the verbal stage of deliberation.

The third suggestion was identified as one of the two main defences of Socrates' denial of the possibility of conscious last-ditch *akrasia*. It was distinguished from another defence based on the claim that the connection between outright singular value-judgement and intentional non-compulsive action is necessary in both directions, or, to adopt the terminology that has been proposed here, that both the forward and the backward connections are necessary.

VII

PRACTICAL REASONING

There is a risk that anything that is said about all the different forms of practical reasoning will be either false or too general to be of any interest. Sometimes the premisses attribute value to certain goals and sometimes they merely specify what the agent wants. The conclusion may promote a particular action as one of several that would achieve the goal or as the one and only action that would achieve it, or even as a necessary but insufficient step towards its achievement in a case in which nothing more can be done for the time being. Life came before reasoning and reasoning before logic and there is an exuberant variety of styles of practical reasoning.

The place of the topic in this investigation does put some restriction on its treatment. It arose out of a question about the kind of fault that can occur between an agent's concluding singular value-judgement and his action: 'Can the judgement be defied by the action consciously and without compulsion?' That question then led to another: 'Is the action really a move within the agent's reasoning, to be assessed in the same kind of way as his earlier, verbal moves?'

However, concentration on these questions does little to narrow the focus of the inquiry. The verbal moves in practical reasoning are presumably governed by the same rules as theoretical reasoning and so, if we ask whether the action is assessed in the same kind of way as a theoretical conclusion, we are evidently asking whether those rules can be adapted to apply to actions as well as to propositions. But that raises many difficult questions about the relation between theoretical and practical reasoning and threatens to make this part of the inquiry unmanageable.

There is, therefore, some excuse for presenting the topic in a schematic way that will at least be clear, even if it omits some of the details. One way of doing this would be to organize the inquiry like an auction. The starting-point would be a thesis about practical reasoning which many people find acceptable at first sight as nothing but the truth. Then there would be various considerations that might make it necessary to add to this minimal thesis and perhaps to modify it and the question would be, how far the facts would take us. Should we really have to say that an action can contradict a value-judgement in the same kind of way that one judgement can contradict another? Or could we get all the facts for less than this?

A plausible thesis to start the bidding is that practical reasoning is simply theoretical reasoning done with a view to eventual action. The central case is deliberation. Here the agent reasons in order to discover the best thing for him to do in the circumstances.[1] He rehearses his premises, factual and evaluative, and arrives at the theory that an action of a certain type would be best. He then forms the intention of doing an action of that type and, if all goes well, does one intentionally. But it should not be forgotten that there are also other cases: the agent may be reminding himself of his reasons for a decision, or reassuring himself that they are sufficient reasons, or even explaining his decision to someone else.

Whatever the precise orientation of his reasoning, truth is the property that is transmitted from his premises, if indeed they are true, to his outright evaluative conclusion. That requires that his reasoning be valid and its validity is judged by the usual theoretical canons.[2] These two points are essential

---

[1] Deliberation is, as Aristotle says, a kind of search. See *Nicomachean Ethics*, 1112b20-24.

[2] The difference between the conclusion, that a particular action is one good thing to do and the conclusion, that it is the one and only thing that must be done, is a difference in content. Naturally, the appropriate way of arguing for a conclusion with the first kind of content differs from the appropriate way of arguing for a conclusion with the second kind of content, but there is no need to postulate two different logics, each with its own standard of validity. The opposite view is taken by A. Kenny: see *Will, Freedom, and Power*, Oxford, 1975, Ch. V.

to the thesis. Naturally, there is no implication that the truth of his evaluative premisses is established in the same easy, non-controversial way as the truth of his factual premisses. However, that does not alter the function of his reasoning, which is to transmit truth to an outright evaluative conclusion. There is no need to exaggerate the accessible objectivity of values in order to defend the thesis that practical reasoning is merely theoretical reasoning done for the sake of eventual action.

The action, according to this thesis, begins after the reasoning has been completed. It may be rational or irrational, just as any step in the reasoning that precedes it may be rational or irrational. However, the criteria of rationality are quite different in the two cases: a step in the reasoning is rational when it is sanctioned by the rules of theoretical validity, but the action is rational when it fits the specification in the outright evaluative conclusion. If a misfit occurs at that location, the irrationality of the action is not like the irrationality of fallacious verbal reasoning. On the contrary, it is like the unruliness of a person who does not do what he is told. So the whole process involves three different operations. The premisses have to achieve truth, the conclusion has to follow from them, and, finally, the action has to conform to the conclusion. Practical reasoning is a sort of template clamped to the existing structure of a person's life and either dictating or, at least, accommodating the next addition to it.

What need is there to add anything to this minimal thesis? It seems to give an accurate, if unexciting, account of the method used by the agent in his search for the best thing to do or in his review of his reasons for judging it the best thing to do. Also, if he fails to do what he finds it best to do, it explains his fault in a way that clearly distinguishes it from a fault committed in the process of the search. Someone who acts against his own better judgement really is, as Aristotle said, like a city with a good legislature but an inefficient executive.[3]

[3] See Ch. III n. 4.

There are many possible adverse reactions to the minimal thesis. One would be to deny that it is nothing but the truth. The usual reason for the denial is that value-judgements are really disguised imperatives and, therefore, incapable of truth and falsehood. The search then begins for analogues of truth and falsehood which will serve as the semantic predicates of value-judgements. This particular adverse reaction is well known and not much need be said about it here. It is, of course, an attempt to undercut the opening bid by claiming that it already goes too far. Perhaps it will be enough to make two brief points against it.

First, even if a class of value-judgements with imperative entailments could be clearly demarcated, that would hardly be enough to show that they are pure imperatives targeted on to actions. In daily life we certainly call them 'true' or 'false' and that does not seem to be an arbitrary choice of semantic predicates, because the judgements themselves are deeply rooted in certain facts about human needs and welfare. Admittedly, the criteria for their truth are disputable and, even when they are agreed, they are hard to apply, but there is no need to yoke a facile epistemology to the theory that truth is the predicate that is transferred down the lines of an acceptable piece of practical reasoning.

Second, the search for another pair of semantic predicates to serve as the analogues of truth and falsehood seems to be doomed to failure. It is, of course, easy enough to find predicates of actions that play a distinctive and important role in practical reasoning. For example, there are the relational predicates 'satisfying the action-specification on the preceding evaluative line' and 'uniquely satisfying the action-specification on the preceding evaluative line'.[4] These are not themselves semantic predicates, but we could, if we wished, construct semantic predicates that corresponded to them, namely 'containing a specification of a type of action satisfy-

---

[4] Kenny's two kinds of practical reasoning rely on these predicates. Loc. cit., pp. 80-91.

ing, or uniquely satisfying the action-specification on the preceding evaluative line'. But it is a disadvantage of these two predicates that they are relational and so cannot belong to the first evaluative line. No doubt, we could modify them to meet this difficulty. We could say, instead, 'containing a specification of a type of action satisfying either the action-specification on the preceding evaluative line or the action-specification that it itself contains'. This semantic predicate belongs trivially to all evaluative judgements. However, that makes it hard to see the point of using it when we are arguing about the best thing to do, because every evaluative line will already satisfy it. If the first evaluative judgement in any argument is not chosen for any other, more substantial reason, it will lack any point of attachment and the whole sequence will hang unsupported like the rope in the Indian trick. That is enough to show that this semantic predicate is not an analogue of truth, but, rather, a transformation of the relation 'following from'.

Let us, therefore, assume that the minimal theory is right in claiming that truth is the semantic property transmitted down the lines of an acceptable piece of practical reasoning, and that the dynamism of value-judgements is located in the evaluative predicates that occur within them. Then there will still be several adverse reactions that the minimal theory has to meet. These further reactions, which are the main concern of this chapter, will take the form of bids that go higher than its opening bid.

They fall into two classes. Either something done by the agent after his concluding singular value-judgement is counted as another step in his reasoning, or else a sentence corresponding to one of the extra things that he does is counted as another line in his argument. It is important to observe the distinction between these two ways of raising the bidding above the point marked by the minimal thesis. The best known theory of the first type maintains that the conclusion of a piece of practical reasoning is the action. This is sometimes developed in a way that was mentioned in the previous chapter: it is claimed that the action is capable of truth or falsity and this, in its turn, is sometimes capped by the claim that last-ditch *akrasia* would be an example of self-contradiction.

It has always seemed rather extreme to maintain that the conclusion is the action, but it is possible to find other theories lying less far out along the same line. Before the agent acts he often forms the intention so to act and the formation of his intention has at least as strong a claim as his action to be counted as a step in his reasoning. Most people would feel that it has a rather stronger claim, because practical reasoning is a preparation for action and so the formation of an intention, which is one way of preparing for the action, is more naturally included in the reasoning than the action itself.

Another theory of the first type would be that, when the agent forms the desire to do a particular action, that too should be counted as a step in his reasoning. This is a suggestion that may need a little more explanation, because there is no great difference between forming a desire and forming an intention to do a particular action. Both seem to be cases of making up one's mind and the difference between them may look so marginal that there is no need for the separate concept of forming a desire to do a particular action. The idea would be that we can get along quite well with unresolved inclinations and actual intentions and that we do not need an intermediate concept.

However, that is not quite right. There is a real difference between forming a desire to do a particular action after weighing up inclinations or valuations and actually forming the intention to do it. In the second case the problem is dismissed, the project is shelved for future execution and the agent believes, to the appropriate degree, that he will in fact execute it. The first case is different because it need not involve anything so firm or final. Perhaps the agent does not yet have to decide to do the particular action, because neither he nor anyone else is going to base any further plans on his doing it. Perhaps he knows that he is not fully apprised of the circumstances or that there is some likelihood that they will change. Some of these possibilities can be covered by the formation of a conditional intention, but all of them can be covered by forming something unconditional but weaker, namely a desire to do the particular action.

If this is so, we have a third theory of the same general type as the well known theory that the action is a step in the agent's reasoning, namely its conclusion. The steps picked out by each of the three theories, forming a desire to do a particular action, forming an intention to do it, and actually doing it, belong to an interesting sequence. Each marks a stage in the escalating transition from thought to action. Of course, that in itself is not enough to show that any of these steps ought to be included in the agent's reasoning and the case for treating them in that way has yet to be sketched and reviewed, and, even if they were included in his reasoning, it would not follow that they were capable of truth or falsity. However, our concern at the moment is only with the classification of the various ways of raising the bidding higher than the minimal theory. If the further bids can be analysed in a way that shows how they are related to one another, that may put us in a position to answer the more difficult questions that they pose.

Theories that belong to the second type are quite different. They include in the agent's argument the sentences corresponding to the extra things done by him that are picked out by theories of the first type. The most extreme theory of the second type would be that the sentence 'So I take your queen' would be a line in a chessplayer's reasoning. Probably nobody has gone so far in this direction, but less extreme theories of this type have certainly been held. It is not uncommon to count sentences like 'So I shall take your queen' as lines in the agent's reasoning, and sentences like 'So I want to take your queen' have sometimes been treated in this way even when 'want' does not mean 'need'. The claim, that the intrinsic character of practical reasoning is altered by the fact that the action is its goal, is sometimes based on considerations of this kind.

It may be felt that all these theories should be rejected out of hand because they generate confusions that are neatly avoided by the minimal theory. According to that theory practical reasoning ends with the agent's concluding singular value-judgement and none of the stages of the ensuing transition from thought to action, sentential or non-sentential, belong to his reasoning. Someone who took this view would allow that 'So I want to take your queen' is a line in the agent's reasoning only when 'want' means 'need'.

There are objections to this extreme conservatism. For example, some pieces of practical reasoning deal exclusively with mere desires unsupported by valuations.[5] However, it is not necessary to reach a general verdict. Our concern is only with last-ditch *akrasia* and with questions about practical reasoning that bear on its possibility.

It so happens that those questions are also particularly interesting in their own right. Therefore, the strategy will not be to take up all the questions about the two types of theory that have been distinguished, because there is no need for a complete examination of the further bids that they make or for a general conclusion about the relative merits of conservatism and adventurousness. The questions that will be taken up will only be ones that are relevant to the possibility of last-ditch *akrasia*.

There are three questions of this kind. Two of them have already been raised, but the third one will be new. The first question is whether there is any sense in which the predicates 'true' and 'false' apply to actions so that in last-ditch *akrasia* the agent would be contradicting himself. The discussion of that topic will be deferred to the next chapter. The second question, which will be taken up in this chapter, is about the action and the two non-sentential moves that may precede it, forming a desire and forming an intention so to act. Is there a

[5] See Ch. IX.

case for including these things in the agent's reasoning? That is connected with the third question, which has not been raised before. If the sentences, 'So I want to take your queen' and 'So I shall take your queen' are counted as lines in the agent's argument, is truth the semantic predicate that ought to be passed on to them? If not, and if the sentences are counted as lines in the argument, the minimal theory will lose much of its original neatness, because it will be extended in a way that produces a sharp change in its character. Or, to put the point in the other way, the character of practical reasoning will be altered by the fact that action and the non-sentential moves that lead to action are its goal.

It is best to begin with the third question. It was suggested in the last chapter that the sentence 'So I want to catch the 4.30 train' and the agent's actual desire might exhibit reciprocal sensitivity. But how exactly would they influence one another? And could the reciprocity be explained without the introduction of some analogue of truth for this so-called 'line in the argument'?

First, something needs to be said about the general character of an argument that uses the sentence 'So I want to catch the 4.30 train', where 'want' does not mean 'need'. There are two cases to be considered. The sentence may follow the line 'So it is best to catch the 4.30 train' or it may replace it. The first case is unusual, because it involves a certain redundancy. It is not so much part of the agent's particular plan as a natural consequence of any plan. Why mention it? In the second case, which is more common, it does not meet this challenge, because it is substituted for the line 'So it is best to catch the 4.30 train' and takes over its role of developing the agent's plan. This substitution produces a change in the character of the argument, and it is none too easy to understand the exact nature of the change.

There seems to be a change of a similar kind in certain theoretical arguments. Someone who is arguing to a theoretical conclusion may not draw it in its simple factual form. His conclusion may take instead the slightly different form 'So I believe that such and such is the case'. When this happens, he is expressing the belief that would have been pragmatically implied by the factual form of his conclusion. But it must not be forgotten that he is also connecting this belief with the preceding lines of his argument. That is why he begins with the word 'So', just as he would have done if he had drawn his conclusion in its straightforward factual form. Now if he had drawn it in that form, he would have been claiming that it was true because it followed from true premisses. But when he draws it in the other form, 'So I believe that such and such is the case', is he claiming that this sentence is true? That might be doubted. Indeed, it might be doubted whether he was making any claim with the whole sentence except the claim that whatever he was doing was rational.

But what exactly would he be doing with the whole sentence? One suggestion might be that he would be expressing the belief that it would be rational to hold, because the embedded sentence, 'Such and such is the case', followed from his premisses and because his premisses were true. Or perhaps he would be expressing the formation of the belief. Or possibly the belief-sentence would be performative and his utterance of it would actually be the formation of the belief.

Maybe there is no need to make an exclusive choice between these alternatives. After all, there are several different kinds of situation in which he might use the belief-sentence. He might be stressing the rationality of the belief in a situation in which he found it difficult to form it. That would make the belief-sentence a little like an imperative targeted on to the formation of the belief. There are also situations in which the factual conclusion comes as something new and then it seems more appropriate to say that he is expressing the formation of the belief or actually forming it by his use of the sentence. When this kind of account is adopted, it is essential not to forget the word 'So', which always carries the implication that whatever he is doing is rational.

There is also another kind of situation in which people argue in this way. Quite often the conclusion does not come as anything new because they already hold the belief for the reasons set out in the argument. Perhaps they are rehearsing the argument in order to remind themselves of their reasons for holding the belief. Or maybe they need to reassure themselves. In this kind of case, though the belief-sentence is expressive, it simply reports the existing belief, presumably truly, and endorses its rationality with the word 'So'. This thought-process is easily reconstructed as an inference, but it is an inference with two peculiarities. First, it requires the extra premiss, 'I am rational', because, if that were not so, the truth of the belief-sentence would not follow from the known truth of the premisses and the known validity of the argument. Second, the conclusion, 'So I believe that such and such', is open to instant verification (or falsification).

This way of construing the argument in situations in which the belief is already held for the reasons given in it suggests an interesting possibility. It might be possible to defend the suggestion that in all the other situations a deep analysis of the belief-sentence would use the concepts of truth and validity in the standard way. Of course, this would be without prejudice to the idea that there is considerable variation on the surface in the other situations in which the belief-sentence is used. No doubt, it is often used to express the formation of the belief or actually to form it. But what if the thinker finds that, in spite of everything, it is false that he believes that such and such is the case? The belief-sentence would surely die on his lips and, though the reasons for calling it infelicitous are interesting, the fundamental obstacle is really its falsehood when it is taken as a factual statement.

The most difficult case for this deep analysis of the belief-sentence is the situation in which the thinker stresses the rationality of the belief but finds it difficult to form it. That certainly makes it natural to adopt the theory that the belief-sentence is an imperative targeted on to the formation of the belief. However, it is surely a short-cut to adopt this theory without more ado. Where does the force of the imperative come from? One possible explanation is provided by the suggested deep analysis. When the belief-sentence is taken as the factual claim, that the thinker has the belief, it aims at truth and the extra premiss, 'I am rational', must be included in his argument for it. So given the truth of his other premisses and the validity of his argument, he can draw the hypothetical conclusion 'If I am rational, I believe that such and such is the case'. The force of the imperative is then derived from the fact that he, like everyone else, wants to be rational.

Perhaps it is not necessary at this point to go into the effect of irrationality, the '*akrasia*' of belief-formation. A number of rather speculative ideas have been put forward to explain the character of the shift in the argument to 'So I believe that such and such is the case'. An attempt will be made in a moment to transfer these ideas to the sentence 'So I want to catch the 4.30 train', and that will be the appropriate point for the introduction of irrationality not only in the formation of desires but also in the formation of beliefs. Meanwhile perhaps it does not matter if doubts are felt about the suggested deep analysis of the conclusion 'So I believe that such and such is the case'. The various surface analyses are more likely to be found immediately acceptable, and they are enough to explain the shift that occurs in a theoretical argument in many situations in which the belief-sentence is substituted for the normal factual conclusion.

How is it with the conclusion, 'So I want to catch the 4.30 train'? There seems to be in this case the same kind of substitution of a conclusion about the reasoner's attitude for a conclusion about the objective basis of his attitude, and the shift in the argument seems to be quite like the shift in a theoretical argument that has just been described. Someone who judges it best to do an action of a certain type will want to do one and will continue to want to do one more than any alternative action, provided that he is rational. So it is natural for him to substitute the conclusion, 'So I want to catch the 4.30 train' for the outright evaluative conclusion, 'So it is best to catch it', just as it is natural for him to substitute a belief-sentence for the straightforward factual conclusion of a theoretical argument.

There is, however, a difference to be noted between the two cases. The sentence 'So I want to do so and so' does not commit the speaker to the corresponding value-judgement, whereas the sentence 'I believe so and so' does commit the speaker to the embedded factual statement. This is because some desires of this kind are not supported by valuations and do not even pretend to be supported by them.[6] This is an important feature of the linkage between wanting and valuing, but it does not upset the parallelism that is being developed here with the linkage between believing and stating. For the parallelism does not depend on the false assumption that wanting involves valuing but only on the converse assumption that valuing involves wanting, which really is true of rational agents. So the explanation of the shift to the conclusion, 'So I want to catch the 4.30 train' stands unaffected by this difference between the two cases.

An examination of the semantics of the conclusion 'So I want to catch the 4.30 train' ought to reveal a close parallelism with the semantics of the conclusion 'So I believe that such and such is the case'. First, there is a similar variety of situations in which the sentence is used. Often it will come as something new to the reasoner, and in such cases he will usually be expressing the formation of his desire to catch the train or actually forming it by using the sentence performatively. There will also be cases in which his mind is already made up and he is rehearsing his reasons, perhaps in order to reassure himself. Naturally, if that is what is happening, his conclusion will not come as anything new to him. However, there are other cases quite like these, in which the desire has been formed automatically, without any reasoning, and the agent has not given the matter any thought. In a situation of this kind his conclusion really is almost a discovery: he reasons to a conclusion which, he finds, is already true.

---

[6] This will be argued in Ch. IX.

It is important to notice two points about cases in which the agent's mind is already made up. First, they are extremely common and it is an illusion to suppose that practical reasoning is always exploratory. Aristotle may have been right when he said that deliberation is a search for the best thing to do, but if he was right, that is only because not all practical reasoning is deliberation. The second point is about the last type of case, in which the agent's mind is not only made up before he reasons, but also made itself up without any reasoning. It is a common philosophical prejudice that cases of this kind are rare and that they always have to be given a Freudian interpretation. In fact, they are not rare, because a person's system of desires and beliefs has a natural tendency to sort itself out and to achieve rationality without explicit reasoning. Nor is this kind of automatism buried at all deeply below the surface. It is deep enough to warrant the idea that the reasoner finds out what he already wants to do. But it is only just a discovery and only just a case of preconscious thought. Certainly there is not the depth or the tough archaeological dig that a philosopher's appeal to Freud usually implies.

As in the case of belief, it is possible to adopt a single deep analysis for the conclusion 'So I want to catch the 4.30 train' without prejudice to the variety of its surface uses. The deep analysis simply relies on validity and truth. If the reasoner is rehearsing his reasons for a particular desire that he supposes himself to possess already, his conclusion will be straightforwardly false, if he does not possess it. The outcome will be the same if he is trying to find out what he already wants to do and gets it wrong. The impact of factual falsehood is oblique in the other kind of situation, in which he is trying to make up his mind and uses his conclusion to express the formation of his desire or is actually trying to form his desire by drawing it. However, though factual falsehood only makes an oblique impact on his conclusion in such cases, it is completely devastating. The claim 'So I want' would immediately die on his lips.

The word 'So', in the conclusion, 'So I want to catch the

'4.30 train', always makes a claim to rationality, just as it does in the conclusion 'So I believe that such and such is the case'. That creates a certain problem in a case in which the reasoner finds that he cannot, or does not, form the desire to catch the train. His conclusion then seems to have the force of an imperative instructing him to form it. But how can that force be explained within the framework of a theory that construes his conclusion as a shot at the truth? To put the problem in another way, how can he have argued validly from true premisses to a false conclusion? Surely there must be another way of construing his thought process?

The most conservative solution to this problem would be the same as the solution offered in the case of belief. We keep the idea on which the deep analysis is based, namely the idea that the conclusion simply aims at truth, but we add to the agent's argument the premiss, 'I am rational'. Then it is possible to explain how the imperative gets its force. Suppose that the agent's other premisses are complete and no consideration of fact or value that is relevant to his predicament has been omitted. Suppose too that he has argued validly from his premisses. Then it is legitimate for him to draw the hypothetical conclusion, 'If I am rational, I want to catch the 4.30 train'. The force of the imperative is then derived from the fact that he, like anyone else, wants to be rational.[7]

This suggestion needs more argument to support it. The argument for it that will now be developed will use the idea of reciprocal sensitivity, which was introduced at the beginning of this investigation of practical reasoning. If the sentence 'So I want to catch the 4.30 train' really has to be included in the agent's reasoning, its semantic predicate will still be truth and so the extension of the minimal theory will not radically change its character. However, truth can only be retained at a price. For we shall have to allow for the possibility that the reasoner's actual system of desires and beliefs is recalcitrant

---

[7] Imperatives are a little rough. Perhaps the manoeuvres described by Attribution Theorists come in at this point to smooth the transition from 'ought' to 'is'. See Ch. IV.

and his conclusion turns out to be false. In such a case his conclusion may influence what he actually wants to do, but what he finds that he actually wants to do may also exert an influence on his conclusion. Indeed, it is the latter influence that makes it plausible to retain the main idea of the deep analysis, that his conclusion aims at truth, and that, in its turn, makes it necessary to explain the conclusion's imperative force in a slightly circuitous way.

The argument that will now be developed for the explanation will also analyse the phenomenon of recalcitrant desires and intentions and show when it has to be explained as the result of internal irrationality or *akrasia*, and when it can be explained in other ways. The argument will also establish a connection between these topics and the idea that the agent's reasoning includes his action, or, at least, includes his preparatory non-sentential moves.

So far, only one argument has been offered for the proposed deep analysis of the conclusion, 'So I want to catch the 4.30' and for the consequential, rather roundabout way of dealing with its instructive force. It fits certain uses of the conclusion neatly and, though it does not achieve a surface fit with other uses, it does explain the impact of factual falsehood on them. It is, therefore, an analysis that provides a deep explanation of the various uses of the conclusion without doing any violence to their surface variety. However, the trouble is that it does look a little arbitrary to insert the premiss, 'I am rational', in order to account for the instructive force of the conclusion.

Perhaps the appearance of arbitrariness might be removed by a comparison of practical reasoning with theoretical reasoning from another point of view not yet mentioned. Suppose that someone predicts an eclipse from the orbits of sun, earth and moon. His premisses might be incomplete because he had failed to take account of some new gravitational effect coming from outside the solar system. However, it would be absurd to find fault with his argument because he had failed to include the premiss that the universe is rational. How could it not be? On the other hand, the parallel premiss about the rationality of the reasoner is not at all absurd, and it really does need to be inserted even by the reasoner himself. We may, if we wish, treat it as a common presupposition of all pieces of practical reasoning, but that will not alter the important fact, that in cases of irrationality it will simply be false. So there is nothing arbitrary about the insertion of this premiss in a piece of practical reasoning. Practical reasoning is a thought process concerned with the reasoner's own system of desires and beliefs which may well exhibit irrationality.

Let us go back to the question where the irrationality might be located. So far, two possibilities have been mentioned. The irrationality might occur at some point before the agent's concluding singular value-judgement, or it might occur at the last ditch between that value-judgement and the action, if indeed that is a possibility. We now have to add some variants of the second kind of case. Before acting, the agent may make one of the two preparatory non-sentential moves and that opens up the possibility that he might make one or the other of them irrationally. Or he might find that one of them had already been made irrationally, because his actual desire or intention did not fit his evaluative conclusion and could not be cajoled into conformity. These would be variants of last-ditch *akrasia* and they raise questions which will have to be discussed. How is their occurrence established? Is there not sometimes a case for respecting the recalcitrant desire or intention and finding some fault with the argument rather than diagnosing *akrasia*?

Akrasia is internal irrationality and so it is relative to the agent's factual beliefs and valuations. But to which beliefs and valuations should it be relativized in a given case? The simple answer, which has been presupposed so far, is that it should be relativized to the factual beliefs and valuations that figure as the agent's premisses. However, there is also the possibility that there are factual beliefs or valuations that he has failed to include in his premisses in spite of the fact that he really does hold them. Consequently, when his actual desire or intention is recalcitrant, there is a real possibility that this is not attributable to *akrasia* but, rather, to some deficiency in his premisses. He may have failed to include in them some important consideration of fact or value, and when the omitted consideration is inserted, he may find that his evaluative conclusion is no longer what it was. In such a case the executive part of his psyche would be wiser than its ratiocinative part.

There is, of course, another way of explaining this kind of recalcitrance without invoking *akrasia*: there might be a fault in the agent's reasoning. However, such faults are usually easier to detect than incompleteness in his premisses. So someone who is puzzled by the recalcitrance of the executive part of his psyche will usually search for some incompleteness in his premisses. Now the general rule governing such explanations is that they must pick on an internal fault: he omitted a premiss which was part of his mental equipment. An external inadequacy in the factual beliefs or valuations with which he was equipped would not be relevant. For how could an inadequacy of that kind produce recalcitrance? We are not supposing that he is clairvoyant.

There is, at this point, a connection with self-deceptive *akrasia*. One common form of that failing exploits the possibility that the agent's evaluative conclusion might be altered if his store of factual beliefs or valuations were enlarged.[8] A different, but related, possibility is being used here to explain recalcitrance without irrationality. The point is not that the agent's store of factual beliefs or valuations might be enlargeable, but, rather, that some of the items contained in it might be mistakenly omitted from his premisses. The general description of the phenomenon is a familiar one: practical reasoning is defeasible. The special case that yields an explanation of recalcitrance is the case in which a piece of practical reasoning is defeated by a factor omitted from the agent's premisses in spite of its availability to him.

[8] See Ch. IV.

When an agent is unable to find an omission from his premisses that would explain his recalcitrance and there is no
detectable fault in his reasoning, he can infer last-ditch *akrasia*
in the executive part of his psyche, if, as will be argued later,
that is a real possibility. Of course, it will not be the irrevoc-
able last-ditch *akrasia* of action, but only the revocable last-
ditch *akrasia* of one of the two non-sentential preparatory
moves. However, these faults all belong to the same general
type: the executive is rebelling against the legislature.

In cases where there is no rebellion and the recalcitrance is
attributable to an omitted premiss the executive shows itself
wiser than the legislature. This can even happen at the very
last moment, because the agent acts against his concluding
value-judgement and only later finds the omitted consideration that would have reversed that judgement. It would be a
romantic idea that people discover the best thing to do by
waiting to see what they actually do when the time for action
arrives, but it is an idea that does have a certain application in
the softer and more intuitive types of practical reasoning. For
example, in personal relations the agent is sometimes right to
attach great weight to his final impulse. This is often seen in
cases where deliberation done in advance is likely to suffer
from a deficiency of imagination. At the other end of the
spectrum there are hard calculative cases, like chess moves,
which are less likely to develop in this way. However, automatized reasoning does sometimes occur even in calculative
cases and, when it occurs, it can always produce a recalcitrant
action directly, without any supporting sentential moves.

Recalcitrance normally makes its appearance earlier, when
the agent finds that he does not want to carry out the course
of action that his concluding singular value-judgement com-
mends to him. If he then discovers a consideration that justifies his recalcitrance, he will reject his previous argument in
two distinct ways: he will claim that it is false that he wants to
do what he previously concluded that he did want to do, and
he will claim that it is false that he would want to do it if he
were rational. So he will reject both the detached categorical

conclusion and the detached hypothetical conclusion, 'If I am rational, I want to do such and such'. The latter point could perhaps be put, without too much paradox, by saying that, when an agent rationally wants to do a particular action, his desire is quasi-cognitive. That idea may have been an important element in Aristotle's theory of practical wisdom. Certainly, he thought that the pleasures of well trained agents are quasi-cognitive.[9]

It is worth asking why so much weight should be attached to the resolved desires of an average agent. After all, he might be irrational and his wanting to do a particular action might simply be a manifestation of revocable last-ditch *akrasia*. True, but there are also considerations on the other side. We often do have some idea whether a recalcitrant desire is based on an intuition of value or comes from some other source. It is, for example, less likely to come from an intuition of value when the rebellion is based on the desire for physical pleasure and so Aristotle placed this kind of case in the centre of the concept of *akrasia*. For one reason or another, before we begin our search for an overlooked factor, our idea, that there is one to be found, is not merely speculative. On the other hand, we are not nearly so ready to attribute rationality to a belief that is recalcitrant to an inductive argument for a factual conclusion without yet having any idea why it might be rational. No doubt, intuitions do play a role in questions about matters of fact, but they are based on generalizations that have to be established and, at some level, remembered, whereas intuitions of value are based on generalizations that have simply become part of the agent's character.[10]

The reciprocal sensitivity of sentence and attitude at this point in a piece of practical reasoning is the direct result of the cognitive weight that an average agent attaches to his resolved desires. Suppose that his premises are complete and his reasoning valid. Then he can detach the hypothetical conclusion, 'If I am rational, I want to do such and such' and

[9] See *Nicomachean Ethics*, Bk. X, Ch. 5.
[10] So Aristotle says that practical wisdom is not forgotten, ibid., Bk. VI, Ch. 5.

exert the force of the imperative that is derivable from his desire to be rational. Alternatively, he can assume that his actual system of desires, beliefs and valuations is already rational and detach the categorical conclusion, 'I want to do such and such'. In short, the sentence 'So I want to do such and such' aims at truth on the assumption that the actual system is rational and, in case the actual system is not rational, its aim is to make it so. It is, therefore, a sentence with two different functions and the state of the agent determines which one it exercises, or, if it exercises both, to what degree it exercises each of them. This division of semantic labour is like the distribution of power that is effected by the differential gear in the driving axle of a car.

It might be objected that it is incoherent to assign both these functions to the conclusion, 'So I want to do such and such'. For how can the sentence have the task of fitting the fact and, at the same time, have the task of inducing the fact to fit it? Surely it is only possible to have a single direction of fit between a single pair of items in semantics. One direction of fit is appropriate to instructions and the other is appropriate to factual statements, and this difference is like the difference between fitting a shoe to a foot and fitting a foot to a shoe. Of course, it is also possible to search for any pair of foot and shoe that fit one another, but that does not seem to be like anything that we do with language and facts. Certainly, the semantic tasks that we expect singular sentences to perform always start from a single item.

The assumption, that it is incoherent to suggest that there might be two opposed directions of fit between a single pair of items, has dominated this topic for the last twenty-five years. The model has been a social one: you tell someone that such and such is the case or you tell him to make it the case, but you cannot get a single atomic sentence to perform both these functions simultaneously. But the dominance of this social model really needs to be challenged. Why should the psyche's dialogue with itself be exactly like its dialogue with another psyche?

There really does not seem to be any need for exact similarity here. However, the difficult thing is to identify a difference between the two dialogues that would explain why the inner one can exploit a device that is radically different from anything that is available when two people are involved. First, a concession must be made to the assumption that a single pair of items cannot exhibit both the opposed directions of fit in semantics. Then a case will be made for a theory that goes a long way towards denying the assumption.

What has to be conceded is that in the case that is being examined, strictly speaking, it is not the same pair of items that exhibits the two opposed directions of fit. For when the conclusion 'So I want to do such and such' functions as an imperative, it is at first relativized to the condition 'If I am rational', and later, when it is detached, the detachment is effected on the basis of the agent's desire to be rational. But when the conclusion functions as a factual statement, though the condition to which it is at first relativized is the same, namely 'If I am rational', the detachment is effected on the basis of the agent's assumption that he is, in fact, rational. So, though the conclusion is expressed in the same words, whichever function it is performing, the underlying operation of detachment is carried out on a different basis in the two cases. The conclusion is like a conjuror's hat from which it is possible to extract different objects only if different objects have first been put into it.

This concession to the objection, that a single pair of items cannot exhibit both the opposed directions of fit in semantics, makes a difference to the question that ought to be asked at this point. It is evident that there is a certain amount of elision or syncopation going on when the conclusion 'So I want to do such and such' combines the two functions. So the question that now needs to be asked is 'What makes it possible for a single sentence to rely on two different bases for its detachment when it performs the two functions simultaneously?'

The answer that will be defended here is that this is possible only because practical reasoning is concerned with the reasoner's own system of desires, beliefs and valuations. If this is right, it may provide a solution to the problem about deliberation, advice and history, which was posed in the last chapter: 'Is the character of practical reasoning altered by the fact that its goal is an action, namely the reasoner's own action?' It may also put us in a position to assess theories that treat the action or the preparatory non-sentential moves as parts of the agent's reasoning.

But is it right? Suppose that someone is giving a piece of advice. He starts from evaluative premisses in the usual way, and then he shifts to the conclusion 'So you want to do such and such', meaning by this 'So you desire to do it' rather than 'So you need to do it' (if the second person sentence can be meant in this way). How would that differ from the parallel shift to the conclusion 'So I want to do such and such' at the end of a piece of deliberation? If there is no difference, the theory that is being defended here will face a dilemma: either the conclusion has the two functions when it is a piece of advice, or else it does not have the two functions when it terminates a piece of deliberation. The first alternative might not be too bad for the theory, because it might be extended to certain social situations without too much difficulty, but the second alternative would be fatal to it.

Evidently, the most hopeful strategy would be to reject the dilemma. This might be done in the following way. We could point out that in a case of deliberation what the agent finally wants to do is often the automatic outcome of the beliefs and valuations that figure as the premisses of his reasoning, whereas in a case of advice the beliefs and valuations belong to the adviser and the final desire belongs to the other person. The adviser cannot form the other person's final desire for him any more than he can do his action for him.[11] Nor can he get his own token-beliefs and token-valuations to occur in the other person. The most that he could achieve in that direction would be some sort of immediate transference of his type-

[11] Cf. G. E. M. Anscombe, *Intention*, Oxford, 1957, § 31.

beliefs and type-valuations. However, that only occurs in rare cases of psychological domination and what the other person usually does is to ponder the beliefs and valuations and ask himself whether he can really accept him. If the transference were general and automatic, the adviser could always shift to the conclusion 'So you want to do such and such' just as the deliberator can always shift to the conclusion 'So I want to do such and such'. But the transference is not general and, when it does occur, it does not occur automatically. Consequently, there is no basis for shifting the argument in this way in cases of advice, unless, of course, 'want' means 'need'.

This view of the matter might seem to be threatened by examples of advice based on the valuations of its recipient. When an adviser argues in this way, he often shifts to the conclusion 'So you want to do such and such' and in some of these cases he may seem to mean 'So you desire to do it' rather than 'So you need to do it'. However, it is very doubtful whether an adviser ever does use the second-person sentence with this meaning and, even if this does sometimes happen, it does not pose any real threat to the view that is being defended here, because it is an explicable exception. Such advice is only conditional, because those who give it do not commit themselves to the recipients' valuations, on which they rely, and they usually indicate their detachment, for example, by beginning 'You judge this goal to be worthwhile'. That is why they can conclude 'So you want (desire) to do such and such', if indeed they can mean the conclusion in this way.

If a person could detach himself from the source of his own valuations and, without any commitment, make the parallel statement about himself, 'I judge this goal to be worthwhile', his deliberation would not get under way. But no such detachment from one's own valuations is possible, and it makes no difference whether the agent expresses or reports his valuations. Either way, his value-judgements indicate the source of his resolved desire only because of his own commitment to them. But in conditional advice the valuations that are the source of the recipient's resolved desire can be indicated without the adviser's commitment to them. It is not possible to give ordinary, unconditional advice from this detached standpoint. So the possibility of the shift to the conclusion 'So you want to do such and such' in cases of conditional advice would cast no doubt on the proposed explanation of the difference between deliberation and unconditional advice. In deliberation the valuations and the desire belong to the same person, but in unconditional advice they belong to two different people.

This difference between unconditional advice and deliberation provides the fundamental explanation of the easy shift to the conclusion 'So I want to do such and such' at the end of a piece of practical reasoning and of the reciprocal sensitivity of this conclusion and the agent's actual desire. There is also another factor which makes an independent contribution to the explanation: the agent stands in a very close epistemic relation to his actual desire, namely non-transitional awareness. He simply feels that he does or does not want to do the action specified in his conclusion. This makes it possible for him to check his conclusion against his actual desire immediately in most cases and, when there is a delay, it is usually only a short one. Now this check may lead to a review of his premises, an addition to them and then a continuation of his reasoning, terminating in a different conclusion. In such cases the reasoning will include the check as a temporal stage in its development and that gives some support to the idea that the actual formation of the desire is a part of the reasoning. For the check is sandwiched between two stages of what is essentially the same piece of reasoning, and the formation of the desire precedes the check. Also, the desire is formed by the agent himself.

It seems that this argument locates the most important motive for including non-sentential moves in a piece of practical reasoning. The agent himself forms the desire against which he immediately checks his provisional conclusion 'So I

want to do such and such' before he firms it up and trans-
forms it into an intention and finally acts on it. There are,
therefore, three considerations, one general and two special,
in favour of counting his formation of the desire as part of
his reasoning. The general consideration is that practical
reasoning is defeasible and its defeat can be achieved by
premisses which were part of the agent's equipment but
which were overlooked by him. So it is important not to exaggerate the forward march of practical reasoning but to allow
for the possibility of contraposing the argument and faulting
its premisses for excessive exigency. That in itself does not
provide the thesis with enough support, because inductive
arguments to factual conclusions can be treated in the same
way. However, the two special considerations add their
weight at this point: the agent's actual desire is something
that he himself forms and he can check his conclusion against
it immediately, before he proceeds to the act.

It might be objected that on this view of the matter the
agent's conclusion 'So I want to do such and such' would be
an hypothesis, and that this would obliterate the distinction
between an ordinary inference to a factual conclusion and an
expressive inference. But in fact, the defensible version of this
distinction is left untouched. It is not being denied that the
conclusion can express the formation of the agent's desire or
actually function as its formation. Nor is it being denied that
he stands in the very close epistemic relation of non-
transitional awareness to his desire. All that is being maintained is that the sentence 'So I want to do such and such' has
two distinct bases, non-transitional awareness and inference,
and that, even when it is used expressively or performatively,
the worst outcome for it is factual falsehood. Of course, the
extreme version of the thesis, that such sentences are incorrigible, has to be abandoned, but that is an acceptable casualty.
For though the agent cannot make a mistaken identification
of the project that he is considering, he evidently can make a
mistaken assessment of the strength of his attitude to it.

There is, however, another more serious objection to this argument for treating the agent's formation of his desire as part of his reasoning. The argument ought to be equally convincing when it is applied to the other two non-sentential moves, the formation of the intention and the action itself, but its application to the action is not convincing, and doubts might be felt about its application to the formation of the intention.

This is easily seen. The nerve of the argument is that the agent's desires are quasi-cognitive and so he should not treat his conclusion 'So I want to do such and such' as his only measure of rationality, but should check it against his actual desire before he proceeds any further. However, the action fails the second test for inclusion in the reasoning: it is not a preparatory step but the end of the drama. So, though in speech and personal relations there is often some point in treating the action as quasi-cognitive, it cannot be counted as part of the reasoning, which extends no further than the preparations for the action. Against this simple fact the observation that the action, like the desire or the intention, is quasi-cognitive and, therefore, not necessarily irrational when it fails to conform to the agent's evaluative conclusion, seems to be powerless.

The application of the argument to intention-formation fares differently. The formation of an intention is a preparatory step and so it passes the second test. Also, the intention to do a particular action is as quasi-cognitive as the desire to do it and so it should be treated with the same respect. However, one of the points made about the desire may not be so readily applicable to the intention. It may be felt that intentions must be formed explicitly and responsibly and that they cannot be formed automatically. If this were accepted, it would only make a small difference to the argument for treating the formation of the intention as part of the reasoning. We would merely have to delete the possibility that the agent might discover that his intention to act against his evaluative conclusion had already been formed automatically. Otherwise the argument would proceed as it did in the case of the desire.

Perhaps there is no need to adjudicate the question, whether these two non-sentential moves are part of the agent's reasoning. What matters is that they are the beginning and the middle of the escalating transition from thought to action. It is particularly important that the sentence corresponding to the first of these two moves, 'So I want to do such and such', combines two distinct functions, report and instruction, and that what makes the combination possible is the fact that the agent's desire is very often the automatic product of his own valuations and sometimes quite evidently so. This is the connection that explains the frequency of the shift to the conclusion 'So I want to do such and such' at the end of a piece of deliberation.

It may be felt that it is too clumsy and confusing that this sentence should both fit and be fitted by the same item, namely the agent's resolved desire. Certainly it would be clearer if he first drew the hypothetical conclusion 'If I am rational, I want to do such and such' and then derived the two categorical conclusions, 'I want, and I ought to want to do such and such', separately and distinctly in the way that has already been analysed. But the issue is not whether this is the underlying structure of the agent's thought-process. That is agreed and the question is only whether it is possible to express this thought-process in a single sentence, which aims at truth by making itself true if it is not already true. In fact, this piece of syncopation does not seem to be an impossible feat for language. People certainly sometimes express beliefs partly in order to fortify them or even to acquire them.[12] There is no reason why they should not do the same with desires, especially when it is rational to do so and they have an argument supporting both the functions of the sentence 'So I want to do such and such'.

---

[12] This strategy for irrational belief-formation was described in Chapter IV.

This inquiry has been presented in the form of an auction. It started with the minimal theory, and the question was whether the bidding has to be raised above it. Do we have to include non-sentential moves in the agent's reasoning? And do the sentences corresponding to them count as lines in his argument? Or can we get all the facts for less than this? It seems that we could still regard the argument as terminating with the agent's outright singular value-judgement, but that the natural shift to sentences like 'So I want to do such and such' in practical reasoning suggests that this might be too conservative. However, if these sentences are included in the agent's argument, the alteration to the minimal theory will not be radical, because in their deep analysis truth will still be the property at which they aim. Nor is it really necessary to count the agent's non-sentential moves as part of his reasoning, although it is true that the immediate availability of the check that they provide does distinguish deliberation from advice.

* * *

The aim of this chapter has been to deal with a limited set of questions about practical reasoning. The starting-point was last-ditch *akrasia*, which involves a fault between the agent's concluding singular value-judgement and his action, and attention was focused on to questions about the transition from thought to action that occurs at the end of a piece of practical reasoning.

The inquiry took the form of an auction. The opening bid was the theory that practical reasoning is simply theoretical reasoning done with a view to eventual action. According to this minimal theory, truth is the property that is transmitted from premisses to conclusion in an acceptable piece of practical reasoning and, if the agent fails to act in conformity with his concluding value-judgement, his irrationality is not like the fallaciousness of sentential reasoning but, rather, like the unruliness of a person who does not do what he is told. The central case of practical reasoning is deliberation, but the agent may also review his reasons in order to remind himself of them or, perhaps, in order to reassure himself that they are sufficient.

One reaction to the minimal thesis is to deny that it is nothing but the truth, on the ground that value-judgements are really disguised imperatives. It is claimed that this makes it necessary to find some analogue of truth to be transmitted down the lines of a practical argument. This claim was discussed briefly, because it lay outside the main area of the inquiry, and it was rejected for some very general reasons.

When the minimal thesis is accepted as nothing but the truth, adverse reactions to it take the form of bids for supplements to it. These bids were divided into two classes: either something done by the agent after his concluding value-judgement is counted as another step in his reasoning, or else a sentence corresponding to one of these extra things that he does is counted as another line in his argument. The best known theory of the first type counts the action as a step in the reasoning, but this treatment is more appropriate to the formation of the intention to do the action or to the formation of the desire to do it. Theories of the second type would count as lines in a practical argument the sentences 'So I shall do such and such' or 'So I want to do such and such', where 'want' does not mean 'need'.

The short way with all these theories is to reject them on the ground that these sentences mark the escalating transition from thought to action after the reasoning has terminated with the agent's concluding singular value-judgement. However, they are worth examining, because they do raise questions that are relevant to the possibility of last-ditch *akrasia*. The discussion of one such question, 'Is there any sense in which the predicates "true" and "false" apply to actions?', was deferred to the following chapter, and the inquiry concentrated on the other two questions: 'Are the sentences "So I want to do such and such" and "So I shall do such and such" lines in a practical argument? And are the two corresponding non-sentential moves steps in a piece of practical reasoning?'

The first of these two questions was connected with the suggestion that the sentence 'So I want to do such and such' and the agent's actual desire might exhibit reciprocal sensitivity. Attention was directed to cases in which this sentence is substituted for the more usual evaluative conclusion of a piece of practical reasoning. This shift in a practical argument was compared with the shift from 'So such and such is the case' to 'So I believe that such and such is the case' in a theoretical argument.

Various uses of this belief-sentence were considered. It might express the belief, or its formation, or else its utterance might actually be the formation of the belief. In the latter two cases the conclusion would come as something new, but in the first case it is possible that the person already held the belief and was reviewing his reasons for it. If that were so, the belief-sentence would be true or false in the ordinary way. But factual falsehood is also the worst outcome for all the other uses of the belief-sentence and, if any one found that he simply could not believe his conclusion, it would die on his lips. This suggested that underneath the various surface analyses of the belief-sentence the deep analysis will use the concept of truth in the standard way.

An objection to this deep analysis was then considered. The word 'So' always makes a claim to rationality, but what are we to say about cases in which the reasoner has not formed the belief because he finds it difficult to form it? In such cases the belief-sentence seems to lack factual content and it looks more like an imperative targeted on to the formation of the belief.

The proposed answer to this objection was that the extra premiss 'I am rational' must be included in the argument. Then, given the truth of his other premisses and the validity of his argument, the reasoner can draw the hypothetical conclusion, 'If I am rational, I believe that such and such is the case'. The imperative is then derived from this with the help of the fact that he wants to be rational. If he had derived the straightforward factual conclusion 'I believe that such and such is the case', he would have been assuming that in fact he was rational.

A similar explanation was suggested for the shift from the normal evaluative conclusion of a practical argument to the conclusion 'So I want to do such and such'. This shift does not presuppose that all desires are derived from value-judgements, but only that all value-judgements generate desires.

The various uses of 'So I want to do such and such' turned out to match the various uses of 'So I believe that such and such is the case'. The situation in which the agent has already formed the desire was examined in detail. Here he will be reviewing the reasoning that produced his desire. Now this reasoning may have been automatic rather than explicit. For a person's system of valuations, desires and beliefs tends to sort itself out and to achieve rationality without the help of explicit reasoning. In such cases there is no need to suppose that the automatic reasoning is deeply buried, as in Freudian theory. When the reasoner realizes what he wants to do, it may be only just a discovery.

It is the prevalence of automatized reasoning that makes the straightforward factual use of the sentence 'So I want to do such and such' so common. But it is also possible to derive from this use a deep analysis, exploiting truth and validity, and applying to all the other uses that differ from it and from one another on the surface. For, as in the case of belief, whatever the surface use of the sentence, its worst fate is factual falsehood.

Here too a problem is posed by examples in which the agent finds it difficult to make his desire conform to his concluding value-judgement. The suggested solution was the same as it was in the case of belief. The agent draws the hypothetical conclusion 'If I am rational, I want to do such and such', and then the force of the imperative is derived with the help of the fact that he wants to be rational. If he had derived the straightforward factual conclusion, 'So I want to do such and such', he would have been assuming that in fact he was rational.

This solution was then developed in more detail, in order to connect it with the problem of last-ditch *akrasia* and with the idea that various non-sentential moves ought to be counted as steps in the agent's reasoning.

First came the objection, that it looks arbitrary to insert the premiss 'I am rational'. The answer was that it is not arbitrary, because the agent is reasoning about his own system of valuations, desires and beliefs. So though there is no need to insert the premiss 'The universe is rational' in an ordinary piece of theoretical reasoning, it is necessary to insert the premiss 'I am rational' in this kind of practical reasoning.

Suppose that it is false that the agent's system is rational. Then he may have formed a desire or an intention that fails to conform to his concluding value-judgement. These would be cases of mental last-ditch *akrasia*, quite like the physical case of last-ditch *akrasia* in action.

Now *akrasia* is internal irrationality relative to the agent's store of valuations, desires and beliefs. But suppose that some relevant valuation in his store has been omitted from his premisses. Then his recalcitrant desire, though it looks like an example of mental last-ditch *akrasia*, may really indicate that his premisses were incomplete. This would be a special case of the defeasibility of practical reasoning. The evaluative conclusion would be revised in the light of a further valuation, specifically in the light of one that was already in the agent's store but had been overlooked by him.

It follows that the agent's detachment of the hypothetical conclusion, 'If I am rational, I want to do such and such', ideally requires the fulfilment of three conditions: his argument must be valid, his premisses must be true and his premisses must include all the relevant considerations in his store. When his desire is recalcitrant to his evaluative conclusion, that can hardly be because one of his premisses is false. Validity in such cases is normally easy to check. So the question in his mind will usually be whether the explanation of the recalcitrance of his desire is mental last-ditch *akrasia* or an incompleteness in his premises in relation to his store of valuations and beliefs, which would sometimes be diagnosable as incipient self-deceptive *akrasia*.

This incompleteness is an interesting possibility. It would be a case of the executive part of the psyche showing greater wisdom than its legislative part. It happens quite frequently in softer, more intuitive examples of practical reasoning, but it can also occur in harder, more calculative cases. A justifiable rebellion of this kind can even occur at the last possible moment, when the action is done, but it usually occurs when the agent makes an internal non-sentential move. We might explain the phenomenon by saying that the resolved desires of a rational agent are quasi-cognitive. So he can trust them and back them against his evaluative conclusions when he believes that they spring automatically from his valuations without any mental *akrasia*.

This yields an explanation of the reciprocal sensitivity of the sentence 'So I want to do such and such' and the agent's desire. He draws the hypothetical conclusion, 'If I am rational, I want to do such and such' and does one of two things with it. Either he assumes that he is rational, derives the factual conclusion and if he finds it to be false, goes back and checks his premises for completeness. Or else he derives the imperative conclusion from his desire to be rational, and then, treating it as a case of mental *akrasia*, tries to bring his desire into line.

If it is objected that it is incoherent to suggest that there are two opposed directions of fit between the single pair of items, sentence and desire, there is a ready answer. The detailed analysis of the argument shows that the sentence combines two different functions only because it is derived from two slightly different sets of premises.

Even when it is allowed that language may conceal this complication and that the sentence may function in the two different ways simultaneously, there is still something that remains to be explained. Why is the shift to the conclusion 'So I want to do such and such' at least more common in practical reasoning than the parallel shift to the conclusion 'So you want to do such and such' in ordinary unconditional advice?

The explanation proposed was that in practical reasoning the reasoner's resolved desires often come from his own valuations, but that this is not the relationship between an adviser's valuations and the recipient's resolved desires. Some contribution to the explanation is also made by the close epistemic relation in which the reasoner stands to his own desires. This makes it possible for him to check a proposed conclusion against his actual desire during his reasoning.

This, in its turn, lends some support to the idea that the non-sentential move of forming a resolved desire is part of his reasoning. The formation of an intention could be treated in much the same way. But the argument for this thesis about these two non-sentential moves is not entirely cogent and it certainly cannot be extended to the action, because the action is not a preparatory move but the final one.

So the case for raising the bidding above the minimal theory did not get very far. It is still possible to regard the agent's argument as terminating with his outright singular value-judgement. If the natural shift to the conclusion 'So I want to do such and such' in practical reasoning suggests that this kind of sentence should be included in the agent's argument, it will still be a sentence aiming at truth in its deep analysis. Also, though the immediate availability of the check provided by the agent's corresponding non-sentential move distinguishes deliberation from advice, there is no need to count such moves as a part of his reasoning.

However, the bids that go above the point marked by the minimal theory do have a certain plausibility. They exploit the differences between deliberation and the same piece of reasoning used in unconditional advice or in retrospective assessment of an action. Perhaps their reaction to these differences is exaggerated but it is not unfounded and it does call attention to some deeper truths.

VIII

TRUTH AND FALSEHOOD, FIT AND MISFIT

The first of the two attempts to outbid the minimal theory of practical reasoning may be developed in a way that takes it very much further than the second one. It may be suggested that a deliberate action is not only part of the agent's reasoning but also, in its own way, capable of truth or falsehood and that, therefore, last-ditch *akrasia* would involve the agent in self-contradiction. The thesis examined in the last chapter, that there is in practical reasoning a gradual, escalating transition from theoretical inference to quasi-inferential performance, might well be accepted without any commitment to the further claim, that actions and theoretical conclusions are assessable for rationality in the same way, or even in the same sort of way. But the further claim is sometimes made.

It is not an easy claim to assess. Perhaps it would be a good idea to begin by looking at its most striking consequence, which is that last-ditch *akrasia* would involve the agent in self-contradiction. Here we need to apply the distinction drawn in Chapter VI between contradicting oneself by acting and contradicting oneself by describing an action, because the claim is that the agent would be contradicting himself by acting.

We may begin by taking another look at the distinction. Someone who said that he travelled to San Francisco without leaving Los Angeles would be describing his own action in a way that could not fit any possible action. If the forward connection between valuing and acting holds necessarily, another example of this kind of self-contradiction would be provided by someone who reported that he had acted consciously against his own better judgement without compulsion and without the help of mental distance. For given the necessity of the forward connection, no such action is possible. A similar effect would be produced by the necessity of the backward connection.[1] But contradicting oneself by action would be quite different. In such a case it is the agent's actual capitulation to the temptation that is supposed to contradict his value-judgement. Here the putative obstacle is in the mind of the agent and not in the mind of the spectator reporting what goes on in the mind of the agent. If the agent becomes his own spectator and reports on his own case, the distinction is easily lost and it must be preserved very carefully. For even when only one mind is involved there is a difference between self-contradictory agency and self-contradictory description of agency.

It must be admitted that the distinction is a slippery one. One thing that makes it difficult to get a firm grip on it is the close connection between the supposed obstacle in the spectator's mind and the supposed obstacle in the agent's mind. The idea is that the agent would be contradicting himself by acting against his own better judgement and that, because it is impossible for him to contradict himself in that way, the spectator would be contradicting himself by describing the agent as acting against his own better judgement, unless, of course, a loophole were provided by compulsion or by some failure of consciousness. But in that case, both agent and spectator would evade the charge of self-contradiction together. When the agent is his own spectator, he may face both charges of self-contradiction: he acted in a self-contradictory way and later he described his own action in a self-contradictory way. But the fact that there is a single defendant as well as a single excuse provides no support for the idea that only a single type of self-contradiction is involved.

Perhaps the best way to appreciate this is to consider the other case mentioned just now. Nobody would say that the only way to get to San Francisco without leaving Los Angeles

[1] The forward and backward connections were distinguished in Ch. VI. See p. 114.

would be to take oneself unawares, so that one could do it without quite realizing that one was doing it. The original obstacle in this case is not in the mind of the would-be agent and yet the obstacle in the mind of the spectator is of the same kind as the supposed obstacle in the mind of the spectator reporting a case of last-ditch *akrasia* in which there is no failure of consciousness in the agent's mind.

However, though this proves that there is a difference between contradicting oneself by acting and contradicting oneself by describing an action, even when the action is one's own, it does not explain what the difference is. We know what a self-contradictory description is, but we still need to be told what kind of self-contradiction acting against one's own better judgement is supposed to be.

Here we encounter a difficulty: the concept of 'contradicting oneself' is vague and it covers several different kinds of faults. When someone acts against his own better judgement, people say that he is acting inconsistently, and, more specifically, that his deeds are inconsistent with his words. They also say that what he does contradicts or belies his value-judgement, and, since it was he who made the judgement, it would be a small step along this line of usage to say that he contradicted himself. Now inconsistency and self-contradiction are among the faults that can be committed in theoretical reasoning. So it seems natural to infer from this usage that actions and theoretical conclusions are assessable for rationality in the same sort of way.

No doubt, this is true if the phrase 'in the same sort of way' is not meant at all specifically, but we must be careful not to exploit the vagueness. If we inspect the assessment of theoretical conclusions and actions, a difference becomes obvious. Sentences, unlike actions, aim at truth and it is inconsistent to put forward two sentences that cannot both be true. Consequently, in theoretical reasoning, when someone draws a conclusion that cannot be true if his premises are true, he is arguing inconsistently or contradicting himself.

There is, of course, another, less extreme way of arguing fallaciously and that is draw a conclusion that may be false even though the premisses are true. However, that is not the model used by those who argue that actions are assessable for rationality in the same kind of way as theoretical conclusions and that, therefore, conscious last-ditch *akrasia* is impossible. Their model is a theoretical conclusion that cannot be true if the premisses are true. But the difference between this kind of fallacious theoretical reasoning and acting against one's own better judgement is obvious. There is no property analogous to truth and such that the action and the agent's final outright value-judgement cannot both possess it.

The reason for this difference is plain. If someone produces a sentence, it is a contribution to his picture of the world, but, if he produces an action, it is a contribution to the world. We may say, if we like, that his action is part of his world, but that will only mean that it is a part produced by him, or, perhaps, that it is a part that is very close to him. It cannot mean that it is part of his picture of the world, because the general function of action is not to portray the world but to alter it.

Admittedly, speaking, writing, and drawing are all actions involving alterations to the world, but the point is that the converse does not hold. Alteration is not even usually portrayal and action is essentially only alteration. It follows that a value-judgement and the corresponding action, provided that it is an ordinary, non-representational action, do not form a couple aimed at the truth and, if they are inconsistent with one another, that will not be because they cannot both be true together. On the other hand, a theoretical premiss and conclusion do form a couple aimed at the truth and their inconsistency, if they are inconsistent with one another, will be explicable as the impossibility of joint truth.

The gulf fixed between theory and practice by these familiar facts seems to be unbridgeable. Naturally, that does not mean that people cannot move rationally from theoretical premisses, factual and evaluative, to practical conclusions and actions and, evidently, they do make these moves rationally. What it means is that we cannot explain them by a philosophical theory that implies that they make them under the aegis of theoretical validity or anything like it. When an agent steps down from the higher level of theory, he does so with both feet. That step is made in its final, conspicuous form at the moment of action, but it is also made in preliminary and less obvious ways when a particular desire or intention is formed. All these things are part of the world, even if they are only part of the agent's inner world. They are not part of his picture of the world, and their rationality is a matter of conformity and not a matter of the kind of consistency that is explained as the possibility of joint truth, or anything like it.

It may be objected that the phrase 'or anything like it' covers a very wide range of possibilities, and that, if we exploited that fact, we might well succeed in bridging the gulf between theory and practice. But the trouble is that any such success would be hollow, because the claim's generality, which would allow it to be true, would automatically reduce its content to a point at which it would have very little interest. This is easily seen. Our language certainly shows that we classify inconsistency and contradiction in action with inconsistency and contradiction in belief-formation, but this classification has to be understood as a very general one, set up from a distance and without any attempt at close discrimination. Any theory that tries to assimilate action to belief-formation has to be so general that it loses most of its content in order to preserve its truth. The risk is that, when we welcome a general theory of this kind, we may give it a more specific meaning than the one that allows it to be true.

One way of doing this would be to admit the existence of the gulf between theory and practice and to concede that actions are not true in the same way as sentences, but to argue that they are true in their own way. This is the line taken by Professor Anscombe in an article on Aristotle's account of practical reasoning and action.[2]

---

[2] G. E. M. Anscombe, 'Thought and Action in Aristotle', in *New Essays on Plato and Aristotle*, ed. R. Bambrough, London, 1965. But Anscombe does not claim that conscious last-ditch *akrasia* is, therefore, impossible.

Any theory of this kind has to be tested for its precise meaning. It will be convenient to call the truth that is proposed for actions 'quasi-truth'. Then the test must be carried out in two stages. First, we have to ask whether 'quasi-truth' is just another name for the action's conformity to the agent's outright value-judgement. If so, the theory short-circuits itself and is back in the extreme generality of the undiscriminating idea underlying the original classification. Now there is nothing wrong with that result, provided that it is made clear that the apparent specificity of 'quasi-truth' was not really intended. After all, one of the established senses of the word 'true' is 'agreeing with a standard, pattern or rule; exact, accurate, precise; correct, right', and so, more generally 'of the right kind, such as it should be, proper'.[3] Given this definition, there can hardly be anything wrong with calling an action that conforms to the agent's outright value-judgements 'quasi-true', provided that the width of the gulf between quasi-truth and the truth of sentences or pictures of the world is appreciated.

However, if this is the result of the first stage of the test, the theory will not have any explanatory power. For it will assign the quasi-truth of actions and the truth of sentences to a genus so broad that the assignment explains nothing. Later in this chapter the similarities and differences between the truth of sentences and the conformity of actions will be examined in detail and it will be shown that 'quasi-truth' is not really an appropriate name for the conformity of actions.

Now suppose that the first stage of the test produces the opposite result: 'quasi-truth' turns out to be not just another name for the action's conformity to the agent's outright value-judgement, but the name of another property of the action underlying its conformity and explaining it. That might give the theory a substantial content. Certainly, it would not be short-circuited back into the generality of the original classification, which merely placed irrationality of action and

---

[3] See *Oxford English Dictionary*, vol. XI, p. 417.

irrationality of theoretical conclusion in the same broad genus of inconsistency or self-contradiction. This version of the theory would identify a specific property of actions, quasi-truth, which would explain why their combination with value-judgements is, in certain cases, contradictory.

However, the gain in specificity of meaning would be accompanied by a loss of likelihood of truth. For this version of the theory is, to say the least, unlikely to survive the second stage of the test. The second stage is to ask for an identification of the underlying property of actions in addition to, and independent of, the claim made for its explanatory power. But, if quasi-truth has to be a distinct, underlying property of actions, what property can it possibly be?

There is a very strict constraint operating here. If quasi-truth is anything like the truth of sentences, it ought to be ascribable to an action independently of the reasoning that preceded it. For we discover from their truth-conditions that two sentences form an inconsistent couple, and so, if the analogy really does extend to specific similarities, we ought to be able to discover from the truth-conditions of a value-judgement and the quasi-truth-conditions of an action that they form an inconsistent couple. But where should we look for the material to meet the demands of this ambitious schema? There seems to be no available source, because actions do not in general point beyond themselves in the way that would be required if their consistency or inconsistency with value-judgements were at all like theoretical consistency or inconsistency. This version of the theory really has gone over the edge into the kind of empty analogical extravagance that Wittgenstein often diagnosed.[4]

The possibilities of manoeuvre in this area are limited and the dilemma is sharp. The first alternative is that quasi-truth is simply conformity to an outright value-judgement, but that puts it under the special sense of 'true', already quoted from

---

[4] See L. Wittgenstein, *Philosophical Investigations*, Oxford, 1953, §132.

the dictionary, 'agreeing with a standard, pattern or rule, etc.' and so deprives it of any explanatory power. The other alternative is to treat quasi-truth as an underlying property of actions which produces their agreement or disagreement with value-judgements, but, though this would yield a genuine explanation if only the property could be identified, the search for it is like the search for the North-west Passage.

It is worth taking an example of a theory of quasi-truth and watching how it fares. Professor Anscombe has put forward a theory belonging to the first of the two types that have just been distinguished, but without the further claim that it demonstrates the impossibility of conscious last-ditch *akrasia*.[5] Her problem is to give the theory substance and explanatory power and it is interesting to see how she goes about it.

Her theory is that an action possesses quasi-truth, or, as she calls it, 'practical truth', when it makes the agent's sentence 'I am doing such and such' true, where 'such and such' is the specification of the action in his outright value-judgement. If, as is usually the case, this value-judgement is reached by practical reasoning, there are three further conditions that have to be met before practical truth can be ascribed to the action. First, the value-judgement must be a conclusion that is correctly drawn from the agent's premisses. Second, it must be drawn intentionally under the specification that makes it correct. Third, the premisses themselves must be true.

This sounds like a description of the best possible outcome for the agent. He will do the right thing, and he will do it not by luck but as the result of consciously correct reasoning from true premisses. To include all this in the conditions of the practical truth of an action that is preceded by deliberation is evidently to make practical truth unlike the truth of a sentence. It also makes it unlike the validity of a theoretical inference, because the last condition of practical truth is that

---

[5] Loc. cit. In her book, *Intention*, which was published eight years before the article, there is an approximately parallel theory of 'practical knowledge'. See §32 and §§45-8.

the premisses themselves must be true. However, the theory certainly belongs to the first of the two types distinguished above, because it makes the conformity of action to outright value-judgement a necessary part of the criterion of practical truth.

The basic condition of practical truth in this theory is the first one: the action must make the agent's sentence 'I am doing such and such' true, where 'such and such' is the specification of the action in his outright value-judgement. The reason why the requirement that the action should conform to the value-judgement is put in this rather complicated way is important. It is that the conformity must not be achieved accidentally. For example, it would be achieved accidentally by a chess-player if, after judging 'So it is best to take the queen', he inadvertently put the wrong specification in his judgement about his imminent action, 'So I am taking the queen's knight', but then actually took the queen, which is what he had concluded that he ought to do. In that case his second mistake would cancel the effect of his first one and he would be lucky. This sort of luck obviously has to be excluded if the conformity of action to outright value-judgement is going to be intentional rather than accidental. Admittedly, the agent will welcome the conformity, even if it is accidentally achieved, but Anscombe's point is that it will not be intentional unless the specification under which it is done intentionally is the specification that occurs in the outright value-judgement. So she expresses the requirement of conformity, which must be met by an action that is practically true, in a complex way that ensures that the conformity is intentional.[6]

A similar distinction can be drawn between intentional and accidental success in a second type of case, in which the mistake that is cancelled is made within the agent's reasoning. Naturally, this is possible only when the action is preceded by

---

[6] See 'Thought and Action in Aristotle', p. 157: 'the description of what he does is made true by his doing it'. Cf. *Intention*, p. 57.

deliberation, and again the chess-player will provide an example. Suppose that he looks at the position on the board and makes the wrong inference, 'So it is best to take the queen's knight', but then, with the thought, 'So I am taking the queen's knight' running through his head, he actually takes the queen, which is what he ought to do and ought to have inferred that he ought to do. Here the action accidentally conforms to the conclusion that ought to have been drawn from the agent's premises. This is another piece of luck that obviously has to be excluded if the conformity of the action to the exigencies of the agent's goal is going to be intentional, and it is excluded by the first of Anscombe's three conditions. If the action actually fits the specification under which the agent does it intentionally and if that specification is the one that occurs in his outright value-judgement, the action cannot conform to the exigencies of his goal unless he makes the correct inference from his premises, which in the case of the chess-player would be, 'So I ought to take the queen'. Thus Anscombe's formulation of the requirement of conformity excludes this pair of cancelling mistakes too.

Evidently, a similar distinction can be drawn between intentional and accidental success in a third kind of case, in which the original mistake and the mistake that cancels it would both occur within the agent's reasoning. Accidental success has to be excluded here too, and Anscombe excludes it by imposing a further condition on actions that qualify for practical truth: 'The judgements involved in the formation of the "choice" leading to the action are all true.'[7] When all these conditions are met, we have what is almost the best possible outcome for the agent.

However, it is not yet quite the best possible outcome. For we still need to stipulate that each step taken by the agent in the verbal part of his practical reasoning is not only correct, but also taken intentionally under the description that makes it correct. The parallel condition has already been imposed

[7] See 'Thought and Action in Aristotle', p. 157.

on the step from outright value-judgement to action by Anscombe's complex way of formulating the requirement that the action should conform to this judgement. But it still remains to be imposed on the verbal steps in the agent's practical reasoning. She takes it for granted, but we must impose it. Then, adding up the whole column of conditions, we really do have the best possible outcome, which is the kind of action that she calls 'practically true'.

There is no doubt that this account of the conditions that have to be met in the best possible outcome is correct. The connection between the three applications of the distinction between intentional and accidental success is particularly important. It constitutes a further point of analogy between theoretical inference and quasi-inferential performance. The move from outright value-judgement to action must be made intentionally under the specification that will ensure conformity with the value-judgement just as the moves within the verbal part of practical reasoning must be made intentionally under the descriptions that make them correct.

The way in which conformity of action to outright value-judgement is stipulated is also interesting. It exploits the agent's immediate knowledge of his imminent action and it is arguable that this kind of knowledge is an essential feature of intentional action. Certainly, our concept of intentional action would be greatly impoverished and life would be much more difficult if intentions went underground after they had been formed, only to surface in action without being monitored during the final moments. It would be extremely inconvenient and rather like giving an order to a poker-faced subordinate who never gave away the fact that he was just about to execute it.

However, though this theory makes some important points about the transition from thought to action, its introduction of the concept of 'practical truth' is questionable. Is this just another name for the conformity of action to outright value-judgement in cases where certain further conditions are fulfilled? If so, does calling it 'practical truth' somehow explain it by drawing attention to a substantial similarity between it and the truth of sentences? Anscombe ascribes her theory to Aristotle and we might get an answer to these questions if we compared her theory with the passage in the *Nicomachean Ethics* that she is interpreting.[8] However, before that is done, we need an analysis of the structure of the theory, which is rather complex, especially in its use of the concept of direction of fit. If we can understand how it exploits this concept, we shall be in a better position to assess its explanatory power.

Practical truth evidently involves two different directions of fit. First, the premises used by the agent have to be true and his reasoning correct so that his conclusion, an outright singular value-judgement, will be true, and that is a case of a sentence satisfying its truth-conditions or, to put it more crudely, fitting a thing. Second, his action has to fit the description contained in his conclusion, and that exemplifies the opposite direction of fit. This double requirement evidently does not pose the problem discussed in the previous chapter, because the value-judgement is related to two different things and it is related to each of them in a different way. However, it does raise another question. Is there really any justification for wrapping up in the single concept of 'practical truth' two requirements that are so very different from one another?

There is a justification of a kind, but hardly an adequate one. When someone deliberates and acts, the best outcome is that his premises should be true, that their truth should be transmitted to his outright singular value-judgement by a valid process that he understands, and that his action should conform to the specification contained in that judgement by another adjustment that he understands. These conditions

---

[8] 1139a21-31. See 'Thought and Action in Aristotle', pp. 157-8: 'The notion of *truth or falsehood in action* would quite generally be countered by the objection that "true" and "false" are senseless predicates as applied to what is done. If I am right there is philosophy to the contrary in Aristotle. And if, as I should maintain, the idea of the *description under which* what is done is done is integral to the notion of action, then these predicates apply to actions strictly and properly, and not merely by an extension and in a way that ought to be explained away.'

are summed up in the requirement that the action should be practically true. But why embed the word 'true', used in a special sense, in the name for a set of relations that include ordinary truth? A handy name is not necessarily explanatory and can be misleading. The justification of the introduction of the term 'practical truth' would be more impressive if it demonstrably helped us to understand the nature of the fit between action and outright singular value-judgement.

Unfortunately, it does nothing of the kind. Anscombe correctly observes that the description of what the agent does, which is, of course, the description contained in his outright singular value-judgement, is made true by his doing it. But why should the fact, that the action confers ordinary truth on something else, persuade us to ascribe practical truth to it? What point is being made by the ascription, if it is not just the point that the conformity of action to value-judgement confers truth on the description contained in the value-judgement, or, more accurately, on the agent's factual judgement about his imminent action because it too contains that description, and confers something else on the action, namely the property of conferring truth on that factual judgement?

If that is all, the theory has to take the first horn of the dilemma. When the property acquired by an action that fits an outright value-judgement is called 'practical truth', that is merely another name for the property of fitting the value-judgement, or, more accurately, the property of fitting the value-judgement provided that Anscombe's further conditions, including the condition that the agent's premises are true in the ordinary way, are all fulfilled. The introduction of the term 'practical truth' does nothing to advance our understanding of the nature of this fit. It certainly does not pick out, and is not even intended to pick out, any independently identifiable property that would explain it. All the exciting implications of the term are misleading.

Anscombe's theory is one of several inspired by the idea that practical reasoning involves quasi-inferential performance. It is hard to do justice to this important idea without being led too far by it. It was ignored by the minimal thesis, that practical reasoning is merely theoretical reasoning done for the sake of eventual action. If we accommodate it by making additions to the minimal thesis, there is a risk that we shall go to the opposite extreme of supposing that practical reasoning must have its own logic, transmitting some analogue of truth, with the opposite direction of fit, down the successive lines of deliberation to the action.[9] That really would be going too far. For it would leave evaluative premisses up in the air, by denying that they are candidates for ordinary truth, when they obviously cannot be candidates for the analogue of truth with the opposite direction of fit.[10] There is also the criticism developed in the previous chapter, that it would fail to explain the semantics of the lines, 'So I want . . .' and 'So I shall . . .'.

Anscombe's theory avoids the first of these two mistakes, because her list of the conditions of practical truth includes not only the requirement that the action should fit the description contained in the outright singular value-judgement, but also the requirement that that judgement be true because it is correctly reached from true premisses. However, anyone who wraps up these two requirements together and labels the package 'practical truth' ought to justify this way of presenting the goods and the justification ought to be substantial. The concept of practical truth should provide a genuine explanation of the fit between action and outright value-judgement. But it does not do so.

It is worth taking a look at Aristotle's view about these matters, because Anscombe attributes her theory to him.

---

[9] e.g. A. Kenny asks 'What is the value which rules of practical reasoning have as their purpose to preserve in the way in which truth is the value preserved by rules of theoretical reasoning?' *Will, Freedom and Power*, p. 71. But he avoids predicating this truth-analogue of actions.

[10] On the other hand, ordinary truth evidently cannot be extended to the action. The two difficulties are exactly symmetrical. No theory can possibly succeed in pulling together under the same specific concept the truth of the premisses and the conformity of the action.

What he says is this:

> What affirmation and negation are in thinking, pursuit and avoidance are in desire: so that, since moral virtue is a state of character concerned with choice and choice is deliberate desire, therefore both the reasoning must be true and the desire right, if the choice is to be good, and the latter must pursue just what the former asserts. Now this kind of intellect and of truth is practical; of the intellect which is contemplative, not practical or productive, the good and the bad state are truth and falsity respectively (for this is the work of everything intellectual); while of the part which is practical and intellectual the good state is truth in agreement with right desire.[11]

The cardinal question of interpretation is 'What does Aristotle think is the possessor of this "truth in agreement with right desire"?' A general answer is easily found. 'The part which is practical and intellectual.' But the precise identification of the thing that Aristotle takes to be true is less easy. Anscombe evidently supposes that his idea is that the action possesses it. According to her, the action is called 'true' in the best outcome because it makes the agent's report of his imminent action true. He reports 'I am doing such and such', where 'such and such' is the specification of the action in his outright singular value-judgement and that judgement is supported in a way that he understands by true premisses, and his action makes his report true. The merits of this line of thought have been discussed and the question now is, whether it is really to be found in the passage quoted from Aristotle's *Nicomachean Ethics*.

The case for the attribution rests mainly on Aristotle's two statements, that 'what affirmation and negation are in thinking, pursuit and avoidance are in desire' and that 'the [choice] must pursue just what the [reasoning] asserts'. Anscombe's inference is that the choice must go for something that is true, just as affirmation goes for a sentence that is true, or, to put the point in her way, that the action ought to be practically true, just as the sentence ought to be true in the ordinary way.

However, this interpretation of Aristotle's two statements

---

[11] Aristotle, *Nicomachean Ethics*, 1139a21-31, tr. W. D. Ross, Oxford, 1925: reprinted in The World's Classics in 1954.

about affirmation and pursuit is questionable. Truth is introduced in the first part of the quoted passage as a property of the agent's reasoning (*logos*) and the property that is ascribed to his desire is rightness. The truth of the agent's reasoning is offered as part of the explanation of the parallelism between affirmation and pursuit and between negation (denial) and avoidance. How, then, can Aristotle have intended to explain the parallelism by invoking the truth of the agent's action? It is, of course, tempting to jump to this conclusion, because, if it were the correct interpretation, Aristotle would be offering a simple, albeit rather empty, explanation of the parallelism. But his appeal to truth is only part of a more complex and substantial explanation of the parallelism and it is, quite explicitly and unmistakably, an appeal to the truth of the agent's reasoning. His idea is evidently that the edict of reason comes first and has to be true, and that the desire acquires a different property, rightness, by conforming to it. Then and only then will the choice be good.

It might be felt that this explanation of the parallelism is too complex and, perhaps, that it really destroys the parallelism by lining up two properties, truth and conformity, opposite the single property, truth. But who are we to say that the parallelism is any simpler than Aristotle says that it is? He takes Anscombe's central conditions of 'practical truth' and treats them as conditions of goodness of choice without wrapping them up in a package with that misleadingly simple label. Even if he had introduced a second concept of truth, the truth of good actions, the underlying complexity of its criteria would affect the parallelism in exactly the same way that they affect it when the second concept is not introduced. Aristotle should, therefore, be taken to be doing exactly what he seems to be doing, namely leaving the complexity on the surface in order to make his explanation of the parallelism clear: when we affirm propositions we aim at truth and when we choose actions we aim at goodness, which depends on conformity and, by an intelligible convolution, on truth.

This interpretation is confirmed by what he says in the

second part of the quoted passage. Action, he explains, is the work of a partnership between intellect and desire and the good state of this partnership is 'truth in agreement with right desire'. If he had meant this truth to be a property of actions, or even of desires, he would certainly have said so at this point. For the only truth mentioned so far is the truth of the *logos*, and it is scarcely credible that in the development of his thesis he would suddenly take it for granted that truth is also a property of the action. His point must be that it is the truth of the *logos* that is in agreement with right desire because, in general, the *logos* is a specification of right desires for human agents and because, in a particular case, an agent's desire will acquire the property, rightness, by conforming to this specification.

The argument for taking the passage in this way does not depend on translating the versatile Greek work '*logos*' by the English word 'reasoning'. Perhaps Anscombe's translation 'judgement' would be better[12] because it would allow for the fact that what the desire or action fits is the agent's outright singular value-judgement. However, that would not affect the argument against interpreting Aristotle in her way. Incidentally, Aristotle does not mention the agent's factual judgement about his imminent action and he does not even hint at the possibility that, when one thing confers truth on another, it might achieve a kind of truth for itself.

But why, it may be asked, does Aristotle specify the good state of the partnership as 'truth in agreement with right desire'? Does that not show that he supposed that the right desire comes first and that something else achieves truth by conforming to it? If so, what could the other thing possibly be but the action?

The answer seems to be 'The *logos*'. Right desires set the standard of fit for the *logos*, because the *logos* is a general specification of right desires for human agents expressed in value-judgements that possess ordinary truth. This is entirely

---

[12] See 'Thought and Action in Aristotle', p. 156.

compatible with Aristotle's idea that the *logos* also sets the standard of fit for desire and action in particular predicaments, and there is no need to credit him with the belief that either desires or actions achieve a special kind of truth by conformity.[13]

It is worth remarking that the translation 'truth in agreement with right desire', which seems to imply that it is desire that always sets the standard of fit, is questionable. The words used by Aristotle mean 'truth with the same *logos* as right desire'. This does not imply that right desire always comes first and sets the standard of fit. Identity of *logos* is a symmetrical relation, like identity of length.

It may be objected that this is scarcely intelligible. For how can a judgement or indeed anything intellectual share a *logos* with a desire or with anything non-intellectual? Granted that the judgement achieves truth because it specifies the right desires for human agents and that a particular desire achieves rightness by fitting the true judgement, how can this be explained by identity of *logos*?

The answer to this question may be that the desire shares the *logos* by conforming to it. This sounds strange when the word *'logos'* is translated 'specification', because we never reify a specification or treat it as an essence. But perhaps the Greek word *'logos'* is more adaptable, at least when it is embedded in certain adjectives. If so, the concept of a shared *logos* is not one that comes naturally to us, and we are likely to protest that a definition of mayonnaise, even if it is a serviceable recipe, is one thing and the essence of the sauce itself is another thing, and there is no way of combining the two under a single concept. Be that as it may, when Aristotle is analysing the right way to live, he certainly uses the concept of a *logos* in a way that allows him to derive his system of values from human nature by exploiting the truth-conferring direction of fit like the author of a cookery book doing the

---

[13] This does not involve the simultaneous operation of two opposed directions of fit between the same two items. The general standard for right desires is first deduced from human nature and then applied to desires in particular predicaments.

necessary research, and at the same time allows him to explain how an agent decides what to do in a particular predicament, by exploiting the opposite direction of fit, like a chef at work.

Enough has been said about the second of the two types of theory that represent last-ditch *akrasia* as a way of contradicting oneself by acting. Both types assign a kind of truth or falsity to actions. The distinction between them, drawn at the beginning of this chapter, turns on the question whether this 'quasi-truth' is a property belonging to actions independently of the value-judgements that precede them, or whether it is merely another name for conformity to those value-judgements. The first option leads to a type of theory that has not been discussed in much detail. The second leads to the type exemplified by Anscombe's theory (not, however, applied by her to the problem of last-ditch *akrasia*). If, as has been argued here, Aristotle did not ascribe any kind of truth to actions, this theory was not shared by him.

Has any philosopher ever taken the first option? Apparently, not. However, in the history of ideas the extreme position at the end of any line usually finds a taker and the apparent absence of one in this case may well be an illusion that further research would remove. Certainly, the first option is tempting. Unlike the second, it would lead to a genuinely explanatory theory, if only it would work. However, there is, for reasons already given, no real hope that it could be made to work. The agent's outright singular value-judgement has to be true, and it is scarcely imaginable that there should be a property ascribable to his action independently of that judgement and such that the action could not possess it if the judgement were true. The action and the judgement do not form a representational couple purporting to be true like the conjunction of two beliefs, and it is impossible to see what material could be used to construct the analogical account of the self-contradiction required by this version of the theory. The idea, that in last-ditch *akrasia* the agent would be contradicting himself in a truth-based way by acting, is the kind of idea that Wittgenstein called 'a dream of language'.

So far, the results of this part of the inquiry have been mainly negative. However, it may be possible to extract something positive from them. Perhaps we can do this by going back to the basic idea on which Anscombe built her theory and developing it in a different way. Her basic idea was that there are certain analogies between fitting a sentence to a thing and fitting a thing to a sentence.[14] The analogy that she selected for development was an analogy between the two properties that result from these two fits, the truth of the sentence and a property of the thing that she calls 'practical truth' when the thing is an action. If, as has been argued, this is not viable, it may be possible to replace it by an analogy between the two operations of fit rather than between the two resulting properties. This would be a less ambitious theory, because it would not imply that any kind of truth is conferred on actions by their conformity to outright value-judgements. Instead, it would trace certain similarities between the ways in which people struggle to achieve the two kinds of fit and also between some of the causes of their not infrequent failures.

Consider, for example, the distorting effect of salience that was mentioned in Chapters III and IV. Experiments have shown that the salience of a weak piece of evidence leads people to attach too much weight to it and that this is a common cause of irrational belief-formation. In Chapter II a distinction was drawn between biased inference, which counts as irrationality, and biased sense-perception, which does not count as irrationality. Now it seems that the salience of certain cues can have the same biasing effect on perception that it often has later on inference when the cues have been noted and stored in the mind as evidence. If this is so, it may be possible to take a further step. We may be able to develop a real analogy between the biasing effect that the salience of certain cues exercises on perception and the biasing effect that the intensity of desires exercises on action in many cases

---

[14] The theory that she develops in *Intention* from p. 56 to the end of the book is based on this idea.

of last-ditch *akrasia*. The key to understanding these cases must be that there are two candidates for the privileged position of setting the standard of fit, the value-judgement and the rebellious desire, and so any property that explains why the latter carries more weight than reason would allocate to it will contribute to the explanation of the phenomenon.

This would be an interesting similarity between the causes of failure in the two opposed cases, trying to fit sentences to things and trying to fit things to sentences. It might even turn out that a detailed examination of the two causes of failure would help to settle the question whether the two failures themselves differ in the probability or in the possibility of their occurrence. Is there less possibility of conscious misfit of sentence to thing than of conscious misfit of thing to sentence? It is a natural intuition that there is indeed less possibility of conscious misfit of sentence to thing and, if that really is so, it is probably a consequence of the point already established, that last-ditch *akrasia* is not a case of contradicting oneself by acting. The question is worth examining in more detail. For what we need now is a viable positive theory about the nature of the misfit in cases of last-ditch *akrasia*. If it is not like contradicting oneself in belief-formation, what is it like?

The suggestion is that it is like misperception caused by the salience of a perceptual cue. It would be as well to begin the development of this suggestion with a clear example of the biasing effect of a visual cue. An ornithologist sees a bird fly past at high speed and identifies it as a falcon, but he is wrong. At the time his thoughts were elsewhere and he did not attach much importance to the sighting and he was not even aware of the precise nature of the visual cues to which he automatically reacted. In fact, he reacted to the speed of the bird's flight, which is salient but inconclusive, because falcons are not the only species capable of the speed of the bird that he saw. He might have reacted, instead, to the bird's shape, which, we may suppose, was quite wrong for a falcon and, therefore, a conclusively negative indication, but, of course, it is less salient and so he did not react to it.

It is risky to invent complex examples and not much research seems to have been done into the biasing effect of salience on sense-perception.[15] However, the example does illustrate a fairly common human experience, for what that is worth. Naturally, it would be worth more if the case did not involve a theory that really needs to be established by experiment. So perhaps the next question should be formulated in a cautious way: 'If the salience of a cue can produce this effect in perception when someone is trying to fit a sentence to a thing, can the intensity or urgency of a desire produce an analogous effect in action when someone is trying to fit a thing to a sentence?'

There can be no doubt about the existence of certain similarities between the ways in which the failures are caused in the two cases, salience-induced misperception and intensity-induced last-ditch *akrasia*. In the first case the subject's judgement is captivated by the eye-catching property, salience, and in the second case the executive part of his psyche is captivated by the will-catching property, urgency, which is really a kind of emotional salience. Also, both take-overs often occur in the rush of the last moment. This is not to say that it is only at the last moment that salience captivates judgement, but that is certainly what happens in the cases that yield the closest analogy, which are examples of salience-induced misperception. Nor, of course, is last-ditch *akrasia* always produced by intensified desire or by heightened emotion intervening at the last moment, but those are certainly its most frequent causes. When examples of these two kinds are compared with one another, their similarities are impressive.

That said, it is immediately necessary to mention a striking dissimilarity between last-ditch *akrasia* and misperception caused by the salience of visual cues. The observer's task is to make a judgement that is true of what he sees, but the

---

[15] See R. Nisbett and L. Ross, *Human Inference: Strategies and Shortcomings of Social Judgment*, pp. 45-62.

agent is not given the impossible task of ensuring that his action makes his outright value-judgement true, but only the feasible task of ensuring that it conforms to the specification contained in that judgement. Now we may follow Anscombe here and express this reasonable requirement by saying that he ought to make the sentence 'I am doing such and such' true, where 'such and such' is the specification of the action that occurs in his value-judgement. However, if we do put it in that way, it is evident, but nevertheless needs emphasizing, that the real source of the onus of fit on the action is the value-judgement, which is not made true by the fit.

The point needs emphasis because the comparison that is being developed is a comparison between acting under the constraint of a value-judgement and judging under the constraint of a perceived object. It is, therefore, important that the two constraints are quite different in character. In the first case success does not consist in making the value-judgement true, whereas in the second case it does consist in producing a true perceptual judgement. The natural intuition here being defended is that conscious failure to make an action fit a value-judgement is easier than conscious failure to make a perceptual judgement fit an object.

Perhaps the defence would be helped by consideration of a different pair of cases which, like intensity-induced last-ditch *akrasia* and salience-induced misperception, exhibited the two opposed directions of fit, but which, unlike that pair, were both attempts to achieve truth. Of course, the ornithologist in the first of the two examples was attempting to achieve truth, but in the second one, the agent's goal was performance of the best action. If we took a different pair of contrasting examples, both of which were attempts to achieve truth, we might succeed in strengthening the defence of the natural intuition. For it might turn out that the difference in direction of fit does not make misfit easier in one member of the pair than in the other, provided that the goal is always truth. That would support the natural intuition, because it would suggest that what makes intensity-induced last-ditch *akrasia* easier than salience-induced misperception is the special character of the onus imposed on the action.

So suppose that the ornithologist is set an examination to test his competence for fieldwork and that in it he is required to carry out two multiple-choice tasks. First, he is given a verbal description of a species of bird, shown a room full of stuffed birds, and asked to choose the bird that fits the description. Second, he is given a stuffed bird, shown a page of descriptions, and asked to choose the description that fits the bird. In both tests he has to achieve truth, but the directions of fit are opposite.

Would the difference in direction of fit make failure in one of these multiple-choice tasks more likely than failure in the other? It seems that there could not be any significant difference in the probabilities of failure because success consists in achieving the same kind of match in both cases. But when someone is required to perform an action that fits his outright singular value-judgement, that is a different kind of match and the difference may well make failure easier. It may even make conscious failure a real possibility. Certainly, it must be easier than consciously forming a false belief about one's own action or, indeed, about anything else. In the original example, if the ornithologist realized that he was mis-classifying the bird as it flew past, his consciousness of his error would instantly lead him to correct it.

Socrates and his modern followers would comment that it is an understatement to say that the agent would find it easier to yield to the temptation consciously, because the truth would have to be that it was impossible for him to resist it. Consequently, on their view, the case would not be one of last-ditch *akrasia* but, rather, one of compulsive action.

That comment will be taken up in Chapter X. The point being made here is that, if conscious last-ditch *akrasia* is a possibility, it is easier than conscious formation of a false perceptual belief, but that there is no significant difference between the difficulty of the two tasks set to the ornithologist. In daily life we accept the first difference and the absence of the second difference as obvious and it would be tedious to rehearse them. Who could doubt that conscious misdescription is always more difficult than conscious last-ditch *akrasia*, or that the probability of failure in the two tasks set to the ornithologist is much the same, because the reversal of the direction of fit hardly affects their difficulty? However, the reason why we accept these points so readily is not entirely obvious, and we must be importunate and ask for it.

The explanation has to start from the fact that in perception there is only one thing that can possibly set the standard of fit, namely the world. Truth is the goal and it makes little difference whether it is achieved by the choice of the thing that makes a sentence true or by the choice of the sentence that is made true by a thing, provided that all the items are put before the subject, as they are in multiple-choice tasks.

The situation is quite different in deliberation and action, because there is often more than one candidate struggling for the position of authority. When there is an outright valuation, that is obviously the candidate that ought to win, but, when *akrasia* is in the offing, there will always be another candidate on the list. For in a case of *akrasia* the agent's psyche will harbour a desire that opposes his outright valuation and aspires to set the standard of fit for his action and so he will be divided against himself.

The world, which sets the standard of fit for theory, harbours no such sources of conflict. Admittedly, in a theoretical matter judgement may be baffled because the evidence is evenly balanced and the task of achieving the truth-conferring fit is not always as easy as it was in the ornithologist's examination. However, it does not make sense to project this conflict into the world. When truth is at issue, the thing that sets the standard of fit cannot be divided against itself. Truth is one.

That, in its turn, explains, or, at least, dramatizes the fact that conscious acceptance of two logically incompatible beliefs is impossible without the help of mental distance. Now a special case of this impossibility would be the formation of a perceptual belief by a person who was conscious that it did not fit the thing perceived. That must be an impossible achievement because it would require him to form a perceptual belief that contradicted another that he was already holding before his mind.

There is, here, a sharp contrast with conscious last-ditch *akrasia*. If an agent could act consciously against his own outright singular value-judgement, he would have to remember the judgement while he was acting and he would have to appreciate the demand that it made on his action. However, the belief, that his value-judgement was so and so and that it made such and such a demand on his action, would not involve him in self-contradiction if he combined it with the wrong action. This is the point that was established earlier in this chapter.

There is nothing surprising about this vindication of the natural intuition that it is easier to fail to make one's action fit one's value-judgement than it is to fail to make a perceptual judgement fit a thing. Full consciousness of the second failure would make it impossible, but that is not the effect of full consciousness of the first one. This is simply a consequence of the fact that action and belief do not form a couple aimed at the truth, plus the fact that there is no other way in which the agent could be contradicting himself by acting, unless the meaning of the phrase 'self-contradiction' is diluted to the point where it becomes just another way of saying that his action does not conform to his value-judgement.

* * *

The first part of this chapter was entirely negative. One of the two attempts to outbid the minimal theory of practical reasoning can be developed in two further stages: it can be argued that deliberate actions are capable of truth or falsehood and that, therefore, last-ditch *akrasia* would involve the agent in self-contradiction. Both developments were criticized.

It was conceded that acting against one's own better judgement and holding two logically incompatible beliefs are both, in some broad sense, examples of self-contradiction. However, any attempt to narrow the sense of 'contradicting oneself' and so to pull the two kinds of irrationality closer together was countered with a dilemma.

One alternative offered was that the 'quasi-truth' of actions is merely another name for the property of conforming to the agent's outright singular value-judgement, given certain further conditions. But in that case the theory of 'contradicting oneself by acting' would have no explanatory power.

The other alternative was that 'quasi-truth' is the name of an underlying property of actions such that their quasi-truth-conditions make it impossible to perform them in cases of would-be last-ditch *akrasia* without contradicting oneself in something like the way in which the truth-conditions of two logically incompatible beliefs make it impossible to combine them without ordinary self-contradiction. But though this would be a theory with explanatory power, if a suitable underlying property of actions could be found, no such property was identified.

This failure was not surprising. For the agent's outright value-judgement and his action do not form a representational couple aimed at the truth, like the conjunction of two beliefs. Nor is there any other material available for the construction of a theory that would pull the two kinds of irrationality together under a narrow concept of 'contradicting oneself'.

Anscombe's theory of 'practical truth' was used to illustrate the working of this dilemma. She does not apply her theory to the problem of last-ditch *akrasia*, but concentrates on normal deliberate actions. Her specification of the conditions of success for such actions was accepted. All that was rejected was her idea that these conditions should be wrapped up and labelled 'the practical truth of actions', and her claim that Aristotle presented the package in this way.

The second part of the chapter was more positive. The aim

was to find a viable way of developing Anscombe's basic idea, that there are points of similarity between the fit that confers rationality on actions and the fit that confers truth on sentences. However, the similarities only extended so far: both are fits between sentence and thing and each can be frustrated by a property of an element on the standard-setting side, intensity or urgency of desire in the first case and salience of cue in the second case.

Beyond that point the difference between the two kinds of fit proved to be more important than their similarities. For when the intensity of a desire that captivates the will was compared with the salience of a cue that captivates judgement, a striking difference emerged. In the case of action there is conflict on the standard-setting side, because the agent's psyche harbours more than one candidate for the authoritative position, but in the case of perception it makes no sense to project any conflict into the world, which sets the standard of fit.

It is a compliment to call an agent 'integrated', but it is not one that is appropriate to the world. The nicest thing of that kind that one can say about the world is that it is intelligible. Of course, people are more intelligible if they are integrated, and there is a degree of irrationality that would make them completely unintelligible, but what makes the world intelligible is not its integration or its rationality.

This obvious, but important point was also put in another way: in a theoretical multiple-choice problem there is no great difference between the difficulty of finding a description that fits an object and the difficulty of finding an object that fits a description, but in a practical predicament there is a great difference between the difficulty of describing one's own action and the difficulty of ensuring that it is rational.

The senselessness of projecting conflict into the world was used to dramatize the absolute impossibility of consciously accepting the conjunction of two contradictory beliefs. It then turned out that, if misperception induced by salience were conscious, it would involve the subject in literal self-contradiction, but if last-ditch *akrasia* caused by the intensity of a desire were conscious, it would not produce the same effect.

This difference simply followed from a point already established, but marking it was a step forward in the line of march of the argument. For it became possible to draw a limited conclusion about conscious last-ditch *akrasia*: Socrates may have been right to deny its possibility, but at least it does not find its way blocked by the insuperable obstacle that stands in the way of conscious malformation of perceptual belief.

This comes out very clearly if we contrast an agent who discovers that what he is just about to do would be last-ditch *akrasia*, produced by the intensity of a desire, with the ornithologist who, we may now suppose, realizes that the identification of the bird that he is just about to make would be a mistake caused by the salience of a misleading visual cue. It is certain that the latter would change his mind, but far from certain that the former would do so.

It is one thing to argue against the existence of a particular obstacle standing in the way of conscious last-ditch *akrasia* and quite another thing to demonstrate that, all obstacles considered, it is a real possibility. Theories belonging to the other genus, which simply find a contradiction in the description of conscious last-ditch *akrasia*, still remain to be confronted.

IX

DOING AND VALUING:
THE BACKWARD CONNECTION

The territory traversed in the last two chapters has been a little
arid and low in human interest, unlike the earlier topic, irrational belief-formation, and it is worth asking what the
explanation of this difference is. We might try to explain it by
pointing out that a topic only establishes itself gradually in
popular consciousness and that self-deception and wishful
thinking have made more progress in that direction than irrational action performed without any intellectual distortion.
One sign of this difference is that, when last-ditch *akrasia*
comes under discussion, there does not seem to be very much
to say about the intrinsic nature of the fault. There is, of
course, a popular theory about its cause, which is so widely
taken to be weakness of will that this has almost come to be
used as another name for it, and weakness of will is a topic
that is well established outside the books and articles of philosophers. But the invitation to look more closely at the nature
of the final move from thought to action seems more tedious.
It strikes people as likely to be one of those occasions for
philosophers to raise a lot of dust over a previously perspicuous matter. What could possibly be clearer than the agent's
move when he makes, or fails to make, his action conform to
the specification in his outright singular value-judgement?

However, that is not a very deep explanation of the difference between the two problems. For why is it that self-
deception and wishful thinking have established themselves
as discussable topics outside the circle of philosophers, but
downright irrational action has not done so to anything like

the same extent? And why is it that psychologists have done much more research in the first area than in the second?

There seem to be several reasons for this situation, some of them historical and others less accidental. The main historical influence has been the part of Freudian theory that has been absorbed into our culture, namely the theory of the unconscious and the preconscious. We find it entirely natural to assume that any lapse between thought and action must be explained as the result of some intellectual fault, and the popular explanation is that the lapse is kept out of consciousness.

However, it is arguable that a failure of consciousness is only a special case of functional failure,[1] and, if that is so, why should there not simply be a functional failure between thought and action? A failure at that point is no more damaging to the person in whom it occurs, although it may be more shaming. In any case, even if we do rule out conscious last-ditch *akrasia* by always invoking Freudian theory to explain the phenomena, there is still a question to be asked about the normal course of deliberation and rational action. What is the nature of the link between final, outright value-judgement and action? It is not only deviations that excite our curiosity and demand explanation.

There must be some intrinsic feature of this subject which makes it seem like a non-subject. In fact, the explanation of this impression is not far to seek. It is what might be called 'the inarticulateness of action'. A value-judgement is something quite explicit, but an action can be taken in various ways, depending on the intention with which it is done, and, even when the intention is known, as it usually is by the agent himself, the action is still a very lumpish thing, which only

---

[1] The argument would be that, when an element is unconscious or preconscious, it fails to produce any reflection of itself in the main system and it is assigned to a sub-system because this is a functional failure. Freud's theory of systems would then be seen as a special case of a functional theory, drawing the line between main system and sub-system in the same general way as the kind of functional theory that was discussed in Ch. V, but only relying on one specific type of functional failure.

has two possible relations to the value-judgement, conformity and defiance. The logic of sentential inferences is quite different. It is subtle and variegated and has been studied for centuries and there have also been treatises on its fallacies, because people need to know not only the correct procedures but also the many deceptively similar deviations from them. Nothing like this can be done for the final move from outright value-judgement to action.

Nevertheless, there are two angles from which this move can be examined. First, it is possible to trace its similarities with other moves, such as the formation of a particular desire or intention, and it is possible to describe the gulf that is fixed between all these moves and the formation of a belief, which is something capable of truth or falsehood. This was done in the two previous chapters and it inevitably involved a quest for the explanation of things that seem utterly perspicuous in daily life and are simply taken for granted.

Second, we may inquire whether there is any contradiction in the description of conscious last-ditch *akrasia*, even if the agent does not contradict himself by so acting. This part of the investigation was marked off at the end of Chapter VI for later undertaking. It will be the last stretch of this inquiry into the irrationality of action and it will differ from the rather dry discussions of the last two chapters. It will be much closer to the ordinary way in which we look at these matters and so it will not be necessary to be a philosopher in order to be immediately convinced that it is a viable topic with a lot to be said about it.

In fact, it is not really necessary to be a philosopher in order to see the point of the earlier, more arid part of the same inquiry. It is just that its point is not immediately evident, because it is not a development of the natural way in which we think about reasoning and action. There is a discontinuity in that territory between ordinary thinking and philosophy and it can be disconcerting. But there is no such discontinuity in the approach to the question, whether the connections between valuing and acting put a contradiction in the description of conscious last-ditch *akrasia*, even if the agent does not contradict himself by so acting. We can move smoothly and without any perceptible break from ordinary, everyday imputations of motive and assessments of character to a philosophical analysis of the connections that underlie them.

The reason for this is easily appreciated if we start from an everyday example of an imputation of a motive. A chess-player makes a move which, fairly obviously, risks the loss of a rook, but which, less obviously, leaves him in an improved position if the rook is taken. Given his competence and, of course, his desire to win, any spectator with sufficient knowledge of the game would impute the motive that makes his move a rational one: he accepted the possibility of the loss because he thought that it would be worth it. That is a prudential value-judgement. The philosophical inquiry begins at this point with the question, 'Is it possible to state conditions under which a non-compulsive, intentional action must have issued from a supportive value-judgement?' Here the connection between philosophy and the way we think about people outside the study in our daily contacts with them is very close. Philosophers are simply trying to analyse the connections that underlie our ordinary imputations of motives.

This enterprise can be connected with the earlier discussion of Attribution Theory.[2] The main thesis of Attribution Theorists is that people tend to rationalize not only their own actions but also those of others, because they want to understand them and the simplest way to understand them is to attribute motives that make sense of them. A subsidiary thesis is that this natural tendency often leads to over-simplification, because the explainer wants a quick result, which is most easily achieved by the attribution of the obvious motive. The idea is that the explainer may fail to allow for other, more complex possibilities and go straight for his preferred simple explanation in order to be rid of the problem as quickly as possible.

---

[2] See pp. 46-50 and 55-9.

In the earlier discussion of this topic the examples used to illustrate this kind of impatience with the facts were cases of failure to allow for the complexity of the agent's circumstances. But even if the explainer does allow for the full complexity of the circumstances, he may simplify the case in another way: he may fail to allow for the possible things that might go wrong within the agent. One important possibility in this area is compulsiveness and another is irrationality. Now when the explainer succumbs to the temptation to oversimplify, he is himself being irrational. In fact, the faults diagnosed by Attribution Theory are malfunctions or perversions of reason. So the explainer who neglects the possibility of irrationality, hot or cold, in the agent is himself exhibiting cold irrationality.

The aim of the philosophical inquiry can be expressed in a way that relates it to Attribution Theory. Its aim is to discover whether the backward connection, running from action to value-judgement, can be formulated in a way that forces us to regard it as a necessary connection.[3] For example, is it necessarily true that, if someone performs an action intentionally and without compulsion, then it must have been preceded by a supportive value-judgement? If this were necessarily true, it would set up a kind of landmark in the territory of Attribution Theory. For it would guarantee the validity of some inference of the kind made about the chess-player in all cases of non-compulsive intentional action.

Naturally, the philosophical thesis would not guarantee the correctness of any specific inference or the attribution of any particular supportive value-judgement. It would only guarantee that some supportive value-judgement could be attributed to the agent of any non-compulsive, intentional action. However, that would be an important result, if it really could be established. For it would follow that, if there were any irrationality in the psychological antecedents of such an action, it must have occurred before the agent's concluding

[3] See p. 114.

value-judgement. There would be no possibility of conscious last-ditch *akrasia*, because that would involve a fault between his conclusion and his action, and the thesis is that the value-judgement that necessarily accompanies the action is always a supportive one, a kind of *alter ego* with which conflict is unimaginable.

This thesis about the backward connection between acting and valuing is exploited by Davidson in his much discussed argument against the possibility of conscious last-ditch *akrasia*.[4] He also exploits the thesis that the forward connection, running from valuing to acting, is necessary, but the examination of that thesis will be deferred to the next chapter. It is one thing to argue that non-compulsive, intentional action necessitates a supportive outright value-judgement, and another thing to argue that an outright value-judgement necessitates a conforming action, if anything is done in the matter intentionally and without compulsion.

First, something needs to be said about the general strategy of Davidson's exclusion of the possibility of conscious last-ditch *akrasia*. Many people, perhaps most people, would say that it is possible to act consciously and without compulsion against one's own better judgement, but, if the backward connection is necessary, they are wrong. However, if so many people make the mistake, there must be something in the phenomenon that misleads them. Davidson's idea seems to be that they are misled because, though the fault does not occur where they think that it occurs, namely between the concluding value-judgement and the action, it does occur at a location so close to that one that it is easily confused with it, namely just before the conclusion. In the example used earlier, the guest appears to jump the rails between his judgement that it is better to stop at two drinks and his acceptance of a third one, but Davidson's suggestion is that what really happens is that he reviews his reasoning at the party, redoes it

----

[4] D. Davidson, 'How is Weakness of the Will Possible?' See Ch. V n. 7.

under bias, and comes to the opposite conclusion, that it is better to go on drinking.

Davidson's theory is in two parts and each of them poses important problems. The first part contains the argument against the possibility of conscious last-ditch *akrasia*, and here it must be remembered that *akrasia* is non-compulsive action done against one's own better judgement. This argument raises two questions, one easy and the other difficult. The easy one is, 'How does the necessity of the backward connection rule out the possibility of conscious last-ditch *akrasia*?' and the difficult one is, 'Is the backward connection really necessary?' Both questions need to be answered here.

The second part of Davidson's theory is not directly relevant to this inquiry, because it contains his reconstruction of what really happens in apparent cases of conscious last-ditch *akrasia*, and the conclusion that is going to be drawn here is that what really happens is very often conscious last-ditch *akrasia*. Now it might be thought possible to argue for this conclusion by demonstrating that Davidson's reconstruction is incoherent. But the view that will be taken here is that it is not incoherent and that *akrasia* does sometimes occur in the way that he describes, namely through conscious last-ditch self-deception, but not always. In any case, even if something could be proved wrong with his reconstruction, that would hardly suffice to establish the possibility of conscious last-ditch *akrasia*, because there would be no reason to suppose that his alternative to it was the only one that needed to be eliminated. So not much will be said about the second stage of his theory and the focus will be mainly on its first stage.

However, if nothing were said about the second stage, the discussion would be too restricted and remote from real life. For even if Davidson is wrong in thinking that apparent cases of conscious last-ditch *akrasia* are always to be explained in his way, his explanation, or something quite like it, certainly applies to some cases. So the two main questions that it raises will be discussed here, but briefly. One is, 'Why should the agent deceive himself that it is better to go on drinking when "all right to go on" would have been enough?' and the other is, 'Is there any incoherence in Davidson's reconstruction?' These two questions will be taken before the main business, which is the alleged necessity of the backward connection.

In Davidson's reconstruction why is the agent not content with deceiving himself that it is all right to go on drinking? Because the argument is that every non-compulsive intentional action must be accompanied by a supportive value-judgement and not merely by a permissive one. That is Davidson's formulation of the necessity of the backward connection and it will be examined in a moment. The point to be made about it now is that it seems to limit the application of his reconstruction of apparent cases of conscious last-ditch *akrasia* in a way that is neither necessary nor realistic. It does not look realistic because people often do deceive themselves that it is all right to do something and then do it, without going so far as to deceive themselves that it is better to do it. It seems to be unnecessary, because it would be enough for his purpose that the action should be accompanied by a permissive value-judgement. For that too would enable him to locate the fault just before the outright value-judgement instead of between it and the action. The fault would be a switch from 'better not' to 'all right' instead of a switch from 'better not' to 'better', but it would occur at the same location.

However, he has an answer to this and in it an issue of cardinal importance makes its first appearance on the scene. So far, the assumption has been that there is a difference between wanting to do something because one judges it best to do it and wanting to do it without judging it best to do it. But he would answer the criticism of his reconstruction by rejecting this assumption and maintaining that any desire is appropriately expressed by a value-judgement.[5]

---

[5] *Actions and Events*, p. 86: '. . . evaluative sentences express desires and other pro attitudes in the same way that the sentence "Snow is white" expresses the belief that snow is white.'

Suppose, for example, that the guest's original attitude to a third drink is neutral: he merely judges that, in relation to safety, it is all right to take a third one. Then if he does so, that must be because he has an independent, positive desire to go on drinking and, according to Davidson, that desire, whatever its nature and origin, will be appropriately expressed by a positive supportive value-judgement. It is clear that, if the phrase 'value-judgement' is used in this way, there will almost always be a positive value-judgement supporting any intentional, non-compulsive action, even in cases in which there might not be one if the phrase were used as it has been hitherto. Given Davidson's usage, the only possible counter-example to his thesis would be a case in which the agent had no preference of any kind between two alternative courses of action, like Buridan's ass halfway between the two bales of hay. However, that would not be a very damaging counter-example, because any theory would need a special development to meet it. For example, the remedy might be to say that in this exceptional case the agent does not choose but picks, and that is why his intentional action is not uniquely supported by his value-judgement.[6]

This defence of Davidson fuses the traditional concept of valuing with the concept of merely wanting, which it is customary to set over against it and contrast with it. The result is a new, but weaker, concept of valuing which has proved fruitful in Decision Theory.[7] This is a move of cardinal importance and its effects will be analysed later. The point to be made about it now is that, if the guest's outright singular value-judgement necessarily expresses something stronger than a mere desire, it does not have to be positive and may be merely permissive. Indeed, it will be argued later that there is not even any need for a permissive value-judgement of this stronger kind supporting every non-compulsive intentional

[6] See E. Ullmann-Margalit and S. Morgenbesser, 'Picking and Choosing', *Social Research*, xliv, 4, 1977.

[7] See P. G. Moore and H. Thomas, *The Anatomy of Decisions*, Harmondsworth, 1976.

action. On the other hand, if the guest's outright singular value-judgement does not necessarily express anything stronger than a mere desire, it is much more plausible to suppose that it is needed and, if it is needed, it is evidently not enough for it to be permissive and it must be positive.

The second question about Davidson's reconstruction of apparent cases of conscious last-ditch *akrasia* was whether it is incoherent. The case for an affirmative answer will first be sketched and then rejected.

The background to this controversy is the theory of latitude. Davidson's idea is that, when the guest redoes his reasoning under bias at the party, and comes to the perverse conclusion, that it is better to go on drinking, he is not contradicting himself. He is, of course, changing his mind about the relative values of the two courses of action open to him, but he can do this without revoking the preceding line in his reasoning. For the preceding line was 'In relation to safety and pleasure and in the circumstances, as far as I know them, it is better to stop at two drinks'. This can stand, because it allows him the latitude that he needs in order to draw his perverse conclusion without contradicting himself. He can evade the charge of self-contradiction in one of the ways that were explained earlier.[8] Maybe he is not sure that courtesy does not require him to accept the third offer, or perhaps he is uncertain of the strength of the drink or the correctness of current medical opinion.

This is an important point and most people have been persuaded by it. Controversy begins at the next stage. Having granted that the agent in a case like this would not be contradicting himself, some claim that, nevertheless, his thinking would be so incoherent that it would be almost unintelligible. For he would be rejecting the outright value-judgement that he had a plausible, albeit not conclusive, reason for making, and the outright value-judgement that he would be substituting for it would be one that he had no plausible reason

[8] See pp. 109-11.

for making. Furthermore, he would know all this, because he would have adjudicated the claims of safety and pleasure in the opposite way on the preceding line of his reasoning and nothing would have changed. That, it is objected, is unintelligible. It is also said to be unintelligible that after this switch of judgement he should act intentionally, because acting intentionally is acting for a reason and he has no reason for his action.

These criticisms are mistaken. The first step towards seeing this is to note the difference between the point that is conceded and the point that is disputed. The conceded point is that the agent would not be contradicting himself by making his perverse value-judgement. The disputed point is whether the irrationality of his thought-process makes it so incoherent that it is scarcely intelligible.

But why should this be so? The critics seem to have forgotten that the whole point of Davidson's reconstruction of these cases is that in them the agent is supposed to be thinking irrationally. It is a mistake to protest that he ought to have a reason for his irrational thought and that, if he lacks one, his thinking it is unintelligible. On the contrary, given the biasing tendency of his desire for the pleasure of another drink, it is entirely understandable that he should go against his previous reasoning and make this unsupported guess at the objective value of taking it. All that he needs is latitude and he has it. As for the second criticism, after he has made his irrational guess it supplies him with a reason for his action, which, therefore, may well be, and presumably is, intentional.

That is all that needs to be said about the second stage of Davidson's theory. It is its first stage that lies in the main path of this inquiry. Does it really succeed in ruling out the possibility of conscious last-ditch *akrasia*? Just now this question was split up into two: 'How does the necessity of the backward connection exclude the possibility of conscious last-ditch *akrasia*?' and 'Is the backward connection really necessary?'

The first of these two questions is easy to answer. If the

non-compulsive intentional action of taking the third drink did require a supportive value-judgement, the guest would be contradicting himself if at the same time he concluded that it would be better to stop at two. It follows that either he never drew that conclusion or he drew it but later revised it. Either way, there would be no possibility of conscious last-ditch *akrasia*, which would require him to draw the conclusion that it is best to stop at two drinks and then, without revising it, to defy it by taking a third one. This argument works whichever concept of 'valuation' is used, weak or strong. The only possible loophole would be provided by mental distance. If the two contradictory conclusions could be kept sufficiently far apart, they might both be drawn and both stand unrevised, but in a case like this it is difficult to see how mental distancing could ever be achieved.

The second question was whether the backward connection really is necessary and the rest of this chapter will be spent answering it. It certainly looks necessary when the weaker concept of 'valuation' is used and the consequences may seem to be far-reaching. It is not only that conscious last-ditch *akrasia* seems to be excluded. It is also a striking fact that it would be excluded by a theory of human agency that is, as far as it goes, maximally rationalizing. Any non-compulsive intentional action would be traced to a supportive value-judgement. It is true that the rationality that would be attributed in such cases would only extend a very short way back into the hinterland behind the action, and beyond the supportive value-judgement irrationality would be allowed to flourish. Nevertheless, the universality of this limited rationality certainly looks impressive.

However, before we allow ourselves to be too impressed by it, we should inquire whether the backward connection holds necessarily between non-compulsive intentional actions and both kinds of value-judgement, weak and strong. It seems scarcely credible that all such actions are derived from strong valuations. We do not need the critical diagnoses of Attribution Theorists to arouse our suspicions of this extreme idea.

Does the human psyche really only have a single line for the production of non-compulsive intentional actions? Does the thrust behind such actions always go through the narrow gate of reason? Is the only hope for a rebellious desire that the check-point of strong valuation will be inefficiently operated and not that it can be bypassed?

The argument that will now be developed will lead to a negative answer to these questions. There are indeed other ways of producing intentional actions without compulsion. If that is right, Davidson's argument for the necessity of the backward connection and the rejection of conscious last-ditch *akrasia* that he bases on it will be unsuccessful when it uses the strong concept of 'valuation', however successful it may be when it uses the weak concept. For if the last stage in the production of non-compulsive international actions is not universally rational, the backward connection will be necessary only if the supportive value-judgement need not express anything stronger than a mere desire.

However, it still would not follow that conscious last-ditch *akrasia* is a real possibility. It has been confronted by a series of possible obstacles to its success and the removal of one more of them, namely the necessity of the backward connection between non-compulsive intentional actions and strong value-judgements, would still leave the forward connection to be reckoned with. For suppose that the argument now to be developed does succeed in establishing that an action of this kind may issue from something other than a strong supportive valuation. That will still leave it an open question whether a strong adverse valuation can be defied by such an action. If the forward connection between valuing and doing turns out to be necessary, we shall have to agree in the end with Davidson and many other followers of Socrates that conscious last-ditch *akrasia* is not a real possibility. So the forward connection will have to be examined and it will be the topic of the next chapter.

The argument against the necessity of the backward connection between non-compulsive intentional action and strong supportive valuation will be developed in two stages. The weak sense of the phrase 'value-judgement', in which it means 'the expression of any kind of preference', will be considered first. This is the sense that comes from Decision Theory and it is, without any doubt, what Davidson means by 'a value-judgement'. So an interpretation of his defence of the necessity of the backward connection is bound to begin at this point.

However, it cannot stay with it, and the second stage of the argument will show why a full understanding of the scope of irrational action cannot be achieved without the introduction of the traditional sense of 'a value-judgement'. A value-judgement in this strong sense expresses a special kind of preference, based on one's own long-term interests or perhaps on other people's interests, and contrasted both with a desire based on a calculation of immediate pleasure and with a sudden yen for a cup of cocoa. This is the voice of reason and the argument will be that, in many cases of *akrasia*, the desire that rebels against reason's edict does not even pretend to speak with the voice of reason.

In self-deceptive *akrasia* the rebellious desire does pretend to speak with the voice of reason because in that kind of case the agent does persuade himself that, by the original standards of his strong valuation, his action is at least permissible. But the argument will be that this pretence is not universal and that the rebellious desire is often not even irrationally derived from the original considerations of reason and the agent often knows that that is not its derivation. It is, for example, the mere desire to go on drinking, which, without masquerading as a derivative, albeit an irrational derivative, of the agent's original strong valuation, openly defies its edict in conscious last-ditch *akrasia*.

Naturally, the two concepts of 'a value-judgement' do not have to engage in a fight to the finish. They can live together within the same theory provided that they are clearly distinguished from one another. So the general strategy adopted here will be partly concessive and partly combative. It will be conceded that, with a small qualification, the backward connection is necessary when the weak concept of a 'value-judgement' is used, but denied that it is necessary when the strong concept is used.

If this denial can be made good, it will be important, because its effects will extend far beyond the removal of another obstacle to conscious last-ditch *akrasia*. It will be a contribution to a picture of human action that is more realistic than the excessively rationalizing picture that holds so many western philosophers enthralled. Reason does not check, and is not generally believed to check, every desire that issues in intentional action without compulsion. Because reason is known not to operate a check-point through which all desires are filtered, however imperfectly, human agents do not even pretend that their rebellious desires always speak with the voice of reason. True, the introduction of the concept of 'weak valuation' allows us to say that they express themselves in value-judgements. But that is only because this is a different sense of the phrase 'value-judgement'. It is obvious that these weak value-judgements are not rationally derived from the original considerations of reason. It is less obvious, but equally important, that they are often not even irrational side-blows of reason, and so the agent does not claim that that is their origin.

First, then, consider the weak sense of 'value-judgement'. It has already been remarked that Davidson makes it quite clear that he is using the phrase in this sense. Now when an agent does something intentionally, two conditions have to be met: he must know what he is engaged in doing, even if it turns out to be a failure, and he must be engaged in doing it because he wants to do it. This yields the quick result that every intentional action must be accompanied by a supportive value-judgement. For when the value-judgement is a weak one, it merely has to express the desire from which the action issued. The case of Buridan's ass introduces a slight complication, but it is one that can be accommodated without too much difficulty.

However, this is a little too quick, because there is another complication introduced by compulsion. Even in cases of compulsion the first condition of intentional action is usually met and so too is the second one, because the agent wants to do the action in the circumstances that constitute the compulsion. For example, he wants to hand over his money at gunpoint. It is only in the limiting cases of compulsion that wanting is absent or, if present, not the sole cause of the action. These would be cases in which the inevitability of the outcome does not involve, and is not affected by, the agent's desires. For example, he is kept at home by being knocked unconscious or by being locked in a room, but, of course, the first of these two cases is not an example of intentional action and in the second one, even if the person does want to stay at home, that is not the only thing that keeps him there.[9] However, there are also difficult borderline cases. Penfield compelled his patients to make certain movements by stimulating the appropriate area of the cortex, but, though it seems that the movements were intentional, it is not so clear that the patients really wanted to make them.[10]

Evidently, the way to play safe is to avoid these complications by simply restricting the thesis to non-compulsive, intentional actions, which must all issue from the corresponding desires. So when we apply the weak concept of 'valuation' to these cases, the backward connection comes out as necessary with a small qualification to cover choices between two equally valued alternatives. It is, of course, of no consequence that the agent may not pause to formulate the value-judgement. The point is only that his non-compulsive intentional doing, or, rather engagement in doing, the action proves conclusively that, in the weak sense, he puts a value on doing it.

This is impeccable, but if outright value-judgements are interpreted in this way and tied tightly to non-compulsive,

[9] A point made by Locke. See *An Essay Concerning Human Understanding*, Bk. II, Ch. xxi, §10.

[10] See W. Penfield and T. Rasmussen, *The Cerebral Cortex of Man*, London and New York, 1950, pp. 111-14.

intentional actions, it is important to understand the consequences. If we claim that a consequence is the elimination of conscious last-ditch *akrasia*, we must understand that only one type of conscious last-ditch *akrasia* has been eliminated, namely the type in which the rebellion is against any kind of preference. But that type never looked very hopeful, because it was so obviously vulnerable to the objection, that, if the agent acted against one desire, his action would always issue from another desire. So we ought to go on to consider a more interesting, limited class of preferences, namely those based on strong valuations, and ask whether conscious last-ditch rebellion against this more narrowly defined authority has been eliminated. Evidently, that is still an open question.

Here begins the second stage of the discussion of the necessity of the backward connection. Its aim is to show that a full explanation of rational and irrational action needs the strong concept of 'valuation', and that, when this concept is used, the backward connection is not necessary. So one more obstacle to conscious last-ditch *akrasia* will be removed.

Let us start by asking what sort of theory of rational and irrational action can be built on Davidson's foundations. How are rationality and irrationality distinguished from one another when the weak concept of 'valuation' is being used? In order to answer this question, we have to go back to some of the suggestions made about practical reasoning in Chapter VII.

It was suggested there that an agent who starts with strongly evaluative premises will sometimes draw the conclusion 'So I want to do such and such', where 'want' does not mean 'need'. In such cases there is a shift in the line of his argument, a kind of side-step that also occurs in theoretical reasoning when the usual factual conclusion is embedded in a belief-sentence. A theory was then developed to explain the unusual semantics of the conclusion 'So I want to do such and such'. It can function as a plain expression of the agent's desire, already automatically rational, but it often has a different kind of function: either it is a rational instruction to the desiderative part of his psyche, or an expression of the formation of the rational desire, or, perhaps, its actual formation. However, in all cases alike its worst fate is factual falsehood.

This theory was then used to explain what happens when the desire is recalcitrant and the conclusion is factually false. There were two particularly interesting possibilities: it may be a case of internal *akrasia*, revocable if the instruction contained in the conclusion prevails in the end, or it may be a case in which the agent failed to include in the premisses of his argument all the considerations that were available to him. In short, what was emphasized was the reciprocal sensitivity of reasoning and the would-be rational system with which reasoning is concerned at its start and at its finish.

This two-way adjustment is not confined to cases in which the agent draws the conclusion 'So I want to do such and such'. If he draws the usual strongly evaluative conclusion, that it is best to do it, there is the same give and take between this conclusion and his actual intuition of the value of the particular action.

This give and take confers a special character on practical reasoning. The antecedents of action, strong valuation, factual belief, and desire, are rational when they are consistent, and their consistency is partly automatic and partly achieved by the regimentation imposed by explicit reasoning. The forward movement of deliberation to the agent's conclusion is made under the pressure of his premisses and so, when desire refuses to go along with it, it exerts a kind of retro pressure on them. He may doubt his earlier valuations or factual beliefs and, in particular, he may wonder whether they cover all the relevant considerations available in his mind.

This point may be put in another way. It is not enough to achieve validity in a piece of practical reasoning, because the conclusion 'So I want to do such and such' ought to fit what the agent actually wants to do. When there is misfit at this point, brutal regimentation is not always appropriate. For the agent's premisses did not just drop out of the sky into his mind. They came from his past and the strong valuations, factual beliefs and desires that they express ought to maintain a certain constancy through time. This does not rob them of their authority, but it does make it conditional. If the agent's reaction to today's predicament ought to conform to his conclusion, that will only be because his conclusion is validly drawn from premises mentioning elements that have maintained their constancy, and so, in the end, only because his reaction today is consistent with his earlier reactions to similar predicaments.

When a biographer is trying to decipher the psyche of his subject he will use his actual history as well as his diaries and he will make a working assumption of overall consistency. Naturally, he will not exclude all possibility of revision of his subject's strong valuations, desires and factual beliefs. Nor will he exclude all possibility of irrationality in his subject's psyche. Indeed, he would be prudent to allow for considerable variations in irrationality between one person and another. But there are limits.[11]

All this is covered in Davidson's theory of rational and irrational action. In fact, the theory was constructed to accommodate precisely this material and to explain how we use it when we interpret another person's strong valuations, desires and factual beliefs. True, Davidson simplifies things by lumping together strong valuations and mere desires and feeding them both into the system under a single concept of valuation. This is a handy procedure, borrowed from Decision Theory, and it certainly does not exclude any of the necessary material. It merely uses it in a form that avoids entanglement in the complicating distinction between strong valuation and mere desire and it yields a powerful and elegant theory of human choice.

However, the difference between strong valuation and mere desire does not cease to exist when we avert our eyes from it and, if we want to understand it, we need to look into

---

[11] A point often emphasized by Davidson.

it. That will put us in a position to answer the question whether last-ditch rebellion against strong valuation is a real possibility.

The simplest way to distinguish between strong valuation and mere desire is to ask whose interest is being considered. If a desire is just an impulse, or if its object is the immediate pay-off of a particular action, the intended beneficiary can only be the self of the moment and it is a mere desire. If, on the other hand, the object is the agent's long-term interest, the desire will carry the endorsement of one of the two main types of strong valuation, namely prudential valuation. The other main type, moral valuation, includes prudential valuation but goes beyond it, because it considers the interests of other people for their own sakes. It is, of necessity, always the self of the moment that deliberates, but its deliberation need not be egocentric. It can adopt an altruistic stance either towards the agent's own future selves or towards other selves.

Nobody would pretend that this simple schema yields a complete account of the difference between strong valuation and mere desire. However, it is enough to explain the possibility of conflict between them and so it immediately puts us in a position to tackle the question, whether last-ditch rebellion against strong valuation is a real possibility.

There is, however, a point about the concept of rationality that needs to be made first. Near the beginning of this book attention was focused exclusively on to internal rationality, which takes no account of the actual truth or falsity of a person's factual or evaluative beliefs. What matters for internal rationality is not the quality of the input, but only the way in which it is processed. This concentration on the working of the mind and neglect of the quality of the raw materials on which it works probably seemed rather perverse. Not that there is anything wrong with marking off internal rationality and examining it first. But the examination has taken up every subsequent chapter and it might seem to be high time that the scope of the inquiry was broadened. The obvious way to broaden it is to bring a certain type of external rationality within its purview, namely the rationality of considering one's own long-term interests.

The extension of rationality to cover prudence is natural and easily intelligible. Reason must have evolved in us because it provides a very effective way of adapting behaviour to circumstances. Something has already been said about the shortcomings of emotions like fear and anger, which do take account of a creature's long-term interests, but only by reacting in an inflexible way to a limited range of cues. Now reason uses internal simulations of different possible actions and internal reactions to their different outcomes. The obvious point, that this is less risky than practical experiment, was made earlier. Two further advantages need to be mentioned now. Reason is not restricted to a limited range of cues, because it is able to process any relevant information, and its internal simulations give it maximum flexibility.

All this is obvious, but it is worth mentioning, because it explains the extension of the concept of rationality to cover prudence. The explanation is that the internal processes of reason have a natural function, self-preservation, and so the concept of rationality applies not only to the internal processes themselves but also to the selection of material that is essential if they are going to perform their natural function successfully. The further extension of the concept to morality is another, more difficult matter.

It is important to notice that there are two possible ways of extending the concept of rationality to cover prudence. One is simply to require that an externally rational agent should make true judgements about his own long-term interests. Another, less stringent requirement is that he must, at least, aim at his own long-term interests and understand the difference between the kind of consideration that is conducive to them and the kind that is not conducive to them. This easier requirement is concerned with truth-conditions rather than with truth. The agent only has to understand the difference between the truth-conditions of prudential valuations and the truth-conditions of expressions of mere desire. When the concept of external rationality is set up in the second less demanding way, it ties in very neatly with the distinction between mere desire and one type of strong valuation, namely the prudential type.

Davidson does not use the distinction between strong valuation and mere desire because he finds it simpler to work with a single type of building-block when he is constructing his theory about the rationality and irrationality of the antecedents of action. Consequently, his theory says nothing about the special character of the truth-conditions of an agent's strong value-judgements but lumps them together with his expressions of his mere desires. If his neglect of the distinction is challenged, he can always point out that it is a difference that will manifest itself in behaviour. For an agent who satisfies the less demanding criterion of external rationality will show by his actions that his strong valuations occupy a higher position on his list of preferences than his mere desires. However, it is almost inevitable that, when this theory focuses on to the sensitivity of the agent's behaviour to his mere desires and strong valuations alike, it will neglect the sensitivity of his strong valuations to the actual values of their objects. So the only truth that will appear on the horizon will be the truth of behaviour-based ascriptions of weak valuations and factual beliefs to the agent.

The fact, that we do make strong value-judgements, is enough to prompt the question whether the backward connection remains necessary when they are substituted for weak value-judgements. The question simply becomes more urgent if the distinction between strong and weak valuation is, as has been argued, essential to the concept of rationality. What is the answer to it? Must the guest's non-compulsive intentional acceptance of the third drink always be accompanied by a strong value-judgement that is either supportive or, at least, permissive?

There are three different types of case to which we might go for the answer. One type would be actions that do not normally raise any question of strong valuation. For example,

someone walking along a beach sees what may be the keel of
a surf-board or a dead fish and curiosity leads him to go and
find out which it is. The second type would be actions that do
raise a question of strong valuation, but the values are evenly
balanced and so the agent makes his choice on other grounds.
An athlete, for example, might face a choice between two
equally suitable diets and he might choose the one that tasted
better. The third type of case is, of course, apparently conscious last-ditch *akrasia*.

In cases of *akrasia* it is difficult to disentangle an answer to
the question about the necessity of the backward connection
because the forward connection is also involved. For example,
it looks as if the guest's craving for alcohol might lead to an
excessive intake without reason's endorsement of the permis-
sibility of the action. However, though this may be unexceptionable when the intake is not excessive and the case belongs
to the first type, there may well be doubts about it in cases of
akrasia, when the intake is excessive. For if there were no
self-deception and so no spurious endorsement by reason, the
action would fall foul of the forward connection.

Let us, therefore, start with the first and simplest case.
There really does not seem to be any doubt that idle curiosity
can lead to the investigation of an enigmatic object without
the endorsement of strong valuation. The agent need not
even put a strong value on doing, in general, whatever he
feels like doing or whatever he thinks will give him pleasure.
He may just do it because he feels like doing it or because he
thinks he will enjoy doing it or get some immediate satisfaction from doing it. These would be mere preferences and they
are enough to account for non-compulsive, intentional action
in this type of case.[12]

The second type of case yields a more complex result. The
difference is that there is strong valuation operating, but it is
evenly balanced between the two alternative courses of action.
So we cannot say that strong valuation plays no part in pro-

[12] See S. Schiffer, 'A Paradox of Desire', *American Philosophical Quarterly*
1976.

ducing the action. On the contrary, the evaluative part of the agent's reasoning is essential and it ends with the permissive judgement that it is all right to do whichever of the two things the agent wants to do on other grounds. However, from this point onwards the case develops in the same way as the first type. For at this point the agent starts, as it were, from a zero base-line of strong valuation and his mere preference comes in and accounts for his choice.

It looks as if the backward connection between action and strong valuation is not necessary. However, before this conclusion is firmly drawn, there are several features of the argument that require some comment. First, it may seem puzzling that Davidson's discussion of the backward connection is concerned with the supportive value-judgement 'It is better to do such and such', while the discussion here is concerned with the permissive value-judgement 'It is all right to do such and such', and its upshot is that a non-compulsive, intentional action does not even require a permissive value-judgement. Why is there this difference between the ways in which the two discussions are set up?

The reason for the difference is simply that Davidson is using the weak concept of 'valuation'. This concept covers every kind of preference and so, if the agent's outright conclusion were that each of the two available alternatives was all right in this sense, there would be no further source of motivation and his will would be hung like the will of Buridan's ass. Therefore, his outright conclusion has to support one alternative rather than the other and so it has to be 'It is better to do such and such'. The situation is quite different when the strong concept of 'valuation' is being used. This concept does not cover every kind of preference and, consequently, the value-judgement that would be required in this case, if the backward connection were necessary, would only need to be permissive. For at this point the agent's mere preference would come into the assessment as something extra and tip the scales.

It is worth stressing that the thesis about the first type of case is not merely that the agent did not have to say or think that it was all right to do the action. It is that this strong valuation might play no part whatsoever in producing it. This is important because many actions are done for reasons that are not explicitly formulated. In fact, our lives are run on automatic programmes most of the time and practical reasoning does not have to take over unless there is some difficulty. The point of the argument is that even automatized strong valuation is not a necessary accompaniment of non-compulsive, intentional action.

It may be objected that there is no way of telling that automatized strong valuation is not playing any part in producing such an action. For if it were playing a part, there would be nothing to show for it in the agent's consciousness. This objection is not quite right, because there are varying degrees of awareness of automatized reasoning. However, it is sufficiently worrying that there are cases at the lower end of the scale where the agent would be completely unaware of what was going on. How do we know that, when a non-compulsive intentional action seems to involve no strong valuation, this is not simply because the reasoning is running silently and producing no effect in consciousness?

Fortunately, we do have an indirect indication that strong valuation is not always playing a silent role in such cases. Suppose that the person in the first example was over-scrupulous and asked himself afterwards whether it really was all right for him to have indulged his idle curiosity and came to the conclusion that it was. There are two different things that he might mean by this. He might mean that it lay within the province of strong valuation and was permissible, or he might mean that it lay outside the province of strong valuation because it was not even the type of thing that might affect his welfare in the long term.[13] If he meant the latter, it is plausible to infer that what went on in his mind before the action did

[13] See Philippa Foot, 'Moral Beliefs', *Proceedings of the Aristotelian Society*, vol. 59, 1958-9, reprinted in *Theories of Ethics*, ed. Philippa Foot, Oxford, 1967.

not involve any strong valuation. What happened was simply what seemed to him to happen: he went and took a look at the object because he wanted to know what it was and there was no silent programme of strong valuation running in his mind or tacit advice that it was all right to take a look at it.

Admittedly, there is no firm line to be drawn between actions that lie within the province of strong valuation and are permissible and actions that lie outside the province of strong valuation because of their type. However, we do use this distinction and it is plausible to infer that it corresponds at the automatized level to the difference between the occurrence and the non-occurrence of a preconscious process of strong valuation with a permissive outcome. If someone objects that strong valuation always holds a watching brief, that will merely be tantamount to saying that the agent has the concept of strong valuation and so a programme of this kind always could have been run in his mind. It would not follow that a mere desire's only outlet to intentional action would be through the check-point of strong valuation. So this way of defending the necessity of the backward connection between non-compulsive, intentional actions and strong permissive value-judgements does not work.

There is nothing surprising about this result. On the contrary, it would be very surprising if every mere desire that issued in intentional action must have received some kind of endorsement, supportive or only permissive, from strong valuation. If that were so, to express such a desire would be to speak, or purport to speak, with the voice of reason. But who would make such a bold claim for all his intentionally fulfilled desires? It seems obvious that they are not necessarily derived from strong valuations even in a faulty or biased way.[14]

The third type of case mentioned just now raises a more complex problem. Can a desire for alcohol lead to an excessive intake without reason's endorsement? This is the case of

---

[14] So in Ch. VII it was only suggested that rational desires are quasi-cognitive.

the guest at the party. The first point to note about it is the obvious one that, if reason's edict were permissive in a case of this kind, it would be a case of self-deceptive *akrasia*. There is no suggestion that the desire might speak correctly with the voice of reason. But must it speak with reason's voice at all?

The argument for a negative answer to this question is simply an extension of the argument used in the first kind of case. If idle curiosity can produce a non-compulsive intentional action without the endorsement of strong valuation surely the same is true of a desire for alcohol. However, in this case the argument will meet an objection: the agent originally judged it better to refuse the third drink and, against that background, things cannot develop in the simple way that the argument suggests. If he is going to take the third drink intentionally and without compulsion, he must irrationally substitute a different outright value-judgement, either a supportive one or a merely permissive one.

That may be so. But, if it is so, it will be the result not of the necessity of the backward connection, but of the necessity of the forward connection. If there are any intentional non-compulsive actions that issue from mere desires, the backward connection is not necessary. It is, therefore, a mistake to suppose, that, if the guest cannot take the third drink intentionally and without compulsion, that is attributable to some special feature that makes the backward connection necessary in this kind of case. The truth is simply that, if the guest's *akrasia* has to be self-deceptive, that will be because the forward connection is necessary. The question, whether it really is necessary, will be taken up in the next chapter.

The structure of this discussion of strong and weak valuation is remarkably similar to the structure of the controversy about psychological hedonism. The thesis maintained by psychological hedonists against all criticisms is that any intentional action is necessarily done for the sake of the pleasure that the agent expects to get from it. It is clear that their best strategy is to weaken the concept of 'acting for pleasure'. For example, they can point out that, when the agent of any intentional action is asked for his reason, he can always say 'Because it pleased me to do it' or 'Because it gave me satisfaction'. That, of course, trivializes the thesis, but the history of the controversy shows how easy it has been to confuse its trivial versions with more substantial versions, which certainly cannot be established in such a simple way, if indeed they can be established at all.

The two versions of the thesis that the backward connection is necessary, which is roughly the opposite of hedonism, are equally easy to confuse with one another. When Davidson uses the word 'desirable' in his formulation of the value-judgements that, according to him, necessarily accompany any intentional, non-compulsive action, he is careful to give it a weak meaning. But it is only too easy to accept his argument for the necessity of the backward connection with the weak concept of desirability and then to give its conclusion the strong meaning that it will not bear.

The analogy between the two discussions is very close. There is even an argument against psychological hedonism that is the counterpart of the argument that has been used here to establish that the concept of 'weak valuation' cannot provide a sufficiently discriminating account of rational and irrational action. The argument against psychological hedonism is that the concept of pleasure cannot yield a complete account of human motivation, because sometimes the only pleasure that an agent can expect is subsequent satisfaction when he reflects on what he has done, and in such cases he must also be motivated by whatever feature of the action he expects to yield subsequent satisfaction. For how could he expect satisfaction from that feature unless he were directly attracted by it before the action?[15] The argument against the adequacy of the concept of 'weak valuation' was that human agents must sometimes want to do things because they are advantageous.

·

[15] See J. Butler, *Sermons*, in *British Moralists*, ed. L. A. Selby-Bigge, Oxford, 1897, pp. 191-3 and pp. 227-36, and H. Sidgwick, *Methods of Ethics*, Bk. I, Ch. 4.

If the case against the necessity of the backward connection with the strong concept of 'valuation' has been made, two general conclusions follow from it. First, one more obstacle to conscious last-ditch *akrasia* has been removed. Second, a picture of human agency that is commonly taken for granted by western philosophers is beginning to look less convincing. Even if the authority of reason ought to make itself felt at the point of origin of every intentional, non-compulsive action, it is becoming more and more clear that in fact it does not do so. It is not just that the voice of reason is not always obeyed. The point is, rather, that the rebel often does not even purport to be speaking with its voice.

These conclusions may be developed in more detail. The first one is by now a rather obvious effect of the breaking of the backward connection. Of course, that in itself is not enough to establish conscious last-ditch *akrasia* as a real possibility. There is still the forward connection to be reckoned with. However, several interesting details are beginning to emerge.

First, the fact that in an ordinary piece of prudential reasoning the agent aims at his own long-term interests, puts a restriction on the type of consideration that can figure in his strongly evaluative premisses. A more complex and controversial restriction is required for moral reasoning. Second, since the interests of the agent almost always extend beyond the moment of the action, the beneficiaries are his future selves. Insurance companies use advertisements designed to stimulate the reader's sympathy with his future selves and Sidgwick seems to have been the first philosopher to argue that that feeling is no more rational than altruism.[16] Third, the deferment of benefits, which is a characteristic, but not universal, feature of prudence, ties in very neatly with the explanation of conscious last-ditch *akrasia* developed in Chapter VIII, which exploited certain similarities between the intensity of desires and the salience of perceptual cues.

---

[16] See H. Sidgwick, *Methods of Ethics*, Bk. IV, Ch. 2.

It is a striking fact that this connection, like so many others in this area, can be described most perspicuously in Aristotelian terms. Aristotle's account of *akrasia* is based on the distinction between mere desire and strong valuation. He treats the defeat of strong valuation by physical appetite as the central type of *akrasia* and he extends the term quite readily to cases in which the rebel is an angry impulse and more hesitantly to other cases.[17] Evidently, he is placing in or near the centre of the concept of *akrasia* those cases in which the rebel is a desire that is able to push its way through to its own satisfaction largely because the benefits are reaped by the self of the moment.

It is at this point that the explanation of conscious last-ditch *akrasia* that relies on the analogy between intensity and salience finds its foothold. It is because the frustration of such desires produces more and more discomfort as the moment for action approaches, and because the pleasures of indulgence can be expected immediately, that these rebels get such a grip on the executive part of the psyche. They speak with loud and urgent voices and the salience of what they say against the background of prudential considerations can be very powerful at the moment of action, even though the agent still remains conscious that what he is doing goes against his own outright singular value-judgement. This is not to say that all *akrasia* is caused in this way. That would be a great over-simplification. The point is only that this is how it is caused in the cases that were central for Aristotle and, perhaps, still are central for us.

The second general conclusion is more far-reaching. If mere desires sometimes have independent access to non-compulsive, intentional action, then one much thumbed map of the human psyche needs to be redrawn. Reason's control does not extend to the origins of all such actions. This is not just because it always operates a check-point but is sometimes defied. The question whether it can be openly defied is, in

---

[17] *Nicomachean Ethics*, 1148b9-14.

any case, an arguable one and it will be argued in the next chapter. But the present point is more radical. It is that mere desires have ways of achieving gratification without any reference to reason. Consequently, if, as Aristotle thought, reason is the legislature that issues commands to appetites and emotions, there are no-go areas in which these subjects run their own affairs. Even where reason is in more or less effective control, it may have to work through persuasion rather than through command. Certainly, it often tries to make its proposals attractive to the more primitive elements in the psyche and it is likely that it has to rely on their support far more often than is commonly supposed.[18]

None of this is surprising given our long psychological evolution. The behaviour of animals that lack reason is prompted by physical appetites and by emotions like anger or fear, which have laid down simple patterns of behaviour for standard predicaments. It is a moot point at what stage consciousness emerged, but any creature that can adjust the movement that it is making to its next movement has the rudiments of intentional action. Anyway, it would be quite implausible to suppose that the advent of intentional action had to wait until reason began to exercise control. So it is only to be expected that, after reason took its seat, the more primitive systems within us should retain their independent access to non-compulsive intentional action.

There is, finally, a topic which lies to one side of the main line of the argument of this chapter, but which needs to be discussed briefly in order to forestall two possible confusions.

Davidson has a theory about intending which might seem to throw some light on his views about the backward connection.[19] He holds that the formation of an intention in advance of the action is the same event as the making of the supportive outright value-judgement. He is inclined to extend this theory to actions done intentionally but without the

---

[18] See M. Toda, *Man, Robot and Society*, The Hague, 1982, pp. 185-6.
[19] *Actions and Events*, Essay 5.

advance formation of the intention: in such cases the intentional doing of the action may be the same event as the making of the outright value-judgement. However, he is less sure of this identification.

This is a reductive theory, designed to evade an ontological dilemma: either the formation of an intention is a totally mysterious act of will or it is nothing. He is suggesting the third possibility, that it is something familiar, namely the making of an outright value-judgement, but, of course, only a weak one. Someone who was unconvinced by this identification would protest, 'But how can the making of value-judgements be fused with the formation of intentions?' On the other hand, it must be observed that the fusion is easier with the weak concept of 'a value-judgement', because an intention is really only a crystallized desire.

However, the crystallization does seem to be a detectable event, unlike an act of will, if acts of will really have to be regarded as mysterious. Whatever else an intention is, it is a disposition and, when an agent forms one, he ceases to agitate his mind about the pros and cons of the project which he then shelves for future execution. This event is often detectable and its phenomenology is familiar. Consequently, there is no need for the extreme ontological parsimony of Davidson's theory.[20]

If we bring in strong value-judgements, as we must, the theory becomes more questionable. For even if the backward connection between the formation of an intention and the making of a strong supportive outright value-judgement were necessary, these two look even less like the same event. Surely it is possible to make the value-judgement and wait before forming the intention. True, if the value-judgement had been made without any residual doubts or reservations, the agent could not have any specific reason for waiting to form his intention. But it by no means follows that he could not wait.

[20] A point made by H. P. Grice in reply to Davidson's paper *Intending*, later published as Essay 5 of *Actions and Events*, when it was originally given at a colloquium organized by the University of North Carolina in 1974.

Whatever the truth about this matter, there are two points that need to be made about the relation between Davidson's identity-theses and the topics of this chapter and the previous one.

First, it is one thing to maintain that the backward connection between forming an intention and making a supportive outright value-judgement is necessary, and quite another thing to maintain that they are the same event. Davidson began by adopting the first thesis without the second one. Conversely, it might be possible to adopt the second thesis without the first one. It would be necessary to maintain that they are the same event when the two event-descriptions are both satisfied, but to deny that the satisfaction of the description 'formation of the intention' necessitated the satisfaction of the description 'making of the value-judgement'. Perhaps the context would be allowed to determine whether the second description was satisfied as well as the first one.

The second point concerns Davidson's tentative suggestion that, when an action is done intentionally without the advance formation of the intention, the doing of it may be the same event as the making of the supportive outright value-judgement. This sounds like the kind of quasi-propositional theory that was examined in the previous chapter. However, it is not really a theory of that kind. For the action is not supposed to be capable of quasi-truth or quasi-falsity, on the ground that doing it is like putting forward a proposition. On the contrary, doing it is supposed to be, among other things, putting forward a proposition that is capable of literal truth or falsity. So the theory is really much more like the one favoured by Richard Wollaston in the eighteenth century: 'I lay this down as a fundamental maxim, that whoever acts as if things were so, or not so, doth by his acts declare that they are so, or not so; as plainly as he could by words, and with more reality. And if the things are otherwise, his acts contradict those propositions that assert them to be as they are.'[21]

[21] *The Religion of Nature Delineated*, 1724: in *British Moralists*, ed. L. A. Selby-Bigge, Oxford, vol. II p. 364. See Hume's criticism in *A Treatise of Human Nature*, bk. III, Part I, § i.

* * *

The central topic of this chapter has been the thesis that a non-compulsive intentional action must be supported by the agent's outright value-judgement, or, more briefly, that the backward connection is necessary. This is a philosophical thesis, but it is closely related to Attribution Theory in psychology.

The main contention of Attribution Theorists is that people tend to rationalize not only their own actions but also those of others because they want to understand them, and the way to understand them is to attribute motives that make sense of them. They also maintain that this tendency often leads to short-cuts and over-simplifications. One kind of over-simplification would be failure to allow for the agent's irrationality. So the question, whether he can act consciously against his own better judgement, is among those that have to be considered by Attribution Theorists.

Davidson answers the question *a priori* in the negative. His answer is based in part on the following argument: the backward connection is necessary and so, when someone appears to act consciously against his own better judgement, what really happens is that the act issues from another outright singular value-judgement, which is supportive but biased. There is, therefore, a fault in such cases, but it is located in the agent's reasoning, most probably just before his outright singular value-judgement and certainly not between it and his action.

The main question here is whether the backward connection really is necessary. But before it was taken up, two points were made about Davidson's reconstruction of what really happens in apparent cases of conscious last-ditch *akrasia*.

First, it is a little puzzling that the outright singular value-judgement which, according to him, has to accompany any non-compulsive, intentional action, must always be supportive. Would it not be enough for it to be permissive? For example, the guest at the party might merely judge that it would be all right to go on drinking. Davidson's insistence, that the outright singular value-judgement must be supportive, was explained in the following way: he uses a weak concept of 'valuation', which allows value-judgements to express not only the verdicts of prudence or morality but also mere desires. When this concept is used, the agent's mere desire, which is, of course, necessary for a non-compulsive intentional action, is always expressible by a supportive value-judgement.

Second, Davidson's reconstruction of what really happens in apparent cases of conscious, last-ditch *akrasia* was defended against the criticism that it is internally incoherent. Things really do sometimes happen in the way that he describes and the only question is whether they always have to happen in that way or whether conscious last-ditch *akrasia* is another possibility.

His thesis, that the backward connection is necessary, was then examined in two stages. In the first stage the thesis was taken to be concerned with weak valuation, because that is certainly the way that he meant it to be taken. In the second stage strong valuation was substituted for weak valuation, because strong valuation plays an important part in our lives.

On the first interpretation the thesis came out as a necessary truth, just as Davidson claimed, with a small qualification to accommodate the case of Buridan's ass. Intentional action requires consciousness of what one is engaged in doing and, unless it is completely compulsive, causation by a desire. So, given that weak valuation includes mere preferences, the backward connection is necessary and the result is an elegant theory of rationality as consistency, namely Decision Theory.

The second interpretation, which was never intended by Davidson, was introduced by a discussion of strong valuation, about which several points were made. First, if rationality is allowed to cover not only internal consistency but also a due regard to one's own long-term interests, it achieves a connection with strong valuation. Second, this extension of the concept of rationality is a very natural one, given that reason evolved as a faculty for adapting behaviour to circumstances. Third, although Davidson's theory of rationality can connect the difference between strong valuation and mere desire with the agent's behaviour, it neglects the sensitivity of his strong valuations to actual values, and so the only truth that appears on its horizon is the truth of behaviour-based ascriptions of weak valuations and factual beliefs.

When the question of the necessity of the backward connection was formulated in terms of strong valuation, the answer to it was negative. Mere desires do have independent access to non-compulsive intentional action and they do not always have to pass through the check-point of strong valuation.

Some simple examples were used to illustrate this kind of transition from thought to action and the objection, that the agent's strong valuations always hold a watching brief, was answered. If this means that they always operate at least automatically, it is plausible to deny it in cases where the action is not of a type to raise questions of strong valuation. If, on the other hand, it means that they always could operate in one way or another, it is true but insufficient to support the thesis that the backward connection is necessary.

It was stressed that this negative answer must be distinguished from the claim that reason, with its strong valuations, operates a check-point on every line to non-compulsive intentional action, but is sometimes impersonated by rebellious desires. That would amount to less than the claim that mere desires have some independent outlets to such actions. The further point is that mere desires sometimes do not speak, and do not even purport to speak, with the voice of reason.

Two conclusions were then drawn. First, one more obstacle to conscious, last-ditch *akrasia* had been removed and in the process more light was thrown on the suggestion that in central cases it can be explained by the analogy between intensity of desires and salience of perceptual cues. Second, the picture of human agency that was beginning to emerge was not at all in the main western tradition. The writ of reason does not extend so far as is commonly assumed and the more primitive systems of appetite and emotion often run their own affairs. Some of the details of this picture were taken from the writings of the Japanese psychologist, Masanao Toda.

Finally, in an appendix, Davidson's later theory of intending was briefly examined and related to the main topics of this chapter and the previous one.

X

VALUING AND DOING:
THE FORWARD CONNECTION

Philosophers who agree with Socrates' rejection of conscious last-ditch *akrasia* have relied on the necessity of the forward connection between valuing and doing more often than they have relied on the necessity of the backward connection between doing and valuing. Their reason for this preference may have been the idea that valuation derives greater effectiveness from the forward connection than from the backward one. If that is so, it is puzzling, because it is hard to see how there could possibly be any difference between the effectiveness of the two connections.

Consider, for example, the case of the guest who is offered a third drink. He either takes it or rejects it, and, if the backward connection were necessary, then, whichever he did, his action would be supported by the appropriate value-judgement, unless it was either compulsive or not intentional. If the forward connection were necessary, its effect would be the same: whichever of the two value-judgements he made, it would be followed by the appropriate action, unless he were either unable to do it, or unaware of the occasion for doing it. So it looks as if the necessity of the forward connection can do no more to exclude the possibility of conscious last-ditch *akrasia* than the necessity of the backward connection. They both seem to have the same effect, namely total exclusion of the possibility. This is hardly surprising, because Davidson's argument proves that, if the backward connection is necessary, so too is the forward connection. For, given the necessity of the backward connection, any action that appeared to break the forward connection would not really do so, because it would have to be interpreted as the result of a change of mind. How, then, could the forward connection possibly exclude conscious last-ditch *akrasia* more effectively than the backward connection?

However, more needs to be said about this. In the case of the guest it is obvious that the two necessary connections would have the same effect, but it may look as if this is because he has to choose at a definite moment between accepting and refusing the third offer of a drink. It might be supposed that things would be different if there were no definite moment of choice, and even more different if the choice were between action and inaction. For example, someone who has offended a friend judges it best to apologize, but, because he sees him on and off for varying periods of time, there is no definite moment of choice and, in addition, the choice is not between doing two different positive things but between apologizing and doing nothing at all. Consequently, he may end up by never apologizing, but perhaps not intentionally, because he did not know when he was missing his last opportunity. He is like a commuter who lets crowded trains go but has no timetable telling him which is the last train of the day.

In this kind of case the necessity of the backward connection seems to be insufficient to ensure that the agent does what he judges it best to do. For his not doing it is, as it were, spread thinly on a surface with no definite edge and so it hardly counts as intentional. If, however, we bring in the necessity of the forward connection, the effectiveness of valuation seems to be increased. For the agent presumably understands the insidious operation of procrastination and knows that, if he is to make sure of apologizing, he must pick a definite, predictable occasion for action out of the indefinite sequence of equally unattractive occasions. So the necessity of the forward connection will ensure that, if he really judges it best to apologize, he will pick such an occasion and then procrastination will be eliminated.

But, though there is something in this, it does not succeed in establishing any asymmetry. We already know that the forward connection cannot possibly exclude conscious last-ditch *akrasia* more effectively than the backward connection, because its necessity follows from that of the backward connection. So there must be something wrong with the argument, and it is not difficult to see what it is. If advocates of the greater effectiveness of the forward connection are allowed to use the idea of picking an occasion in this way, then advocates of the equal effectiveness of the backward connection should be allowed to use it too. Their argument would be that, if the agent did not pick such an occasion, that would show that he did not think it worth picking one, but then, if he knew that that was the only way of making sure of apologizing, it would follow that he did not really judge it better to apologize. No doubt, this is too simple, but the simplicity does not matter, because the point is the symmetry between the two arguments, simple or complex.

This must be the right way of looking at the matter. The claim, that, under certain conditions, doing is necessarily matched by valuing, cannot be any less successful at ruling out cases of mismatch than the claim, that, under the same conditions, valuing is necessarily matched by doing. It is indeed true that procrastination is the easiest form of *akrasia*, but it does not follow that in such cases there is nothing that the agent intentionally refrains from doing. If those who rely on the effectiveness of the necessity of the forward connection have to identify what the agent is required to do intentionally as picking an occasion, then those who rely on the effectiveness of the necessity of the backward connection can simply follow suit. Symmetry must be maintainable, as it was with the foot and the shoe.

Consequently, if philosophers who agree with Socrates have a good reason for relying more often on the necessity of the forward connection, it may simply be that it is a less ambitious thesis and, therefore, easier to establish. Certainly, the forward connection might be necessary without the backward connection being necessary. So the counter-examples adduced in the previous chapter broke the backward connection without even challenging the forward connection. But, by Davidson's argument, the backward connection could not be necessary without the forward connection being necessary too.

Davidson, who uses both arguments against the possibility of conscious, last-ditch *akrasia*, formulates the necessity of the forward connection in a very simple way: 'If an agent judges that it would be better for him to do x rather than to do y, and he believes himself to be free to do either x or y, then he will intentionally do x, if he does either x or y intentionally.'[1] Here he is carefully refraining from specifying the circumstances in which the agent will do anything about it intentionally. This goes a long way towards securing identity of conditions in his formulation of his theses about the two connections. For they can evidently be combined in the following formula: given that the agent does something about it intentionally, if he judges it better to do x, it will be x that he does, and, if he does x, it will be x that he judges it better to do.

It is true that, for a reason to be discussed in a moment, the conditions do not remain the same in the two cases when an allowance is made for freedom. For in the first case the agent is only required to believe himself to be free to do x or y, whereas in the second the assumption is that he actually does x and, therefore, must actually have been free to do it. However, the immediate point is that the condition about acting intentionally is the same in both theses and Davidson does not find it necessary to take on the task of specifying in what circumstances the agent will do something about it intentionally.

Professor R. M. Hare's formulation is a bolder one.

The test, whether someone is using the judgement, 'I ought to do x', as a value-judgement or not, is 'Does he or does he not recognize that, if he assents to the judgement, he must also assent to the command, "Let me do x"?' . . . It is a tautology to say that we cannot sincerely assent to a command addressed to ourselves, and *at the same time* not perform it, if now

[1] *Actions and Events*, p. 23.

is the occasion for performing it and it is in our (physical and psychological) power to do so.[2]

This is a bolder formulation, because it specifies the conditions under which the agent will do x intentionally without including in them the proviso that he does something about it intentionally. So Hare has to make his conditions stronger in some way. He does so by including in them the agent's actual freedom or power to do x, and, though he does not say so, he must be taking the agent's awareness of this power for granted. Similarly, he must be taking for granted his awareness that now is the occasion for doing x.

There is also another conspicuous difference between Hare's thesis about the forward connection and Davidson's. Hare has a rather complex theory about the link between the making of the value-judgement and the doing of the action. According to him, the value-judgement is a command, and, if the agent sincerely assents to it and the other conditions are met, he will do the action intentionally if now is the moment for it, and, if the moment has not yet arrived, he will form the intention for later execution. Davidson's theory is simpler, because he holds that making the value-judgement is the same event as forming the intention, and thereafter he can rely on the normal functioning of the intention to produce the action, x, if the agent does anything about it intentionally. If, on the other hand, now is the moment for action, and the intention has not been formed in advance, he is inclined to think that making the value-judgement actually is doing x intentionally.[3]

So far, in spite of these obvious differences, there is a general similarity between the two philosophers' versions of the thesis that the forward connection is necessary. However, the similarity dwindles dramatically when we look at them more closely. Hare is defending the necessity of the forward connection between strong valuation and acting, while

---

[2] *The Language of Morals*, Oxford, 1952, p. 20.
[3] *Actions and Events*, pp. 98-9, discussed in the previous chapter.

Davidson is defending the necessity of the forward connection between weak valuation and acting. When this crucial difference is added to the greater cautiousness of Davidson's formulation, it is much less difficult to defend and there can be no doubt that he has vindicated it successfully.

This is easily seen. In the previous chapter it was argued that the backward connection holds necessarily when the weak concept of 'valuation' is being used. But, if the necessity of the backward connection entails the necessity of the forward connection, it follows that, when the weak concept of 'valuation' is being used, the forward connection holds necessarily too. If, for example, the guest must have judged it best to take the third drink before he took it intentionally, and if this is generally true of any intentional action, then an outright singular value-judgement that stands unrevised cannot be followed by an intentional action that fails to match it. To put the point in Davidson's way, if the guest does anything intentionally about the offer of the third drink, he must intentionally do whatever the value-judgement that is currently in force tells him to do. So if he does not refuse this offer, that shows that he has revised his judgement that it would be best to stop at two drinks.

This account of the relation between Davidson's theses about the two connections is slightly over-simplified, because the condition about freedom has to be covered, and it is covered in different ways in the two cases. When he formulates his thesis about the backward connection, it looks as if he ought to stipulate that the action must be done not only intentionally but also freely. However, he does not mention freedom at this point. Perhaps his idea is that he only needs to exclude the most extreme form of compulsion, in which the inevitability of the outcome does not involve, and is not affected by, the agent's desires. But that exclusion is implicit in the requirement that the action must be done intentionally, and so he does not need to mention freedom separately.

On the other hand, when he formulates his thesis about the forward connection, he does have to stipulate that the agent believes himself to be free to take or refuse the third drink. This is because, even an agent who wants, and is free to do x still might not do it if he did not believe himself to be free to do it. But again Davidson thinks that no extra stipulation about actual freedom is needed, because it has already been laid down that the agent does something about it intentionally, and from that it follows that his action issues from a desire, and so that the extreme form of compulsion, which is the only one that could have broken the forward connection, has already been excluded. Both theses are formulated very circumspectly and the conditions inserted in them go no further than is required for the necessity of the two connections when the weak concept of 'valuation' is being used.

However, here, as in the case of the backward connection, we also have to ask what happens when the strong concept of 'valuation' is used. Hare poses this question about the special case of moral valuation. His answer, that the forward connection holds necessarily in this case, is evidently harder to defend than Davidson's parallel thesis about weak valuation. For, with the strong concept of valuation, the backward connection does not hold necessarily and so it is no good pointing out that the necessity of the backward connection would entail the necessity of the forward connection. Nor, of course, is it so easy to demonstrate on independent grounds that the forward connection does hold necessarily with the strong concept of valuation. It is notorious that on this matter people's intuitions differ sharply.

It is clear that the disputed question is not just how high a degree of consistency of the kind analysed by Decision Theory is shown by the choices of human agents. That is only part of what is at issue and the concept of weak valuation covers that part adequately. The other part of the controversy is about the constraints imposed by the concept of external rationality that was introduced in the previous chapter. External rationality finds its natural expression in strong value-judgements. So the question is, 'How successful are human agents in their attempts to achieve conformity to their own strong value-judgements?' This is the problem that exercised philosophers of the past when they questioned the necessity of the forward connection.

Hare asks the question about a particular type of strong valuation, namely moral valuation. Here it is going to be asked about prudential valuation. There are obvious differences between the two and among them there is one that could affect the answer to the question. When moral and prudential values conflict, it is generally assumed that moral values should carry the day, and from this it is sometimes inferred that the intrinsic effectiveness of moral valuation is greater. The premiss of this inference may be conceded with minor qualifications, but the inference itself should be challenged. It may even be more plausible to suppose that the intrinsic effectiveness of prudential valuation is greater.

Anyway, the question about the necessity of the forward connection will here be posed for prudential valuation. Nevertheless, Hare's version of the thesis, that it is necessary, will guide the discussion. This is because it is explicitly concerned with strong valuation and because it identifies the problems accurately.

Hare's version yields a straightforward behavioural test of strong valuation: if the guest really judges it best to stop at two drinks, then he will do so, unless either he is unaware of the relevant facts, because, for example, he has miscounted, or he is unable to stop, because, for example, he is an alcoholic. This identifies two ways in which a valuation, which would otherwise have delivered a matching action, might fail to do so: its effectiveness might be lost through lack of awareness or blocked through lack of ability. Lack of awareness has already been discussed, and so it will now be assumed that the agent is fully aware of all the relevant facts. That will tip the discussion forwards on to the second possible cause of failure, lack of ability, about which little has yet been said.

There is also in Hare's version a theory about the link between strong valuing and doing. The connection is made through the agent's intention and, according to him, it depends on the fact that a strong value-judgement is a self-addressed command. Something was said about this kind of theory in Chapter VII, but not really enough.

Hare's account of the forward connection also raises a general question about the nature of this kind of philosophical theory. It is offered as a theory known *a priori* from the analysis of concepts. Yet it conveys a definite message about the way in which the human psyche ought to be organized. How does it achieve substantial content as an ideal without losing its *a priori* status? This question can also be asked when the substantial message conveyed by a philosophical analysis is factual rather than instructive. How, for example, are philosophical theories about the mind related to psychological theories? This topic was touched on in Chapter I, but it needs to be taken up again before the book ends.

The first of the three topics that remain to be discussed is lack of ability. Is Hare right in supposing that when a strong valuation fails to deliver a matching action, but does not fail through any deficiency in the agent's awareness, the failure must be attributed to lack of ability and not to last-ditch *akrasia*?

One argument for this thesis was mentioned in Chapter III. The agent's strong valuation comes from his reason. In fact, it is the only contribution that his reason can make towards keeping him on the rails. So if derailment occurs in spite of it, there is nothing more that his reason could have done to stop it. But the agent is his reason, and so there is nothing more that he could have done to stop it. Therefore, he could not have stopped it.

This argument, which is not Hare's, is naïve. It assumes that, if the derailment can be avoided, that must be because it is possible to do something as a result of which it will be avoided. But though this is generally true of obstacles in the external world, it is not generally true of the world within. When the guest is offered a third drink, he can just refuse it. The argument also assumes that an agent can be identified with his reason for all purposes. But though he identifies himself with his reason because in a cool hour he wants to be the way it tells him to be, it would be naïve to take the identification literally and infer that, if reason cannot control him, he cannot control himself.

However, though the argument would probably convince nobody, its assumptions are interesting, because they introduce two important ideas, alienation and unavoidability. If the agent is identified with his reason, he will be alienated from his ordinary emotions and appetites, because they will be treated not as parts of himself but as things in a kind of external world. Moreover, when one of these things causes *akrasia* after reason has done all that it can, the *akrasia* will appear to be unavoidable, if it is supposed that it could have been avoided only if it would have been avoided had reason been able to do something more.

The thesis of the previous chapter was that the mere wanting of appetites and emotions sometimes has independent access to intentional action. But some intentional actions are done not only independently of reason but also in defiance of reason and the question is whether any of these actions are free. Now in order to be free, they would have to issue spontaneously from something that was really a part of the agent and they would have to be, at the very least, avoidable. Here avoidability is judged by ordinary, everyday criteria and not excluded *a priori* by overall determinism. But consider the assumptions made by the naïve argument. If they were correct, neither of the two modest requirements of freedom would be met in apparent cases of conscious last-ditch *akrasia*. For in such cases the action would issue from an ordinary appetite or emotion that was not really a part of the agent, and, because reason could do nothing more to stop it, it would be unavoidable. These results would be achieved by shrinking the agent until he coincided with something that is usually supposed to be only a part of himself, namely his reason.

The shrinkage also tends to produce unwelcome side-effects in cases where no strong valuation is involved. One would like to think that intentional actions that simply issue from ordinary appetites or emotions are often done freely. But if the agent is shrunk to the point of detachment from his ordinary appetites and emotions, such actions will not issue from anything that is really a part of him and so they will, at least, be alien. Indeed, they may even be regarded as unavoidable. Kant seems to have been attracted by the extreme view that actions that are caused by feelings are caused mechanically and unavoidably.[4] But even the less extreme view, that they are alien, ought to make us suspicious. There must be something wrong with a theory that treats intentional actions, done without the endorsement of strong valuation, as alien performances, even if it does not add that they are unavoidable. Many actions of this kind are paradigms of freedom. They issue spontaneously from the agent's ordinary feelings or appetites and there is no special reason for believing them to be unavoidable.

However, the home ground of this theory about the place and function of reason in the psyche is really the other kind of case, in which strong valuation is involved. So let us return to apparent cases of conscious last-ditch *akrasia* and ask, what, if anything, is wrong with rejecting the two assumptions made by the naïve theory. To put the question the other way round, what is wrong with the idea that ordinary emotions and appetites are proper parts of an agent, so that intentional actions issuing from them are not alien but, in a full sense, his own? And what is wrong with the idea that, when ordinary emotions and appetites defy reason, the actions that issue from them are often avoidable?

It is really obvious that there is nothing wrong with the idea that human agents are not, in general, alienated from their own ordinary emotions and appetites. If an argument is needed, try to imagine reason guiding action without any reference to any of the desires inherent in human nature. One does not have to be a Hume to find this unthinkable.

The second question, about avoidability, is not so easy to

---

[4] See Kant, *Fundamental Principles of the Metaphysics of Morals*, Third Section.

settle. Before it is tackled, it might be useful to review what has been said so far on this topic. In the earlier chapters of this book various points were made about the concept of 'compulsion'. When compulsion is exerted by one person on another, the victim often has a choice, but an unfairly restricted one. For example, when a bank clerk is held up by a gunman, he can either hand over the cash or take the consequences. In such cases the compulsion is not the kind that prevents the action from being caused by a desire. That is why Davidson only needed to stipulate that the action must be done intentionally when he was formulating his thesis about the backward connection. For that stipulation is sufficient to exclude the extreme form of compulsion in which the inevitability of the outcome does not involve, and is not affected by, the agent's desires, and so, when it has been made, Davidson's thesis, which is, of course, only concerned with weak valuation, can simply romp home.

So far, few examples of the extreme form of compulsion have been given and this end of the spectrum has not been closely examined. Maybe cases in which the outcome is inevitable and its inevitability neither involves nor is affected by the agent's desires, are really off the end of the spectrum and should not be classified as compulsion of any kind. This certainly seems to be the conclusion to be drawn from clear examples of this sort of thing, such as using a flamingo as a croquet mallet. The flamingo's desires clearly contributed nothing to Alice's shots.

However, there are other examples in which it is not so clear that the agent's desires are bypassed by the line that leads inevitably to the outcome. Torture provides borderline cases of this kind. Suppose that the victim betrays his secret because he is literally unable to withstand the pain. Evidently he would not be choosing to betray it in quite the way in which the bank clerk chose to hand over the cash. But would it be his desire to avoid the pain that made him betray it? If so, the inevitability of the outcome would involve the victim's desires and the case might be squeezed on to the end of the spectrum of compulsion. Certainly, there are absolutely clear cases of compulsion originating within the victim and making the outcome inevitable. That is how we regard the final stage of addiction to alcohol or drugs.

But how can we distinguish this kind of case from the case of a person who leaves a burning building? Should we say that this too is a case of inner compulsion, but of compulsion exerted by a normal desire? It is worth noting that we encounter the same difficulty if we ask why we count resistible addiction as compulsive but do not count the resistible pressure of every strong desire as compulsive. We cannot answer that resistible addiction exerts a force that is literally external, like the gunman. So ought we to say that we count it as compulsive for the quite different reason that it is an abnormal, and presumably harmful, desire?

That would introduce a very lax criterion of compulsiveness. For there would be nothing abnormal about the way in which the desire produced its effect. There would often be a choice and it would not be an unavoidable one, unless, of course, determinism is true and all choices are unavoidable. But we are not concerned with overall determinism. What we are seeking is a discriminating criterion of compulsiveness, and, from this ordinary point of view, the only thing wrong with the choice would be that reason would not endorse it, because it came from an abnormal desire. The case may be contrasted with one in which a mildly addictive smoker is prevented from smoking under resistible duress for his own good.[5] That would be a case of compulsion, but capitulation to the mild addiction would not be a case of compulsion. Certainly, no philosopher would use such a lax criterion of compulsiveness to rule out the possibility of conscious last-ditch *akrasia*.

Perhaps this review of the points that have been made about compulsiveness and inevitability has put us in a posi-

---

[5] A more extreme case is described in Italo Svevo's book, *La Coscienza di Zeno*, Bologna, 1923: English translation by Beryl de Zoete, *Confessions of Zeno*, New York, 1930 and London, 1962.

tion to answer the second, more difficult question about conscious last-ditch *akrasia*: 'What, if anything, is wrong with the idea that, when normal emotions and appetites defy reason, the intentional actions that issue from them are often avoidable?' It is easy to see how to test this idea, but not at all easy to carry out the test. The test is to take a case in which an agent makes a strong value-judgement, which stands unrevised, and yet acts against it, and to ask whether the explanation has to be one of the following three: he did not really mean the value-judgement, or he did not know that he was acting against it, or his action was, by ordinary criteria, unavoidable. If the explanation need not be any of these three, it may be conscious last-ditch *akrasia*.

This test has a simple structure, but it is not easy to carry it out, because it involves three different variables, all of which are difficult to tie down. So philosophers usually proceed by describing cases in which two out of the three variables have been tied down successfully and the third one is then pitted against the possibility of conscious last-ditch *akrasia*. For example, Aristotle, in his well known discussion of this problem in the *Nicomachean Ethics*,[6] takes cases in which it is assumed that the agent is committed to his value-judgement and able to act in conformity with it, and he inquires whether his nevertheless acting against it must be the result of some lack of awareness or can be the result of conscious last-ditch *akrasia*. He also sets up the test in a different, but equally appropriate way in a less well known passage in the *Eudemian Ethics*.[7] He takes cases in which it is assumed that the agent is committed to his value-judgement and fully aware of all its implications in the circumstances, and he inquires whether his nevertheless acting against it must be the result of some degree of compulsion or can be the result of conscious, last-ditch *akrasia*. Hare sets up the test in this second way in his book *Freedom and Reason*,[8] but with a difference that will be analysed in a

[6] *Nicomachean Ethics*, Bk. VII, Ch. 3.
[7] *Eudemian Ethics*, Bk. B, Chs. 6-8.
[8] *Freedom and Reason*, Oxford, 1963, Ch. 5.

moment: the first of his two candidates is not compulsion but inability, as it was in the *Nicomachean Ethics*.

It is instructive to compare the results of Aristotle's two tests. But, before that is done, a word of warning is needed. His approach to this topic is not the same as ours. He never considers the possibility of universal determinism but always looks for features that would distinguish compulsive actions from others. Even when he takes the extreme case of irresistible compulsion, he restricts himself to examples in which the cause is a force exerted from outside the agent, usually by another person. Also, he never treats a desire as compulsive merely because it is abnormal, but always sticks to the idea that there has to be something wrong with the way in which the cause of a compulsive action produces it. On this last point he differs sharply from Freud, who did count the resistible force of an abnormal desire as compulsive, simply because reason would not endorse its indulgence. It has already been observed that no philosopher would use this lax criterion of compulsiveness to rule out the possibility of conscious last-ditch *akrasia* and Aristotle is no exception.

It is clear that Aristotle's two tests have to be run separately, but there is a risk attached to the procedure. When each test is being run, attention will be focused on to the variable that is being pitted against conscious last-ditch *akrasia* and not on to the other two variables that have been ruled out as candidates for explaining the particular case by the way in which it has been described. This makes it easy to exaggerate the strength of the argument for excluding the possibility of conscious last-ditch *akrasia*. It is a candidate that has to compete twice and it may fail one stage of the test in spite of passing the other one. That, of course, would show that there was some inconsistency in the operation of the two tests. It would then be premature to draw the conclusion that one failure is decisive and that conscious last-ditch *akrasia* is not a real possibility. We should first have to find out what lay behind the inconsistency.

Something of this sort may explain the difference between

Aristotle's two discussions of the possible explanations of *akrasia* and the view taken by many commentators, that he rejects the suggestion that it might be last-ditch and conscious. In the *Nicomachean Ethics* the description of the cases on which the thought-experiment is run takes for granted the agent's full commitment to the evaluative premiss of his practical reasoning and his ability to conform to the outright value-judgement that follows from it together with his factual premisses. Aristotle then makes a minimal concession to Socrates: there must be some deficiency in the agent's awareness, even if it is only a small one and, perhaps, only one that affects his appreciation of the demand that his outright value-judgement makes on his action.[9] So though the possibility of conscious last-ditch *akrasia* is ruled out, it is only just ruled out, and one of the explanations of the cases considered, namely deficient appreciation of the demand made by the outright value-judgement, is not easily distinguished from a temporary failure of commitment. How can we tell whether the voice of reason is muffled or whether the voice of the rebellious desire is too loud, so that it achieves the salience that it needs even when reason speaks with its normal voice?

In the *Eudemian Ethics* he evidently takes it for granted that there is no deficiency in the agent's commitment to his evaluative premisses or in his awareness. So, in strict consistency with the result of the thought-experiment in the *Nicomachean Ethics*, he ought to say that the agent is not able, or not entirely able, to resist the temptation. For if, in cases of *akrasia* with full commitment to the evaluative premiss, ability indicates some deficiency in awareness, awareness ought to indicate some deficiency in ability. However, he does not say that there must be some deficiency in ability. What he says is that the agent does not act under any compulsion.

If this implies that there is no deficiency in ability, it is a surprising result and it is worth looking at the way in which

---

[9] *Nicomachean Ethics*, 1147a1-b19.

he reaches it. He assumes that compulsion occurs only when an act issues wholly or in part from something outside the agent. The first case would be illustrated by Alice's flamingo and the second by the bank clerk and the gunman. But neither of these two things happens in *akrasia*, because the act issues from an appetite of the agent's, and so his whole psyche is not under compulsion. Of course, it is natural to deny this, because reason, which is the defeated element in his psyche, is put under constraint. But Aristotle argues that the denial would be mistaken, because what is true of a part of the psyche cannot be transferred to the whole psyche. It is obviously impossible for both parts to win in this kind of conflict and that is the agent's problem. However, it is a mistake to suppose that he acts under compulsion when he gives way to temptation, just as it would be a mistake to suppose that he would have acted under compulsion if he had resisted the temptation and his appetite had been put under constraint.[10]

The rejection of the first of the two assumptions made by the naïve argument is quite clear. The assumption was that, because the agent identifies himself with his reason for one purpose, he ought to be identified with his reason for all purposes. He identifies himself with his reason, because in a cool hour he wants to be the way it tells him to be, but it does not follow, nor is it true that, when his reason is put under constraint, the resulting action is not really one that is done by him. Acts that issue from his emotions and appetites are as truly his as acts that issue from his reason. Any theory of alienation that denies this is simply mistaken. So much is clearly Aristotle's message in this text.

However, his inference from it is not so clear. He does not directly deny the second assumption made by the naïve argument, namely that in an apparent case of conscious last-ditch *akrasia* the action is really unavoidable. Instead, he denies the suggestion that in such cases the action is really compulsive. This is because the question about compulsiveness is the one

---

[10] *Eudemian Ethics*, 1224a30-b36.

to which he has been addressing himself in this passage and compulsiveness is not the same thing as unavoidability, and perhaps both these things differ from lack of ability.

This might seem to cast doubt on the suggestion made just now, that there is a certain lack of consistency between the results of Aristotle's two tests. For the candidate for the explanation of apparent cases of conscious last-ditch *akrasia* is compulsion in the *Eudemian Ethics* and in the *Nicomachean Ethics* one of the background conditions is ability, and, if compulsion and lack of ability are two different things, the two texts do not present tests of quite the same things and the inconsistency is dispelled. Or so it seems.

However, there are two answers to this, one short and the other more lengthy. The short answer is that in the *Eudemian Ethics*, if Aristotle had meant that his test showed that there is always some lack of ability in the cases specified, he would surely have said so. He would have said that, though there is no compulsion, there is some lack of ability. But he does not say anything of the kind. Therefore, we can infer from his silence that he did not suppose that his thought-experiment showed that there is always some lack of ability, and the inconsistency with the result of the other thought-experiment in the *Nicomachean Ethics* remains.

But though this seems right, it leaves something unexplained and more needs to be said about unavoidability. Aristotle's reason for denying that there is any compulsion in the cases examined in the *Eudemian Ethics* is simply that there is no alienation from the source of the action. There is, however, another relevant variable, avoidability and unavoidability. Suppose that an action issues unavoidably from one of the agent's ordinary desires, as may well happen when he escapes from a burning building. Or suppose that it is a case of addiction and the desire that makes the action unavoidable is abnormal. Would Aristotle not have to say that, though these cases ought not to be classified as compulsive, they are, nevertheless, cases of unavoidability and, therefore, of lack of ability?

This is an interesting question. But even if it gets an affirm-ative answer, the inconsistency noted above will not be re-moved. For there is absolutely no suggestion in the text that all apparent cases of conscious last-ditch *akrasia* involve the psychological unavoidability that we might classify as com-pulsive, but Aristotle, for the reason already explained, would not classify as compulsive. So the inconsistency would remain, even if Aristotle did think that unavoidability entails lack of ability.

But did he think this? The first step towards answering this question is to recall that throughout his discussion of this topic he is concerned with the way in which the action issues from the desire that is its source and not with the normality or abnormality of the desire itself. From this point of view, the escape from the burning building and the alcoholic's next drink are classified together. The question about both cases is whether, if the action were unavoidable, it would follow that the agent lacked the ability to avoid it.

The second step is to make the obvious point, that neither case is like Alice's manipulation of the flamingo, or, to take Aristotle's less bizarre example, like a man blown by the wind.[11] On the contrary, a desire contributes to the result in both the cases that are under examination.

The third step is more problematical. In the case of addic-tion or escape from a burning building Aristotle seems not to have drawn a distinction that was mentioned above. We see, or at least think that we see, a difference between two ways in which the action might be produced unavoidably by the desire. The desire might operate through reasoning and choice, or it might bypass that channel and save the agent's body from burning or from deprivation of alcohol by some sort of automatism. Either way, the result might be unavoid-able, but the first way would preserve the liberty of spon-taneity while the second way would eliminate it. However, Aristotle seems not to have drawn this distinction.[12]

[11] *Nicomachean Ethics*, 1110a1-4.
[12] See Michael Woods, *Aristotle's Eudemian Ethics*, Oxford, 1982, pp. 142-5.

Maybe he was right not to draw it. Certainly, it is not an easy distinction to apply. For how can we tell that, when the desire bypasses reasoning and choice, it is not a perfectly ordinary case of automatism? It was pointed out earlier that large parts of our lives are controlled by automatized epitomes of reasoning and there is no reason to suppose that we lose the liberty of spontaneity whenever we switch to that channel. If it is argued that the addition of unavoidability produces that effect, there is the ready retort, that it does not even seem to produce it on the escape from the burning building. If it is suggested that, though such automatism does not always eliminate the liberty of spontaneity, it does sometimes eliminate it, we need to know how to tell when it does, and when it does not eliminate it. But where is the material for constructing a criterion? Maybe Aristotle was right.

Be that as it may, he seems to have been aware of the difference between the unavoidability of failure to execute a decision that the agent is unable to execute and the unavoidability of the decision itself. The fourth and last step is to suggest, rather tentatively, that he did not count the latter as an example of lack of ability.

That completes the answer to the question about Aristotle's view of the connection between unavoidability and lack of ability. But suppose that the answer is not found convincing. Then, as was pointed out earlier, before this digression, there will still be an inconsistency between the results of the two stages of his thought-experiment on the possibility of conscious last-ditch *akrasia*. For nothing can alter the fact that his result in the *Eudemian Ethics* is that no degree of compulsion is necessary, and so, whatever he thought about the limiting case of compulsion, namely unavoidability, it is impossible to represent him as concluding that apparent cases of conscious last-ditch *akrasia* really always involve some lack of ability.

So which of the two results represents his real view, and which one should be discounted? The simplest way of achieving some sort of reconciliation would start from the observation that the discussion in the *Nicomachean Ethics* is not a demonstration of the total impossibility of conscious last-ditch *akrasia*. On the contrary, it is a careful attempt to discover the minimum concession that has to be made to Socrates. Its result, that only a very small deficiency in awareness is needed, is not thought to be sufficiently important to be recorded at all the points in the text where it would be appropriate. For example, in the same Book, Aristotle says that, when *akrasia* is caused by weakness, the agent does not abide by the results of his deliberation, and nothing is said about any deficiency in his awareness of those results or the demand that they make on his action.[13] Similarly, when the test is being run on compulsion in the *Eudemian Ethics*, the agent's awareness is simply taken for granted and the fine point, that, by parity of reasoning, there should be some deficiency in his ability, is overlooked. Or, perhaps, as was suggested earlier, the truth is that Aristotle was ambivalent about conscious, last-ditch *akrasia*, and not that he usually forgot his minor concession to Socrates. Or, perhaps, he just failed to mark the difference between the faintness of the voice of reason and its indistinctness. What is unacceptable is the view that he firmly and consistently placed it well beyond the bounds of possibility.[14]

Hare, in *Freedom and Reason*,[15] relies mainly on the test that he runs on lack of ability. The result that he reports is that, if a person really means a value-judgement and yet acts against it without any deficiency in awareness, he must have been unable to avoid acting against it. Since ordinary physical ability can usually be established in this kind of case, the burden of explanation falls on psychological ability or, in cases of addiction, on a mixture of both kinds of inability.

---

[13] *Nicomachean Ethics*, 1150b19-28.

[14] The minor concession to Socrates occurs in Book VII of the *Nicomachean Ethics*. This book also belongs to the *Eudemian Ethics*. If, as Kenny argues, it was originally part of the Eudemian treatise, the incompatibility between the results of the two tests would really be surprising. See A. Kenny, *The Aristotelian Ethics*, Oxford, 1978.

[15] *Freedom and Reason*, Ch. 5.

This result goes far beyond anything that Aristotle envis-
aged when he ran his test on compulsiveness in the *Eudemian
Ethics*. He considered, and rejected, the possibility that there
might always be some degree of compulsion, but it seems
never to have occurred to him that there might always be
complete psychological unavoidability. On the other hand,
the result of his other test, in the *Nicomachean Ethics*, is mar-
ginally less distant from Hare's result.

How does Hare reach his extreme result? He does not, of
course, invoke universal determinism. That is a theory that
produces overkill in this area and the special force of strong
valuation is lost in it. Hare's claim is that this special force is
strong enough to overcome all internal obstacles except sheer
psychological impossibility. When, therefore, there appears
to be a case of conscious last-ditch *akrasia*, which was not
physically unavoidable, the explanation will always be that it
was psychologically unavoidable. He supports this claim by
quoting two descriptions of apparent cases of conscious last-
ditch *akrasia* and pointing out that in both the agent pleads
inability to resist the temptation.[16] He accepts the plea and
concludes that in 'typical cases of moral weakness' the explanation is always psychological inability.

There are several objections to this. First, weakness is not
the only cause of such lapses. The point was made in Chapter
III, but it is worth repeating, because it has a certain importance. It is easy to be misled by the assumption, that weakness
is the only cause, and to infer that an agent who is too weak
to resist a temptation is psychologically unable to resist it,
just as a Japanese wrestler, who is not strong enough to push
his opponent out of the ring, is physically unable to push
him out.

Second, although some addicts in some circumstances are
literally unable to resist temptation, it does not follow that
this is the explanation of all, or even of typical, apparent
cases of conscious last-ditch *akrasia*. In fact, the claim is

---

[16] Ibid. pp. 78-80.

self-evidently implausible once its extreme character is clearly understood.

Third, even if we always had to believe the agent's excuse, 'I could not resist the temptation', there would be no need to suppose that it always means, 'It was literally impossible for me to resist it'. There is a common use of 'I could not' in which it only means 'Because it was difficult, I did not succeed', just as 'I could' often means 'I did succeed in spite of the difficulty'.

It would not be premature to draw a conclusion which would have been something of an anticlimax even if it had been drawn earlier: conscious last-ditch *akrasia* is a not uncommon human failing, and an understandable one. However, here, as in so many cases, it is the way in which we succeed in understanding it that is important. So something will now be said about the second topic on the final list, Hare's account of the link between strong valuing and doing.

His theory is that a strong value-judgement entails a command addressed, when appropriate, to oneself.[17] This command is, of course, an instruction to do the valued action, and not an instruction to form the particular desire or intention to do it. However, acceptance of the command is supposed to involve the formation of the appropriate intention. In this theory the word 'command' is used to cover any use of an imperative sentence and it is not restricted to the specific speech-act for which the word is usually reserved. Now if someone really means an ordinary command addressed to another person, he intends him to carry it out. So if he really means a quasi-command addressed to himself, he must intend himself to carry it out, and must, therefore, intend to carry it out. This intention then takes over in the usual dispositional way and constitutes the final link in the chain connecting valuing with doing.

The use of the word 'command' suggests that there is opposition, or at least inertia, that has to be overcome by the

---

[17] See R. M. Hare, *The Language of Morals*, Ch. 2.

value-judgement. For one person usually addresses an ordinary command to another when he would not have done the
action without it. However, this suggestion is no part of the
theory, which is meant to cover all uses of value-judgements,
including cases where all the agent's desires point in the right
direction. That is one reason why the internal performance is
only a quasi-command, and in this kind of case it would really
be more appropriate to call it an 'endorsement'.

However, the interesting cases for this investigation are
those that involve conflict. What happens when the guest
very much wants a third drink but tells himself that it is best
to stop at two and really means it? According to this theory,
he intends himself to stop at two and, therefore, intends to
stop at two. However, though the smooth inference from the
first intention to the second one would be acceptable in a case
where all the agent's desires pointed in the same direction, it
is questionable in a case of conflict. For if the conflict is at all
severe, he will not intend to stop at two drinks and that is
precisely why he will tell himself that it is best to stop at two
with the intention that, as a result, he will form the intention
to stop at two and then stop at two. It is obviously legitimate
to ascribe this complex intention to him even though he does
not yet have the intention to stop at two drinks. In fact, it is
the absence of the intention to stop at two drinks that explains the presence of the complex intention.[18] So the smooth
inference only works when there is no conflict.

It is worth noting that this objection to Hare's account of
the link between valuing and doing does not depend on the
assumption that he is using the word 'command' to mean an
ordinary self-addressed command. In fact, there cannot be
much wrong with the assumption in cases of conflict, but the
objection does not depend on it.[19] It depends on the distinction between two different intentions. One is intending
oneself to stop at two drinks and the other is intending to

[18] See my *Predicting and Deciding*, Proceedings of the British Academy, 1964.
[19] See R. M. Hare, *Wanting: some Pitfalls* and my comments on this paper in
Agent, Action and Reason, ed. R. Binkley *et al.*, Toronto, 1969.

stop at two drinks. The point is about a situation in which the latter intention is absent, and, of course, that does not mean that the guest actually intends to take a third drink, but only that he has not screwed his resolution not to take it to the sticking point that is appropriately signified by the verb 'intend'. So he steps back from the situation and does something else with the intention that, as a result, he will form the firm intention of stopping at two drinks and will actually do so. This other thing that he does is to address a quasi-command to himself.

This is a coherent case-history and a common one. It follows that Hare's account of the link between valuing and doing is mistaken. However, we do need to understand why the story is coherent. How, in general, can a person intend to produce an intention in himself without immediately generating it? Two types of case need to be analysed. One is the type with which we are concerned here, involving conflict, and the other type involves no conflict.

Consider, first, an example of the latter type. A person may plan a holiday in such a way that it will put him in a position to do something that he really rather wants to do. He arranges to break a journey at Nice because that will give him an opportunity to see the Matisse Chapel at Vence. Now it is possible for him to make this plan and buy the air-ticket with a stronger intention, namely the intention that, once he is in Nice, he will form the intention to see the Chapel. But in that case must he have already formed it? Obviously not. This is a holiday and, though he intends the stop-over in Nice to generate the intention, he wants that day to take care of itself and so he has not yet firmed up the plan within the plan.

Evidently, this person's state of mind when he buys the air-ticket is perfectly coherent. If there were any threat of incoherence in forming the outer intention without the inner intention, it would be removed by the difference between the dates of their formation. The outer intention, formed today, is to do something that will produce a situation next week in which the inner intention will be formed. Why not?

But is there perhaps a real threat of incoherence in cases of conflict? If there were any incoherence, it would not begin until the outer intention had actually produced the situation that was supposed to lead to the formation of the inner one. However, in the case of the self-addressed command, that happens immediately. For the guest simply tells himself that it is better to stop at two drinks, thereby producing the situation that is supposed to elicit the inner intention. However, it does not elicit it while the conflict is going on and it is in this period that there may be incoherence. Perhaps the inner intention is never formed, in which case the problematical period will last as long as the active execution of the outer intention.

It is clear that what we have here is a problem that might have to be solved by the functional version of the theory of systems that was sketched in Chapter V. Let us inquire whether that really is so. One way of posing this question would be to take a leaf out of Plato's *Republic* and to divide the guest into two parts, the drinking man and the driving man.[20] What we want to know is whether, at the party, when the conflict is actually occurring, the drinking man and the driving man should be regarded as two distinct systems.

Now, we certainly do not get two systems here when we use the Freudian criterion, failure of consciousness. For if there is any incoherence in having the outer intention without the inner one, it is evidently not so severe that it could not occur openly. The best way to see this is to contrast this case with a more extreme case of conflict. Suppose that a person intends to achieve a certain goal, believes that there is only one method of achieving it, but intends to avoid that method. This would be a case very near the top of the scale of irrationality introduced in Chapter III, and it would enforce a Freudian separation of main system from sub-system,[21] because it

---

[20] See Plato, *Republic*, 435-9.
[21] See Ch. V.

would be so obvious that it was impossible to fulfil the first intention without frustrating the second one.[22]

The case of the guest is quite different. He does not yet intend to stop at two drinks but he has just reminded himself that it would be better to stop at two, intending, by this reminder, to produce in himself the missing intention to stop at two. This is not at all like intending the end without intending the necessary means. On the contrary, the outer intention in this case belongs to a level that is different from the level of the missing inner intention. Consequently, it would be an understatement to say that the objects of the two intentions are not linked in a way that produces an incompatibility. The truth is that the difference in level makes it impossible for them to be linked in that way. The point is a general one. Another example would be wanting to want something that one does not yet want. It is true that wanting does not have the exclusiveness of intending, but the difference in level is enough to eliminate the incompatibility in both cases alike. It would, therefore, be a mistake to regard the drinking man and the driving man as two systems separated from one another by the Freudian criterion.

Would they come out as two separate systems, if we used the functional criterion? It might be thought that they would, because, when the outer intention fails to produce the inner intention, its failure is a failure of function rather like the

[22] Plato's argument for the division of the psyche relied on the concept of 'wanting' rather than the concept of 'intending'. He did not use the Freudian criterion for drawing the line between systems, because he was concerned with desires and it is never impossible for one system to be conscious of another system's desires without sharing them. However, he did argue from cases of incompatibility, because he wanted to prove that the psyche is divided. Unfortunately for his proof, wanting lacks the exclusiveness of intending. Survivors in a lifeboat can both want and not want to drink sea-water, because drinking it has the two different properties of slaking thirst and accelerating dehydration and death. It is, of course, true that in this particular case the sources of the two desires are different, namely appetite and reason. However, that cannot be proved in Plato's way. If his proof were valid, it would enforce a further division within the appetitive part of the psyche in a case in which thirsty people disliked the taste of the drink that they were offered.

failure of the cautionary belief to stop the formation of the irrational belief in wishful thinking.

However, there is an important difference between the two cases. The cautionary belief is supposed to produce its rational effect in the mind directly, but the direct effect of the outer intention is the situation in which the inner intention is supposed to be formed. When it has produced that situation, it has shot its bolt, and, if the inner intention is not formed, that is certainly a failure, but not a failure in rational function. Is it then required to intervene directly?

Even if it were legitimate to distinguish two functional systems in the case of the self-addressed command, that would provide no support for the thesis that conscious last-ditch *akrasia* is impossible. The reason for this is plain. If the Freudian criterion had enforced the division between the drinking man and the driving man, the value-judgement could not have been made consciously with the outer intention. But the criterion that is supposed to enforce the division is only functional, and so it does not exclude the possibility of conscious last-ditch *akrasia* but, rather, explains it, just as the functional theory explains, but does not exclude the possibility of conscious irrational belief-formation.[23] Therefore, Hare's link between valuing and doing is too weak to hold and understanding its weakness is one way of understanding why the forward connection is not necessary.

If it is true and understandable that conscious last-ditch *akrasia* is a real possibility, why has anyone ever denied it? It is noticeable that the denial is commonest among philosophers, who are less exposed to empirical facts than psychologists. When philosophers set up their examples, it is only too easy for them to project their own assumptions into the characters that they create. Of course, their thought-experiments are supposed to be controlled by what they find it natural to say when they are describing human agents and their vicissitudes. But there are so many opportunities to idealize, and

---

[23] See Ch. V.

even to idealize consciously, thus providing an example of the very irrationality about which they are so sceptical. The motive is the glorification of reason, which does not encounter much opposition, because reason itself is being used by the philosopher who is presenting his characters in *akrasia*. His reason is quietly projected into them and he feels that he is talking about himself.

Something similar happens in the description of glaring intellectual errors. 'You cannot really have thought that': 'You must have imagined it'; 'You imagined it'. This progression means, 'Since I have to imagine it, when I am describing your case, you too must have been consciously fantasizing.' This idea has even been absorbed into the meaning of the verb 'to imagine' when it is used to signify 'supposing falsely'. A gross failure must really have been an attempt of a different kind. 'You must have been deceiving yourself' is one step further down this line of thought. There is, in philosophical rejections of conscious last-ditch *akrasia*, the same tendency to overlook the difference between a cool use of reason in the study and its use in the heat of real life.

One more question remains to be discussed. What exactly is the nature of this kind of philosophical theory? It was pointed out in Chapter I that philosophy sets a limit to the possibilities within the framework of our conceptual scheme. It sets this limit *a priori*, because the framework is deduced from an analysis of the concepts out of which it is constructed. This sounds very definite and it seems to give philosophical investigation a certain purity and independence of human vagaries.

In fact, things are not so simple. The *a priori* knowledge has to be derived from careful thought-experiments designed to discover how we would describe various cases of *akrasia*. This is not a straightforward factual inquiry, because the question is 'How would we describe them, if we described them correctly?' However, the only way to get an answer is by asking the factual question, 'How would we, the reposi-

tories of the conceptual scheme, actually describe them?'
This is a limitation felt by those who do the research on which
dictionaries are based.

There is, therefore, some latitude allowed to philosophers.
An innovation may be permissible if it is not too great and a
concept may be stretched if it is not stretched too much. But
what is the source of the pressures to which a philosopher
would be responding? It is not like the pressure on compilers
of dictionaries to include the latest slang. More is at stake,
because the philosopher must be responding to the conceptual needs of psychology, both technical and popular. For
that is the discipline dealing with the phenomena to which the
conceptual scheme is applied. The give and take between psychology and philosophy was discussed in Chapter I.

However, there is a complication at this point. Psychology
is not the only discipline related in this way to the philosophical investigation of irrationality. There is also ethics. Now
ethics aims at good behaviour and it is arguable that people's
behaviour would be improved if they accepted from philosophers a stretched version of the concept of 'really meaning
a value-judgement'. For if they could be persuaded that,
provided they really meant what they said, their value-
judgements would necessarily overcome all internal obstacles
except psychological impossibility, there might well be less
akrasia in the world. The idea is that it is obvious that most
conscious last-ditch cases cannot be attributed to anything
like addiction, and so, if people could be persuaded to accept
the stretched concept of 'really meaning value-judgements',
they might be shamed into stronger commitment.

This is a sophisticated idea. The calculation is that stricter
standards for the use of the language that guides behaviour
might lead to stricter conformity in the behaviour itself. The
theoretical rejection of conscious last-ditch *akrasia*, which
would begin by being factually false, would then make itself
true by winning general acceptance. That would be a social
variant of the way in which practical reasoning was said to

operate in Chapter VII. For the suggestion is that people·
would toe the line partly as a result of accepting a theory
which would be false if they did not do so.

There is, however, a conspicuous difference between the
trick played by practical reasoning and the trick played by the
social variant. In practical reasoning the agent seeks a theory
about the best thing to do in a particular predicament, and,
since he wants, in general, to do the best thing, it is not surprising that he sometimes draws his conclusion in the form
'So I want to do such and such', where 'want' does not mean
'need'. This conclusion aims at factual truth, which it may
achieve either with folded hands or by making itself true. But
when the social variant imitates this mixture of description
and regimentation, the reasoning that is supposed to produce
a beneficial effect is reasoning about the way in which ordinary practical reasoning produces conformity in particular
desires, intentions, and actions. Can it really be true that
idealization of this process would make it more effective?

Hare admits that his defence of the necessity of the forward connection is not strictly factual, because it involves a
certain idealization of our concepts and language. In his
discussion of the tension between strong valuation and
rebellious desires he writes: 'So great is the strain . . . that
something has to give; and this is the explanation of the phenomenon of moral weakness. Not only do *we* give, because we
are morally weak; we have found for ourselves a language
that shares our weakness, and gives just where we do.'[24] He
then contrasts our actual language with another, ideal language, which would not have 'any of the escape-routes for
back-sliders which are so amply provided in our actual moral
language'.

He does not actually say that acceptance of this ideal language would lead to an improvement in behaviour. He only
says that it would suit angels, because they would not have
any rebellious desires, but 'we are not angels . . . and we

[24] *Freedom and Reason*, p. 73.

shy at this rigorous and austere simplicity, and, in our vain struggle to find a more comfortable way of speaking, have introduced complexities into the logic of our moral language . . .'[25] However, he does give a strong hint that he means not only that the ideal language would suit agents who behaved perfectly because they never felt any temptation to do anything else, but also that agents who are plagued by conflict would behave better if they adopted it. For what he says about back-sliders is that our actual language amply provides them with escape-routes. But to what haven are these escape-routes supposed to lead? One answer to this question would be, 'They lead to comfortable acceptance of the theory that some bad behaviour is the result of conscious last-ditch *akrasia*.' Another, quite different answer would be, 'They lead to comfortable acquiescence in actual bad behaviour.' Since Hare does not distinguish between these two prognoses, there is, in what he writes, at least a hint that adoption of the ideal language would lead to an actual improvement in behaviour.

The two answers are evidently quite different from one another. In fact, it is tendentious to formulate the first one in a way that suggests that it is at all like, or even closely associated with, the second one. Why should acceptance of the theory, that conscious last-ditch *akrasia* is a real possibility, be described as 'comfortable'? One would have thought that the best reason for finding it comfortable would be its evident truth. Certainly, the idea, that it provides an escape-route to complacent bad behaviour, is completely mistaken. If a doctor discovers yet another way of developing a certain malady he is in a better position to cure it.

However, in the case of *akrasia* the patient is his own doctor, and so it is conceivable that a factually false diagnosis might lead to a cure, or, at least, to an improvement. Is this really so? Now, by the criteria of our actual language, a factually true diagnosis of many apparent cases of conscious last-ditch *akrasia* is 'Conscious last-ditch *akrasia*', and in

---

[25] Ibid. pp. 74-5.

those cases there would be two different factually false diagnoses, 'Psychological inability' and 'Deficient commitment to the value-judgement'. Suppose that, by the criteria of actual language, one of these cases is wrongly classified as 'Psychological inability'. That really would encourage acquiescence and complacency in a familiar way. But the diagnosis, 'Conscious last-ditch *akrasia*', apart from being true of the supposed case, has the advantage of encouraging belief in the possibility of improvement, and, since the patient is his own doctor, actual efforts to achieve self-improvement.

So far, there seems to be no reason to erase this diagnosis from our check-list. However, the suggestion is that self-improvement would be even further encouraged if it were replaced on our check-list by 'Deficient commitment to the value-judgement'. This suggestion would be correct if it were easier to increase one's commitment to one's own value-judgements than to overcome internal obstacles that are not insuperable. Now this might conceivably be true when cases are classified according to the check-list of actual language. But even if it is true on that basis, how could it possibly remain true when the heading 'Conscious last-ditch *akrasia*' is erased and the cases listed under it are transferred to the column headed 'Deficient commitment to the value-judgement'?

If, *per impossibile*, this manœuvre did work, we would face an interesting question of a kind discussed in Chapter V. Granted, for the sake of argument, that Hare's idealization of language would produce an improvement in behaviour, ought we to accept it on that ground or ought we to treat truth as paramount? To put the question more fairly, ought we to treat factual truth by present criteria as paramount, or ought we to prefer, on pragmatic grounds, a theory that would make itself true? However, though there are cases in which we really do face a dilemma of this kind, this is not one of them.

* * *

This chapter opened with the question why philosophers who have rejected the possibility of conscious last-ditch *akrasia* by arguing from the necessity of the forward connection between valuing and doing are more numerous than those who have done so by arguing from the necessity of the backward connection. Several possible reasons for this strategy were discussed, all but one of them inadequate. The exception was the consideration that the necessity of the backward connection would entail the necessity of the forward connection, but not vice versa, and so it is easier to argue for the latter.

However, Davidson is certainly able to establish the necessity of the backward connection, because he uses the weak concept of 'valuation'. Having established it, he can exploit the entailment to prove that the forward connection holds necessarily too. But since the history of the problem of *akrasia* shows that it has traditionally been taken to be a problem about the concept of strong valuation, attention was switched to Hare's theory, which uses that concept.

The first step was to sketch a naïve argument, not Hare's, for the necessity of the forward connection. The agent's strong valuation comes from his reason and it is the only contribution that his reason can make. Consequently, when *akrasia* occurs in spite of it, there was nothing more that his reason could have done to stop it, and, since he is identifiable with his reason, there was nothing more that he could have done to stop it.

Two assumptions underlie this argument. One is that the true agent is the agent shrunk to exclude his emotions and appetites. The other is that, if *akrasia* is then avoidable, that must be because he, the shrunken homunculus, could have done something to avoid it, and not because his emotions and appetites might have co-operated.

Next, a framework was set up for testing the possibility of conscious last-ditch *akrasia*. Two things were held constant: the agent really meant his value-judgement and yet he acted against it. There were two variables that had to be pitted against the possibility of conscious last-ditch *akrasia*, lack of awareness and lack of ability. Each of these variables could be tested separately.

The strategic situation was illustrated from the writings of Aristotle, who in the *Nicomachean Ethics* assumes ability and pits lack of awareness against conscious last-ditch *akrasia*, and in the *Eudemian Ethics* assumes awareness and pits compulsion against conscious last-ditch *akrasia*. The result of his first test was that, when ability is not impaired, apparent cases of conscious last-ditch *akrasia* always involve some lack of awareness. So the result of his second test ought to have been that, when awareness is not impaired, they always involve some deficiency in ability.

However, when he ran the second test, he substituted compulsion for inability. That raised the question, how he thought that these two things are related to one another. It also raised the question, whether the results of his two tests are inconsistent. They certainly would have been inconsistent if the result of the second test had been that there is no deficiency in ability.

His views about lack of ability, compulsion, and unavoidability were explored. The two main points made were that he certainly did not think that there is any lack of ability in the middle range of cases of compulsion, and that he probably took the same view about extreme cases in which the action is unavoidable. However, even if these interpretations were rejected, it would not follow that the result of his second test was that there is always some lack of ability in the cases on which the test was run. For his result was that there need not even be any degree of compulsion. There is, therefore, a certain inconsistency between the results of the two tests, and some explanations of the inconsistency were suggested.

When Hare pits inability against conscious last-ditch *akrasia*, he reaches a much more extreme conclusion. Given that the agent really meant his value-judgement and that there was no deficiency in awareness, it must have been impossible for him to avoid *akrasia*, and usually the impossibility is psychological.

It was pointed out that this conclusion is not derived from universal determinism. There has to be something special about the impossibility to which Hare appeals. Then it was argued that, once it is clear that the psychological impossibility that Hare needs is not universal but extremely strong, his appeal to it is self-evidently implausible. Two contributory errors were diagnosed: a misuse of the concept of 'weakness' and a misunderstanding of the plea 'I could not resist the temptation'.

His theory about the nature of the connection between valuing and doing was then examined. He maintains that a value-judgement entails a self-addressed command, and that really meaning this command entails intending that, as a result of it, one should form the intention to do the action commanded, and eventually, given certain further conditions, do it.

Against this it was argued that in cases of conflict the smooth inference from the outer intention to the inner one is not justified. This objection did not depend on mistaking Hare's 'self-addressed commands' for internalized versions of ordinary commands. It depended on the difference in the level of the two intentions.

The next step was to examine the suggestion that having the outer intention without the inner one is sufficiently incoherent to force us to attribute each to a different system within the agent. It was argued that this suggestion is certainly mistaken, if the criterion of schism that is being used is Freudian, and probably mistaken if it is functional. Anyway, even if the functional criterion did enforce a division into two systems in this case, that would provide no support for the thesis that conscious last-ditch *akrasia* is impossible.

Finally, an attempt was made to explain why anyone should deny the possibility of conscious last-ditch *akrasia*. There were two suggestions. First, philosophers tend to project their own cool awareness and rationality into the characters described in their thought-experiments. Second, there is some give and take between philosophy and other disciplines operating in this area, notably psychology and ethics.

The interaction with ethics was illustrated by the sophisticated thesis, that an idealization of our actual conceptual scheme which excluded the possibility of conscious last-ditch *akrasia* might lead to an improvement in behaviour, if it were generally accepted. Against this two points were made. One was that it is difficult to see how this could possibly be the effect of erasing the diagnosis 'Conscious last-ditch *akrasia*' from our check-list. The other was that, even if it might be the effect of the erasure, there would also be, on the other side, the nagging claim of factual truth.

ENVOI

It is customary to apologize for an unrelieved discussion of deviations and abnormalities, but perhaps there is no need when the subject is intrinsically interesting. If the topic of this book did need an excuse, it certainly would not be the common one, that the investigation of the abnormal throws light on the normal. That is not true of the kind of irrationality that has been examined here. When a wish distorts normal processes of thought or the normal transition from thought to action, it works like an expert in demolition. The methods used may be interesting but they reveal very little about the structure that buckles and collapses under the attack. There is here a marked contrast with the unmotivated perversions of reason. A thorough study of those faults would lead in many cases to an analysis of logical fallacies sufficiently detailed to throw some light on valid reasoning. If the topic of this book did need an excuse, it would be that western philosophy has always puffed the pretensions of reason, which, therefore, can do with a certain amount of deflation.

INDEX